THE WEBSTER'S
CHILDREN'S
THESAURUS

THE WEBSTER'S
CHILDREN'S
THESAURUS

By John Bellamy
Illustrated by Peter Stevenson

BARNES
&NOBLE
BOOKS
NEW YORK

This edition published by
Barnes & Noble Inc., by arrangement with
Larousse Kingfisher Chambers, Inc.

1996 Barnes & Noble Books

LIBRARY OF CONGRESS CATALOGING-IN-PUBLICATION DATA
Bellamy, John.
    The Doubleday children's thesaurus presenting over
    6,000 word entries accompanied by synonyms and antonyms,
    and homonyms.
    1. English language – Synonyms and antonyms –
    Dictionaries, Juvenile.
    [1. English language – Synonyms and antonyms]
    1. Stevenson, Peter. ill. II. Title.
    PE1591.B43 1987

ISBN 0-7607-0200-4

10 9 8 7 6 5 4 3 2 1

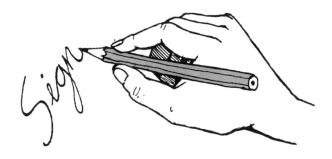

I·N·T·R·O·D·U·C·T·I·O·N

The entries in this Thesaurus are in normal alphabetical order. Each entry is printed in **bold type** and is immediately followed by an abbreviation in *italic type* telling us whether the word is a noun (*n*.), verb (*v*.), adjective (*adj*.), and so on. There then follow, in ordinary type, one or more words which have the same or a similar meaning to the entry word. These are the synonyms. So after the word **ask**, for example, you will find the words demand, request, question, interrogate.

Words sometimes have more than one meaning. The different meanings are given after a number and the appropriate abbreviation. Take, for instance, the word **coach**. This is how it appears:

coach 1. *v*. instruct, train, drill. 2. *n*. vehicle, carriage, bus.

If a word has an antonym – a word with an opposite meaning – this is shown at the end of the entry in ***bold italic***. So, for instance, at the end of the entry **cold** *adj*. and its synonyms icy, chill, wintry, frosty, bleak, raw we find the antonym ***hot, warm***.

If a word has a homonym – a word with the same sound but a different spelling – this appears at the very end of the entry, after any antonym and is printed in SMALL CAPITAL LETTERS. So the word HOARSE appears at the very end of the entry **horse**.

We hope you find, discover, locate the word you are searching, looking, hunting for! And we hope you have a lot of fun doing it.

abandon

abandon *v.* 1. desert, forsake, leave 2. give up, surrender *join*.

abandoned *adj.* 1. deserted, cast off 2. sinful, wicked, depraved.

abash *v.* shame, disconcert, put down.

abbey *n.* priory, church, monastery, convent.

abbreviate *v.* shorten, cut short, reduce, condense *lengthen*, *extend*.

abdicate *v.* resign, surrender, renounce, forgo *usurp*.

abide *v.* stay, dwell, remain, continue.

ability *n.* dexterity, skill, knack *inability*.

able *adj.* talented, clever, skillful, capable, qualified *unable*, *incompetent*.

abnormal *adj.* odd, peculiar, unnatural, unusual *normal*, *usual*, *average*.

abolish *v.* erase, cancel, quash, make void *keep*, *retain*.

abominable *adj.* hateful, horrible, unpleasant, nasty, odious *noble*, *admirable*.

abominate *v.* detest, hate, loathe *love*, *admire*.

about *prep.* 1. around, near, close to 2. concerning, touching.

above *prep.* over, beyond, higher than, superior to *below*, *under*.

abridge *v.* condense, shorten, reduce, diminish *expand*, *extend*.

abroad *adv.* 1. widely, expansively 2. overseas *home*.

abrupt *adj.* 1. unexpected, sudden, blunt *His manner was unfriendly and abrupt* 2. steep, broken *gradual*.

absence *n.* non-attendance, privation, want *presence*.

absent *adj.* not present, gone, away, missing *present*.

absolute *adj.* perfect, true, actual, ideal *partial*, *qualified*.

absolutely *adv.* completely, definitely *perhaps*, *uncertain*.

absolve *v.* acquit, clear, free, discharge *accuse*, *condemn*.

absorb *v.* consume, exhaust, swallow, take up *leak*, *drain*, *exude*.

A bridge

abstain *v.* refrain, desist, give up, hold back *indulge*.

abstract *adj.* vague, unreal, hypothetical *concrete*.

absurd *adj.* silly, foolish, stupid *sensible*, *reasonable*.

abundance *n.* wealth, plenty, more than *lack*, *poverty*.

abundant *adj.* full, plentiful, lavish, much, ample *scarce*, *scant*.

abuse *v.* mistreat, hurt, injure, misuse *respect*, *honor*.

accelerate *v.* hurry, quicken, expedite *slow down*, *decelerate*.

accent *n.* emphasis, stress, voice, tone.

accept *v.* admit, take, receive *refuse*, *reject*, *ignore*.

access *n.* approach, entry, admission *exit*.

accessible *adj.* approachable, reachable *inaccessible*.

accessory *n.* detail, supplement, extra *principal*.

accident *n.* mishap, casualty, misadventure, chance.

accidental *adj.* casual, chance, fortuitous, incidental *deliberate*, *intentional*.

acclaim *v.* applaud, cheer, praise *denounce*, *reject*, *disapprove*.

Abridge

accommodate *v.* furnish, house, oblige, assist *inconvenience*.

accompany *v.* escort, follow, go with *desert*.

accomplice *n.* confederate, helper, partner, associate *opponent*.

accomplish *v.* achieve, perform, complete, do *fail*, *attempt*.

accomplishment *n.* performance, achievement, completion *failure*.

accord 1. *v.* consent, agree, grant *quarrel* 2. *n.* agreement, harmony *strife*, *discord*.

account *n.* 1. story, report, tidings 2. record, register, invoice.

accumulate *v.* increase, grow, collect, gather *dissipate*.

accuracy *n.* exactness, precision, fidelity *mistake*.

accurate *adj.* exact, precise, correct, true, faithful *inexact*, *mistaken*, *wrong*, *erroneous*.

accuse *v.* charge, impeach, blame, indict *acquit*, *absolve*.

accustomed *adj.* habitual, usual, ordinary, everyday *unaccustomed*.

ache 1. *n.* pain, anguish, agony 2. *v.* throb, pain, hurt *relieve*, *ease*, *comfort*.

achieve *v.* reach, complete, accomplish, execute *fail*.

achievement *n.* performance, completion, attainment *failure*.

acquaintance *n.* 1. familiarity, knowledge 2. friend, person known *stranger*.

acquire *v.* obtain, gain, get, attain *lose*, *forfeit*.

acquit *v.* release, pardon, absolve, forgive *condemn*, *sentence*, *accuse*.

act 1. *n.* action, deed, feat, exploit, achievement 2. *n.* statute, decree 3. *v.* operate, perform, execute, work, behave.

action *n.* 1. contest, battle, skirmish 2. deed, feat, performance.

active

active *adj.* agile, alert, brisk, smart **idle**, **lazy**, **inactive**.

actual *adj.* true, veritable, real, genuine, certain **unreal**, **fake**, **bogus**, **false**, **imaginary**.

acute *adj.* sharp, shrewd, keen, smart **dull**, **obtuse**.

adapt *v.* modify, adjust, fit, suit.

add *v.* join, affix, unite, total, sum up **subtract**, **withdraw**, **deduct**, **remove**, **take away**.

address 1. *n.* place, home, abode, location 2. *v.* speak to, court, greet, accost **ignore**.

adequate *adj.* sufficient, enough, proportionate **inadequate**.

adhere *v.* cling, stick, cleave, hold, attach **sever**, **separate**.

adjacent *adj.* near, adjoining, bordering, next, close to, touching **distant**, **apart**.

adjust *v.* 1. reconcile, settle, pacify *Joe is too old to adjust to a new job* 2. set, regulate, put to rights **derange**, **disturb**.

admirable *adj.* excellent, praiseworthy, superb **abominable**, **despicable**, **hateful**.

admiration *n.* liking, love, regard **contempt**, **disdain**.

admire *v.* respect, regard, esteem, prize, value **dislike**, **loathe**, **detest**, **hate**.

admit *v.* 1. confess, acknowledge, own **deny** 2. give access to, let in **obstruct**, **reject**.

ado *n.* trouble, difficulty, bother, stir, fuss **tranquility**, **quiet**.

adopt *v.* 1. assume, appropriate *She adopted a new way of speaking* 2. foster, take care of **repudiate**, **reject**, **discard**.

adore *v.* love, honor, admire, worship, esteem **hate**, **despise**, **loathe**, **abominate**.

adorn *v.* enrich, decorate, beautify, embellish **mar**, **deface**.

adult 1. *n.* grownup, mature person **child**, **youth** 2. *adj.* mature, grownup, ripe **infantile**, **immature**.

adulterated *adj.* corrupted, impure, contaminated **pure**.

advance *v.* progress, march, move forward, proceed **retreat**, **flee**, **withdraw**, **retard**, **hinder**, **delay**.

advanced *adj.* up-to-date, in front of, modern, technical **elementary**, **rudimentary**.

advantage *n.* benefit, profit, gain, superiority **disadvantage**, **handicap**, **drawback**.

advantageous *adj.* beneficial, convenient, profitable, helpful, useful **harmful**, **inconvenient**.

adventure *n.* exploit, hazard, undertaking, experience.

adverse *adj.* unfavorable, contrary, unlucky, hostile **favorable**, **lucky**, **beneficial**.

advice *n.* counsel, instruction, information, tip.

affable *adj.* cordial, courteous, civil, obliging **reserved**, **unfriendly**, **unsociable**.

affect *v.* influence, alter, change, transform.

affection *n.* fondness, friendliness, liking, tenderness **dislike**, **coldness**, **spite**.

affectionate *adj.* loving, fond, tender, warm **distant**, **unfeeling**, **cold**.

affirm *v.* swear, aver, declare.

afford *v.* endure, support, give, be able to pay.

afraid *adj.* fearful, scared, timid, alarmed, frightened **unafraid**, **daring**, **bold**, **fearless**, **valiant**.

aft *adv.* abaft, astern, behind **fore**.

after *prep.* afterward, behind, following, later **before**.

again *adv.* once more, afresh, often, anew.

against *prep.* facing, opposite to, opposed to, adverse to **away from**.

age *n.* period, date, life, maturity, years **youth**.

aged *adj.* old, elderly, feeble, ancient **young**, **youthful**.

agent *n.* delegate, representative, deputy, middleman **opponent**.

aggravate *v.* 1. exasperate, annoy, irritate 2. intensify, exaggerate, worsen *The strike was aggravated by weather conditions* **soothe**, **diminish**, **lessen**, **mitigate**.

aghast *adj.* appalled, shocked, horrified, amazed, startled **calm**, **placid**.

agitate *v.* shake, toss, jar, stir, excite, rouse **calm**, **soothe**.

agitated *adj.* excited, worried, upset **serene**, **tranquil**.

agony *n.* suffering, pain, torture, torment **peace**, **calm**, **comfort**.

agree *v.* consent, harmonize, assent, match, tally **differ**, **disagree**, **argue**, **contradict**.

agreeable *adj.* pleasant, welcome, gratifying, charming, friendly **disagreeable**, **quarrelsome**, **touchy**, **irksome**.

agreement *n.* treaty, pact, harmony **conflict**, **dispute**, **opposition**.

ahead *adv.* onward, forward, in front **behind**.

aid *v.* assist, help, support, back, succor, relieve **obstruct**, **hinder**, **foil**, **obstruct**.

aim 1. *v.* direct, level, point 2. *n.* goal, object, purpose, intention.

aisle *n.* corridor, passage, way, path ISLE.

alarm *v.* upset, scare, frighten, terrify, startle **calm**, **soothe**, **comfort**.

alert *adj.* nimble, brisk, lively, agile, watchful **stupid**, **slow**, **dull**, **listless**.

alien 1. *adj.* strange, foreign 2. *n.* stranger, foreigner **native**.

An alien

Two aliens alike

alike *adj.* like, identical, similar, same, akin **unlike**, **dissimilar**.

alive *adj.* live, active, alert, sprightly **dead**, **extinct**, **inanimate**, **dull**.

allot

allot *v.* divide, deal, distribute, allocate, apportion *withhold*.

allow *v.* let, grant, permit, admit, approve *forbid*, *prohibit*, *resist*.

ally 1. *n.* colleague, helper, friend, confederate *enemy*, *foe* 2. *v.* combine, *join*, *unite*.

almost *adv.* somewhat, nearly, well-nigh.

alone *adj.* lonely, lone, desolate, solitary *together*, *accompanied*.

aloud *adv.* loudly, noisily, distinctly, audibly *silently*, *inaudibly* ALLOWED.

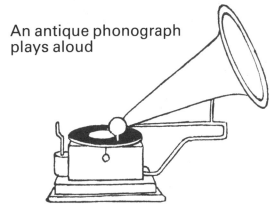

An antique phonograph plays aloud

alter *v.* change, adjust, modify, vary *keep*, *fix*, *maintain* ALTAR.

alternative *n.* choice, selection, possibility.

altogether *adv.* completely, entirely, quite, wholly *partly*.

always *adv.* eternally, forever, evermore *never*, *rarely*.

amateur *n.* nonprofessional, beginner, learner *professional*.

amaze *v.* astonish, astound, surprise, bewilder *bore*, *tire*.

ambition *n.* aspiration, desire, enthusiasm, drive.

amend *v.* revise, correct, improve, rectify, alter *worsen*, *impair*.

amiable *adj.* friendly, obliging, winning, sweet-natured *surly*, *unfriendly*, *cross*, *touchy*, *peevish*.

amount *n.* sum, total, whole, measure, quantity.

ample *adj.* plentiful, abundant, liberal, copious *scanty*, *insufficient*.

amplify *v.* expand, extend, enlarge, develop, increase *curtail*, *abbreviate*.

amuse *v.* please, entertain, interest, divert *bore*, *tire*.

ancestor *n.* forefather, forebear, predecessor.

ancient *adj.* old, antique, aged *new*, *fresh*, *current*, *modern*.

angel *n.* spirit, cherub, seraph *fiend*, *imp*, *demon*, *devil*.

angelic *adj.* entrancing, adorable, heavenly *fiendish*.

anger *n.* rage, wrath, ire, fury, indignation *pleasure*.

angle *n.* 1. bend, elbow, corner 2. viewpoint, standpoint, position.

anguish *n.* pain, agony, misery, suffering, distress *comfort*.

animosity *n.* bitterness, rancor, hate, enmity, grudge *fellowship*.

announce *v.* publish, declare, proclaim, report *suppress*, *repress*, *conceal*, *stifle*.

annoy *v.* bother, vex, irk, irritate *comfort*, *soothe*, *please*, *oblige*.

annoying *adj.* worrying, distracting, hectoring *pleasing*.

answer *v.* respond, reply, retort, rejoin *question*, *query*, *ask*.

antagonistic *adj.* adverse, hostile, contrary *friendly*.

anticipate *v.* expect, forecast, foresee.

anticipated *adj.* expected, foreseen *unexpected*.

antique *n.* rarity, curio, collector's item.

anxious *adj.* uneasy, restless, worried, fearful *composed*, *cool*, *confident*.

apart *adv.* alone, separately, asunder *together*, *adjacent*.

apathetic *adj.* stoical, cold, unfeeling, indifferent ***ardent, fervent***.

apathy *n.* unconcern, indifference, coldness ***interest, passion***.

aperture *n.* hole, gap, opening, cleft.

apologize *v.* excuse oneself, confess, regret.

appall *v.* terrify, frighten, alarm, shock ***reassure, please***.

apparent *adj.* plain, obvious, clear, evident, manifest ***hidden, dubious, secret***.

appeal *v.* pray, implore, beg, ask, plead.

appear *v.* emerge, seem, show, look, arise, arrive ***disappear, vanish, evaporate***.

appease *v.* calm, soothe, pacify, satisfy, allay ***irritate, enrage, provoke***.

appetite *n.* desire, longing, craving, hunger.

applaud *v.* clap, cheer, praise ***denounce, disapprove of, criticize, censure, chide***.

appliance *n.* apparatus, instrument, tool, machine.

apply *v.* utilize, employ, use, avail ***neglect, ignore***.

appoint *v.* select, choose, designate, pick, elect, name ***dismiss, discharge***.

appreciate *v.* value, prize, rate, esteem ***scorn, disparage, abuse***.

approach *v.* draw near, get near, advance ***avoid, elude, shun, evade***.

appropriate 1. *adj.* proper, suitable, fitting ***inappropriate, irrelevant*** 2. *v.* employ, assign, adopt *The occupying army appropriated all houses in the town.*

approval *n.* approbation, praise, liking ***rebuff, veto***.

approve *v.* endorse, applaud, like, commend, appreciate ***disapprove, frown on, oppose, censure***.

approximate *adj.* nearly correct, rough, almost exact ***exact, precise***.

ardent *adj.* passionate, eager, keen, enthusiastic ***cool, unemotional***.

arduous *adj.* 1. steep, high, lofty 2. hard, difficult, laborious ***easy***.

area *n.* region, district, territory.

argue *v.* discuss, debate, dispute, disagree ***agree, concur***.

argument *n.* dispute, controversy, debate.

arid *adj.* dry, parched, barren ***damp, moist, fertile***.

arise *v.* rise, appear, emerge, get up ***sink***.

army *n.* host, force, troops, legions, multitude, throng.

arouse *v.* wake, awaken, excite, stir ***calm, settle, soothe***.

arrange *v.* place, order, group, plan, organize ***disturb, disorder***.

array 1. *v.* adorn, clothe, dress, attire 2. *n.* order, display, arrangement ***disarray, disorder***.

arrest *v.* check, stop, capture, catch, stay ***release, free***.

arrive *v.* reach, attain, get to, come ***leave, depart***.

arrogant *adj.* proud, haughty, disdainful, insolent, imperious ***bashful, humble, modest, meek***.

artful *adj.* cunning, sly, wily, crafty, tricky ***artless, simple, naïve***.

artificial *adj.* synthetic, man-made, unreal, unnatural ***real, genuine, natural***.

artless *adj.* ignorant, unlearned, simple, natural ***canny, foxy, artful***.

ascend *v.* climb, rise, soar, go up, mount ***descend, go down, fall***.

ascent *n.* elevation, rise, slope, gradient ***fall, descent***.

ashamed *adj.* abashed, shamefaced, mortified, embarrassed ***proud, arrogant, self-respecting***.

ashore *adv.* on shore, on land, aground *afloat*.

ask *v.* demand, request, question, interrogate *answer*, *reply*.

aspect *n.* appearance, outlook, view, look.

aspire *v.* aim, desire, yearn, long *reject*.

assault *v.* assail, attack, charge, invade *defend*.

assemble *v.* gather, meet, collect *scatter*, *disperse*.

assembly *n.* company, gathering, collection.

assent *v.* agree, approve, consent *dissent*, *disagree*, *object*.

assert *v.* affirm, declare, maintain, say *deny*, *contradict*.

assign *v.* allocate, allot, appoint, designate.

assist *v.* aid, help, support, sustain *obstruct*, *hinder*, *impede*.

assorted *adj.* various, mixed, divers, miscellaneous.

assume *v.* 1. presume, suspect, suppose 2. adopt, undertake *After her mother died, Mary assumed the role of housekeeper.*

assure *v.* promise, certify, pledge *deter*, *deny*.

astonish *v.* astound, amaze, surprise *bore*, *tire*.

astute *adj.* crafty, cunning, keen, shrewd, clever *slow*, *dull*, *naïve*, *simple*.

athletic *adj.* robust, muscular, strong, brawny *puny*, *weak*.

atrocious *adj.* villainous, heinous, infamous, diabolical.

attach *v.* fix, fasten, affix, connect *detach*, *unfasten*, *loosen*.

attack *v.* assault, charge, storm, engage *withdraw*, *retreat*, *defend*.

attain *v.* reach, achieve, accomplish, acquire *fail*, *lose*, *miss*.

attempt *v.* seek, endeavor, try, struggle *achieve*, *accomplish*.

attend *v.* visit, go to, be present, frequent *be absent*.

attentive *adj.* mindful, heedful, careful *inattentive*.

attire 1. *n.* costume, clothes, garments, raiment 2. *v.* dress, clothe, equip.

attitude *n.* position, pose, disposition, predicament.

attract *v.* entice, allure, enchant, draw, pull *repel*, *repulse*.

attractive *adj.* pretty, beautiful, charming, fascinating, lovely *plain*, *homely*, *ugly*.

austere *adj.* severe, rigid, strict, formal *lenient*, *informal*, *sumptuous*.

authentic *adj.* genuine, real, true, pure *fake*, *false*, *counterfeit*.

authority *n.* power, sovereignty, rule, command *weakness*.

automatic *adj.* self-moving, self-acting *manual*.

avail *adj.* help, profit, use, benefit.

available *adj.* accessible, convenient, obtainable *unavailable*, *unobtainable*.

avenge *v.* revenge, vindicate, punish *forgive*, *pardon*.

average *adj.* normal, usual, ordinary, moderate *abnormal*.

avoid *v.* dodge, avert, escape, shun, elude *meet*, *encounter*.

avow *v.* acknowledge, confess, own *repudiate*.

award *n.* prize, reward, medal, payment.

aware *adj.* mindful, conscious, informed, knowing *ignorant*, *unaware*, *unconscious*.

awe *n.* dread, fear, terror, reverence, veneration *scorn*, *contempt*, *disdain*.

awful *adj.* dreadful, fearful, horrible, dire OFFAL.

awkward *adj.* unskillful, uncouth, clumsy, inept, sloppy *graceful*, *deft*, *elegant*, *skillful*.

babble *v.* prattle, chatter, gibber, jabber, gabble.

baby *n.* infant, child, bairn, tot, toddler.

back 1. *adj.* hind, rear **front**, **fore** 2. *v.* aid, support, abet.

background *n.* 1. framework, setting **foreground** 2. experience, training.

backward *adj.* 1. slow, sluggish, dull, retarded 2. behind **forward**, **advanced**.

bad *adj.* 1. rotten, spoiled 2. wicked, sinful, evil, naughty **good**.

badge *n.* emblem, token, crest, symbol.

baffle *v.* bewilder, confuse, mystify, foil **aid**, **assist**.

bag *n.* sack, pouch, case, wallet.

bait 1. *n.* snare, lure 2. *v.* heckle, tease, pester 3. *v.* entice BATE.

bake *v.* 1. roast, cook 2. harden.

balance 1. *v.* weigh, steady, poise 2. *n.* self-possession, steadiness.

bald *adj.* bare, hairless **hairy**, **covered**.

balk *v.* 1. hesitate, stop 2. baffle, foil, disappoint.

ball *n.* 1. globe, sphere 2. dance, party.

ban *v.* prohibit, outlaw, forbid, stop **permit**, **allow**.

The band is banned

band *n.* 1. belt, stripe, ribbon, strip 2. group, body, gang, society BANNED.

bandit *n.* outlaw, brigand, thief, robber.

bang *v.* thump, beat, strike, pound.

banish *v.* exile, deport, expel, exclude **admit**, **welcome**.

bank

bank *n.* 1. coast, shore, brink, margin 2. accounting office.

bar 1. *v.* stop, block, prevent, hinder ***encourage***, ***aid***, ***permit***, ***allow***

A bare bear

bare *adj.* 1. nude, naked, undressed, unclothed 2. barren, empty BEAR.

bargain *n.* deal, contract, agreement, cheap.

bark 1. *v.* yelp, bay, yap, howl 2. *n.* tree layer.

barren *adj.* bare, sterile, unfruitful ***fertile***, ***fruitful***, ***prolific*** BARON.

barrier *n.* bar, obstacle, wall, barricade.

barter *v.* swap, exchange, trade.

base 1. *n.* bottom, foundation ***peak***, ***top***, ***summit*** 2. *v.* establish, found *Pidgin tongues are usually based on English*, 3. *adj.* bad, low, vile *The criminal had committed a number of base crimes* 4. *adj.* cheap, worthless ***noble***, ***moral***, ***upright*** BASS.

basement *n.* vault, cellar.

bashful *adj.* shy, coy, modest, timid ***bold***, ***immodest***.

basic *adj.* main, root, fundamental ***incidental***.

batter *v.* hit, pound, beat.

battle *n.* combat, fight, war, struggle.

bay 1. *n.* bight, gulf, inlet 2. *v.* yelp, bark, howl BEY.

beach *n.* coast, shore, sands, margin BEECH.

bead *n.* ball, sphere, marble.

beam 1. *n.* girder, truss, joist, balk 2. *n.* gleam, ray 3. *v.* glow, shine, flash.

bear *v.* 1. carry, haul, convey, transport, lift 2. endure, suffer, stand, tolerate BARE.

bearable *adj.* endurable, tolerable ***insufferable***, ***intolerable***.

A bear

bearing *n.* 1. conduct, manner, posture *The old lady was upright and of aristocratic bearing* 2. position, course BARING.

beastly *adj.* brutal, brutish, bestial ***gentle***, ***kind***, ***agreeable***.

beat *v.* 1. conquer, overcome, defeat 2. strike, hit, batter, thrash 3. pulsate, throb BEET.

beautiful *adj.* bonny, lovely, pretty, fair, attractive ***ugly***, ***plain***.

beauty *n.* grace, charm, elegance.

14

become *v.* turn to, change to, be transformed.

becoming *adj.* 1. graceful, neat, pretty **ugly**, **unbecoming** 2. fit, proper, suitable, meet.

before 1. *adv.* previously, earlier 2. *prep.* preceding, in front of **after**, **behind**.

beg *v.* 1. beseech, implore, ask, entreat 2. cadge.

begin *v.* commence, start, originate, found **end**, **finish**, **halt**.

beginning *n.* origin, inception, opening, start **end**, **finish**, **conclusion**.

behavior *n.* demeanor, bearing, manner, conduct.

behind *prep.* after, following, astern **before**, **in front of**.

believe *v.* 1. trust, accept, suppose **disbelieve**, **doubt** 2. imagine, opine, consider.

below *prep.* beneath, under, underneath **above**, **over**.

belt *n.* band, strap, strip, zone.

bench *n.* seat, form, table.

bend *v.* curve, crook, turn, bow, fold **straighten**.

beneath *prep.* under, underneath, below **upon**, **on**, **over**.

benefactor *n.* savior, patron, supporter **miser**.

beneficial *adj.* useful, profitable, helpful, advantageous **adverse**, **evil**.

benefit *v.* & *n.* help, profit, aid **harm**, **injure**, **hurt**.

benevolent *adj.* kind, benign, tender, humane, generous **merciless**, **spiteful**.

besides 1. *adv.* also, yet, too, further 2. *prep.* except, in addition to.

best *adj.* excellent, most good, first-rate, finest **worst**.

bet *v.* wager, gamble, stake.

betray *v.* mislead, lure, delude, divulge, give away, tell **shield**, **guard**, **protect**, **shelter**.

better *adj.* superior, finer, preferable **worse**.

beware *v.* be cautious, take care, mind, look out.

bewilder *v.* puzzle, confuse, mystify, perplex **enlighten**, **clarify**.

beyond *prep.* later than, past, after, yonder.

bias *n.* say, tendency, prejudice **fairness**, **justice**.

biased *adj.* prejudiced, influenced, partial, swayed **fair**, **just**, **impartial**.

bid *v.* 1. offer, propose, tender 2. direct, order, enjoin, command **forbid**, **prohibit**.

big *adj.* great, large, huge, important **small**, **little**, **tiny**.

bill *n.* 1. beak, mandible 2. account, charges, reckoning 3. draft of law.

bin *n.* box, receptacle, crib, container, tub.

bind *v.* fasten, tie, attach, link, join **loosen**, **free**, **untie**.

birth *n.* start, creation, nativity, origin **death**, **end** BERTH.

bit *n.* morsel, scrap, piece, particle, crumb, fragment.

bite *v.* chew, champ, gnaw BIGHT.

biting *adj.* keen, pungent, sharp, crisp, cutting, incisive.

bitter *adj.* sharp, harsh, acid, sour, acrid **sweet**, **bland**.

black *adj.* inky, dark, dusky, murky, dingy **white**, **rosy**.

blame 1. *n.* fault, wrong, disapproval, guilt, responsibility **credit**, **honor** 2. *v.* condemn, reproach, reprehend **forgive**.

bland *adj.* smooth, soft, mild, gentle, kind, insipid **pungent**, **harsh**, **bitter**.

blank *adj.* empty, vacant, void **filled**.

blast 1. *n.* explosion, burst, outbreak, eruption 2. *v.* burst, **explode**, **split**.

blaze *v.* flare, burn, glow, flame.

bleach

bleach *v.* whiten, blanch *darken, blacken*.

bleak *adj.* dismal, dreary, cheerless, desolate, bare *cheerful*.

blemish *n.* speck, defect, mark, flaw, stain, spot.

blend *v.* mix, combine, merge, mingle *separate, divide*.

bless *v.* glorify, exalt, praise, beautify *damn*.

blessing *n.* advantage, boon, glory, honor, benediction *curse, disaster*.

blight *n.* pestilence, disease, sickness, mildew.

blind *adj.* 1. unseeing, sightless, eyeless *sighted* 2. ignorant, unaware, thoughtless, inconsiderate, rash *That film star is beautiful, but I am blind to her charms* *aware*.

blink *v.* wink, flicker, flutter, twinkle.

bliss *n.* happiness, joy, ecstasy, rapture *misery, unhappiness*.

block *v.* impede, hinder, obstruct, bar, stop *aid, further* BLOC.

bloom *v.* flower, flourish, blossom, thrive *wither, shrivel*.

blot *n.* blemish, spot, stain.

blow *n.* tap, thump, rap, hit, cuff, clout, smack.

The wind blew the blues away

blue *adj.* 1. azure, sapphire 2. glum, sad, depressed *happy, cheerful* BLEW.

bluff 1. *v.* trick, delude, deceive 2. *n.* fake, deceit, fraud 3. *adj.* blunt, abrupt, brusque.

blunder 1. *n.* error, mistake, stupidity 2. *v.* flounder, bungle.

blunt *adj.* brusque, curt, bluff, abrupt *subtle, tactful* 2. obtuse, dull *sharp, fine*.

blur *v.* dim, smear, obscure, darken *clear, clarify*.

blush *v.* flush, glow, redden.

board 1. *n.* council, committee, conclave 2. *n.* plank, table 3. *v.* embark BORED.

boast *v.* brag, bluster, crow *be modest*.

boastful *adj.* bragging, blustering.

boat *n.* vessel, ship, craft.

body *n.* 1. collection, crowd, party, band 2. carcass, corpse.

bogus *adj.* fake, spurious, counterfoil *actual, genuine, real*.

boil *v.* seethe, stew, simmer.

boisterous *adj.* loud, roaring, stormy, lively, noisy *calm, quiet*.

bold *adj.* 1. fearless, daring, valiant, hardy, brave *afraid, cowardly, fearful, timid* 2. confident, striking, prominent *Such a scheme as this requires bold action* BOWLED.

bolt 1. *v.* flee, abscond, run off 2. *v.* lock, secure, close 3. *n.* rod, bar.

bond *n.* 1. guarantee, premium, security 2. fastening, tie, rope, band.

bondage *n.* slavery, servitude, captivity *freedom, liberty*.

bonny *adj.* pretty, fair, beautiful, handsome *ugly*.

bonus *n.* reward, award, premium, gift.

boom 1. *v.* roar, drone, hum 2. *n.* pole, spar, beam.

boon *n.* gift, present, grant, blessing *calamity, catastrophe*.

boorish *adj.* rude, rustic, loutish, clumsy, coarse *gallant, suave*.

boost *v.* raise, hoist, lift, elevate, increase, expand *Lower prices helped to boost exports*.

booty *n.* spoils, plunder, prize, loot.

border *n.* 1. boundary, frontier 2. edge, rim, brink, verge, margin BOARDER.

bore *v.* 1. tire, weary, worry, annoy *amuse*, *interest*, *arouse* 2. drill, pierce, perforate BOAR.

borrow *v.* take, adopt, obtain as a loan *lend*, *loan*.

boss *n.* manager, superintendent, master, overseer *employee*, *worker*.

botch *v.* bungle, patch, mend.

bother *v.* harass, worry, tease, annoy, vex, harry, pester *comfort*, *appease*.

bottle *n.* flask, jar, carafe.

bottom *n.* base, foundation, ground, basis *top*, *peak*.

bough *n.* limb, shoot, branch BOW.

bounce *v.* bound, leap, spring, jump.

bound 1. *v.* leap, jump, spring, vault, 2. *n.* limit, boundary, 3. *adj.* trussed, tied, roped.

boundary *n.* border, limit, confine, verge, edge, frontier.

bounty *n.* reward, bonus, premium, gift, bonus.

bow *v.* bend, buckle, incline, yield, submit BOUGH.

bowl *n.* dish, basin, beaker, container, goblet BOLE, BOLL.

box 1. *n.* case, carton, crate, bin, receptacle 2. *v.* smite, punch, hit.

boy *n.* youth, lad, stripling BUOY.

brace 1. *n.* strut, bracket 2. *v.* prop, support, bolster, fortify.

bracing *adj.* stimulating, invigorating *relaxing*.

brag *v.* boast, vaunt, bluster, crow, swagger *deprecate*, *apologize*.

braid *v.* weave, plait, twine, interlace BRAYED.

branch *n.* 1. limb, shoot, bough 2. section, department.

brand *n.* stamp, mark, label, tag, make.

brash *adj.* rash, hasty *coy*.

brave 1. *adj.* valiant, heroic, gallant, courageous, unafraid, bold *cowardly*, *timid* 2. *v.* dare, challenge, defy.

brawny *adj.* stalwart, sturdy, athletic, muscular *weak*, *flabby*.

brazen *adj.* bold, insolent, rude, shameless *shy*.

breadth *n.* width, largeness.

break *v.* shatter, burst, smash, batter, fracture, crack *repair*, *mend*, *heal* BRAKE.

breathe *v.* exhale, emit, inhale.

breed 1. *v.* bear, produce, rear, raise 2. *n.* species, kind, race.

bribe *v.* corrupt, suborn, lure, entice.

brief *adj.* short, curt, laconic, terse *lengthy*, *long*, *interminable*.

Boughs bowing

bright

bright *adj.* 1. keen, acute, ingenious, intelligent *stupid*, *slow* 2. radiant, shining, luminous, gleaming 3. happy, lively, cheerful *boring*, *dull*.

brighten *v.* polish, burnish, illuminate, cheer up *tarnish*.

brilliant *adj.* 1. alert, acute, gifted 2. sparkling, splendid, radiant, bright *dull*.

brim *n.* edge, brink, border, verge.

bring *v.* take, convey, carry, get, fetch.

brink *n.* border, margin, verge, brow, shore.

brisk *adj.* sharp, keen, active, lively, agile, nimble *sluggish*, *slow*, *slothful*, *inert*.

brittle *adj.* fragile, crumbling, weak, frail *flexible*, *supple*, *sturdy*.

broad *adj.* wide, large, ample, extensive *narrow*.

broken *adj.* shattered, rent, imperfect *intact*.

brood *v.* ponder, think, dwell on BREWED.

brook *n.* stream, runnel, burn, creek.

brow *n.* forehead, edge, brink, border.

bruise *v.* squeeze, crush, contuse, squash BREWS.

brusque *adj.* blunt, gruff, rough, rude *polite*.

brutal *adj.* cruel, savage, ferocious, ruthless, mean, coarse *gentle*, *kind*, *humane*.

bubble *n.* froth, blister, blob, foam.

buckle *n.* clasp, brooch, fastening.

bud *n.* shoot, sprout, germ.

budge *v.* move, flinch, stir, go, shift.

build *v.* erect, assemble, construct, raise, fabricate BILLED.

bulky *adj.* huge, large, clumsy, vast *delicate*, *small*, *handy*.

bully 1. *v.* browbeat, intimidate, force *coax* 2. *n.* brute, ruffian.

bump *v.* hit, collide, bang, knock, jar, jolt.

bunch *n.* cluster, group, batch, lot, set.

bundle *n.* package, pack, parcel, packet, bunch, roll.

bungle *v.* botch, mismanage, muff, fumble, blunder *manage*.

burden *n.* 1. trial, trouble, sorrow *consolation* 2. cargo, freight, load, weight.

A burglar

burglar *n.* robber, thief.

burly *adj.* brawny, lusty, bulky, strong, strapping *frail*.

burn *v.* scorch, toast, consume, parch, flame, shrivel.

burst *v.* split, explode, break, crack, rend.

bury *v.* entomb, inter, hide, conceal, secrete *unearth* BERRY.

business *n.* 1. trade, traffic, industry, job, profession 2. office, company, firm.

bustle *v.* fuss, stir, fidget, rush, hurry.

busy *adj.* engaged, employed, diligent, active, brisk, occupied *lazy*, *idle*, *inactive*, *slack*.

buy *v.* purchase, acquire, get *sell* BY, BYE.

bygone *adj.* past, gone by *future*.

C

cab *n.* taxi, taxicab, carriage.

cabin *n.* 1. hut, shack, shed 2. berth, compartment.

cabinet *n.* 1. case, cupboard 2. closet, boudoir 3. council, committee.

cable *n.* rope, wire, line, hawser.

cackle *v.* laugh, giggle, snicker, titter, cluck, quack.

café *n.* coffeehouse, restaurant, bar.

cajole *v.* wheedle, flatter, coax, blandish, persuade *compel*.

cake 1. *v.* harden, solidify, concrete 2. *n.* pastry, bun, tart.

calamity *n.* mishap, accident, disaster, misfortune *blessing*.

calculate *v.* count, compute, reckon.

call *v.* 1. summon, send for invite *I'll call for you on the way home* *dismiss* 2. cry, shout, exclaim 3. term, christen, name.

calling *n.* job, business, profession.

callous *adj.* insensitive, unfeeling, hard *tender*, *merciful*.

calm 1. *adj.* quiet, placid, tranquil, still *disturbed*, *upset* 2. *n.* tranquility, placidity *A great calm settled over the land after the storm* *hubbub*, *turbulence* 3. *v.* soothe, pacify, appease *inflame*.

camouflage *n.* disguise, covering.

cancel *v.* 1. annul, put off, abolish 2. erase, delete, obliterate.

candid *adj.* blunt, frank, just, open, fair *devious*, *cunning*, *biased*.

candidate *n.* nominee, applicant, claimant.

canny *adj.* artful, wise *artless*.

canopy *n.* awning, shelter, cover.

capture

cap *n.* 1. hat, headgear, cover, lid 2. peak, head, top, crown.

capable *adj.* able, clever, competent, gifted *inept*, *incompetent*, *unskilled*.

capacity *n.* 1. content, volume 2. skill, cleverness, ability *incapacity*, *inability*.

cape *n.* 1. cloak 2. promontory, headland.

caper *v.* bound, dance, gambol, hop, skip, jump.

capital 1. *n.* initial letter 2. *n.* cash, money, outlay, wealth 3. *n.* main city 4. *adj.* good, excellent, prime.

capsize *v.* overturn, tip up, upset.

capsule *n.* sheath, pod, case, envelope.

captain *n.* skipper, chief, commander, leader.

caption *n.* chapter, title, heading, picture description, subtitle.

captivate *v.* fascinate, enchant, bewitch, charm.

captive *n.* hostage, prisoner.

capture *v.* grab, arrest, catch, seize, trap *release*, *free*, *liberate*.

A captured burglar

car

car *n.* automobile, streetcar, carriage, vehicle.

carcass *n.* corpse, body.

card *n.* board, sheet, stiff paper, playing card.

care 1. *n.* caution, heed, regard 2. *n.* concern, worry, anxiety 3. *n.* custody, charge, protection *The orphans were in the care of the city authorities* **neglect, indifference** 4. *v.* look after, mind.

career 1. *v.* rush, sweep, course, dash 2. *n.* job, profession, occupation, calling.

careful *adj.* cautious, attentive, discreet, watchful *careless*, *reckless*, *rash*.

careless *adj.* thoughtless, neglectful, rash, unconcerned, heedless, sloppy *careful*, *vigilant*, *scrupulous*.

carelessness *n.* inattention, neglect, negligence *caution*, *precaution*.

caress *v.* embrace, hug, fondle, stroke, kiss, cuddle *chastise*.

cargo *n.* load, freight, burden.

carnival *n.* festival, traveling show, fair.

carol *n.* hymn, song, ditty, chorus, lay.

carp *v.* criticize, cavil, find fault.

carriage *n.* coach, conveyance, vehicle.

carry *v.* bear, convey, transport, move.

carve *v.* sculpt, shape, whittle, chisel, engrave, cut.

cascade *n.* cataract, waterfall.

case *n.* 1. box, covering, capsule 2. action, lawsuit, process, trial.

cash *n.* coin, money, currency CACHE.

cashier 1. *n.* cashkeeper 2. *v.* discharge, dismiss, break *Because of his gambling debts, he was cashiered from the Army.*

casino *n.* gaming house, gambling hall.

cask *n.* barrel, keg, tun, butt.

cast 1. *v.* mold, shape, form, found 2. *v.* hurl, pitch, throw, fling, toss *The fishermen cast their nets into the sea* 3. *n.* actors, players *The new Broadway show has a large cast* CASTE.

castaway *n.* outcast, vagabond.

A castle

castle *n.* palace, château, fortress.

casual *adj.* 1. informal, occasional *formal* 2. accidental, chance *planned*, *regular*.

casualty *n.* accident, disaster, misfortune, calamity.

cataract *n.* 1. waterfall, cascade, fall 2. eye disease.

catastrophe *n.* misfortune, mishap, disaster, calamity *blessing*.

catch *v.* arrest, capture, grasp, seize, clutch, snatch *lose*, *free*, *release*.

catching *adj.* contagious, infectious.

category *n.* sort, kind, class, head, division, rank.

cause 1. *v.* bring about, originate, produce 2. *n.* reason, source, origin *The doctors were unable to find the cause of the outbreak* **result** 3. *n.* enterprise, undertaking CAWS.

caution *n.* 1. heed, care, wariness *rashness*, *carelessness* 2. advice, warning.

cautious *adj.* careful, watchful, wary, prudent *careless*, *foolhardy*.

cave *n.* cavern, hole, den, grotto, shelter.

cavity *n.* space, hollow, void, hole.

cease *v.* end, stop, terminate, finish, desist *start*, *begin*.

celebrate *v.* glorify, extol, keep, praise, observe *disregard*, *ignore*, *grieve*, *mourn*.

celebrity *n.* dignitary, VIP, notable, hero *nonentity*.

celebrated *adj.* famous, renowned, eminent *unknown*.

celibate *adj.* unmarried, single *married*.

cell *n.* room, chamber, den, cubicle, apartment SELL.

cellar *n.* basement, crypt, vault SELLER.

cement 1. *n.* adhesive, mortar 2. *v.* stick, join, attach, unite.

cemetery *n.* graveyard, churchyard, necropolis.

censor *n.* critic, inspector, examiner, snoop, inquisitor CENSER.

censure *v.* reprove, blame, chide, criticize, reproach *praise*, *approve*, *applaud*, *forgive*.

center *n.* middle, heart, midst, midmost *edge*.

central *adj.* middle, chief, main, inner.

ceremonious *adj.* 1. formal, studied, precise, stiff 2. stately, lofty *informal*.

ceremony *n.* rite, pomp, formality, form, service.

certain *adj.* 1. sure, unfailing, positive, assured, confident *uncertain*, *doubtful*, *questionable* 2. particular, special *The birds fly back at certain times of the year.*

certainly *adv.* absolutely, plainly, surely, positively *doubtfully*.

certainty *n.* 1. assurance, surety, inevitability *chance* 2. truth, fact.

certificate *n.* testimonial, voucher, document.

chafe *v.* irritate, rub, vex, annoy *soothe*.

chaff 1. *v.* mock, jeer, scoff, ridicule 2. *n.* rubbish, refuse.

chain *n.* fetter, shackle, manacle, link, bond.

chair *n.* seat, stool, bench.

challenge *v.* dare, defy, brave, threaten.

chamber *n.* room, hall, apartment, cavity, hollow, cell.

champion *n.* protector, winner, victor, defender *loser*.

chance *n.* 1. opportunity, occasion, accident, fate 2. risk, hazard *certainty*.

change *v.* 1. alter, vary, modify *endure*, *remain* 2. replace, barter, exchange.

changeable *adj.* variable, unstable, fickle, fitful *steady*.

channel *n.* duct, conduit, passage, canal, furrow, strait, groove.

chant *v.* sing, recite, intone, warble.

chaos *n.* turmoil, disorder, confusion *order*, *tidiness*.

chaotic *adj.* disordered, confused, muddled, messy *tranquil*, *ordered*, *neat*, *tidy*.

chap 1. *n.* fellow, lad, boy, youth 2. *v.* crack, split, cleave *Wearing gloves will prevent chapped hands during cold weather.*

chapter *n.* 1. period of time 2. book section 3. society branch.

char *v.* singe, scorch, burn.

character *n.* 1. sign, symbol, emblem, letter, mark 2. quality, nature, disposition, reputation *I'll give you a letter which says that you are a person of character* 3. person, individual.

characteristic

characteristic 1. *n*. feature, quality, peculiarity, trait 2. *adj*. special, peculiar, typical, distinctive.

charge 1. *v*. attack, assault *retreat*, *flee* 2. *v*. blame, accuse 3. *n*. cost, price.

charitable *adj*. generous, considerate, kind, liberal *mean*, *stingy*, *petty*.

charity *n*. kindness, goodness, good nature, love *selfishness*.

charm 1. *n*. amulet, talisman, trinket 2. *v*. enchant, delight, attract, fascinate *repulse*, *repel*.

charming *adj*. fascinating, captivating, bewitching, delightful *repulsive*.

chart *n*. map, diagram, plan.

charter 1. *v*. let, hire 2. *n*. bond, deed, right, privilege.

chase *v*. follow, pursue, track, hunt *abandon*.

chaste *adj*. virtuous, innocent, modest, pure *corrupt*, *impure*, *wanton* CHASED.

chastise *v*. beat, punish, flog, whip.

chat *v*. talk, gossip, chatter, prattle.

cheap *adj*. inexpensive, low-cost, inferior, paltry *costly*, *expensive*, *dear* CHEEP.

cheat 1. *n*. trickster, rogue, knave, impostor 2. *v*.defraud, swindle, deceive.

check *v*. curb, hinder, obstruct, halt, restrain *advance*, *continue*.

cheer *v*. 1. comfort, encourage *discourage*, *depress* 2. clap, yell, shout, applaud *hiss*.

cheerful *adj*. jolly, merry, happy, lively, glad *sad*, *gloomy*, *downhearted*, *blue*, *forlorn*.

cherish *v*. treasure, care for, support, value, prize *scorn*, *abandon*.

chest *n*. 1. box, case, trunk, casket 2. bosom, trunk.

chew *v*. gnaw, bite, masticate, munch.

chide *v*. scold, blame, reprove, rebuke *praise*, *commend*, *applaud*.

chief 1. *n*. leader, head, boss, commander 2. *adj*. main, head, leading, principal *minor*, *lesser*.

chiefly *adv*. mainly, principally, especially, mostly.

child *n*. baby, bairn, infant, brat, youngster *adult*.

chill *n*. cold, coldness, frigidity, coolness *heat*, *warmth*.

The chase

A big chest

chilly *adj.* cold, cool, brisk **warm**, **hot**.

chime *v.* ring, peal, sound.

chink *n.* crack, cranny, crevice, gap, opening.

chip *v.* cut, splinter, hew.

chirp *v.* twitter, tweet, cheep, warble.

chivalrous *adj.* noble, valiant, polite, courteous, gallant.

choice 1. *adj.* select, rare, fine, exquisite 2. *n.* pick, selection.

choke *v.* suffocate, smother, strangle, stifle.

choose *v.* pick, prefer, elect, select CHEWS.

chop *v.* cut, slice, mince, hew, fell.

chorus *n.* refrain, tune, melody, song, choir.

chronic *adj.* persistent, constant, deep-rooted.

chubby *adj.* plump, short, thick, round, buxom, stocky **skinny**.

chuck *v.* pitch, hurl, toss, throw.

chuckle *v.* laugh, titter, giggle.

chum *n.* comrade, pal, friend, companion.

chunk *n.* lump, piece, log.

church *n.* temple, chapel, kirk, meetinghouse.

churlish *adj.* brusque, impolite, rude, harsh **polite**, **civil**.

cipher *n.* 1. secret code 2. zero, naught, nothing.

circle *n.* 1. ring, disk, loop 2. group, class, set.

circuit *n.* course, tour, orbit, circle, journey.

circular 1. *adj.* round, annular, ring-shaped 2. *n.* handbill, leaflet, advertisement *Vacancies for the new job were made known by a circular sent around the firm.*

circulate *v.* spread, publish, diffuse, propagate, broadcast.

circumstances *n.* condition, situation, position, factors, background.

cistern *n.* reservoir, tank.

A little chirp

cite *v.* mention, refer, quote, name SIGHT, SITE.

citizen *n.* resident, townsman, inhabitant, dweller.

city *n.* town, metropolis, capital.

civil *adj.* 1. polite, courteous, obliging **impolite**, **rude** 2. public, political **military**.

civilization

civilization *n.* society, refinement, culture.

civilized *adj.* refined, educated, polished, well-behaved *savage*, *uncivilized*.

claim 1. *v.* ask, assert, declare, demand *waive* 2. *n.* right, title.

clammy *adj.* sticky, slimy.

clamor *n.* noise, uproar, din, hubbub *quiet*, *silence*.

clamp *v.* secure, cramp, fasten.

clan *n.* family, tribe, set, group.

clap *v.* applaud, acclaim, cheer.

clarify *v.* clear, purify, explain, define *pollute*, *confuse*, *bewilder*, *blur*.

clash *v.* 1. disagree, oppose, conflict 2. crash, collide.

clasp 1. *n.* hook, pin, brooch, buckle, catch 2. *v.* grip, clutch, hug, grasp.

class *n.* 1. order, set, rank, species 2. set, form.

classical *adj.* elegant, polished, refined, model, master.

classify *v.* order, sort, categorize, arrange, class.

clatter *n.* noise, din, clash, rattle.

claw *n.* talon, nail, hook.

clean 1. *v.* purify, cleanse, wash, scrub 2. *adj.* pure, unsoiled, clear *dirty*, *foul*, *impure*.

clear 1. *v.* free, loose, remove, empty 2. *adj.* lucid, obvious, evident, sure, certain *dubious*, *indistinct* 3. *adj.* unobstructed, free.

cleave *v.* 1. cling, stick, hold 2. divide, split, separate.

cleft *n.* fissure, rift, break, crevice, chink.

clemency *n.* mercy, mildness, leniency, gentleness *severity*.

clench *v.* clutch, seize, grasp, grip.

clever *adj.* apt, skillful, quick, expert, dextrous, smart, adroit *dull*, *stupid*, *dumb*.

client *n.* patron, customer.

cliff *n.* precipice, headland, crag.

climate *n.* weather, clime.

climax *n.* culmination, acme, top, summit *outset*.

climb *v.* ascend, mount, scramble, surmount CLIME.

Climbing high

cling *v.* clasp, grasp, stick, adhere, hold.

clip 1. *n.* fastener, clasp 2. *v.* snip, trim, cut, prune.

clique *n.* crowd, set, party, group.

cloak *n.* coat, wrap, mantle.

clock *n.* watch, timepiece, chronometer.

clod *n.* 1. lump, chunk 2. fool, dolt, dunce, oaf.

clog 1. *n.* wooden shoe, sabot 2. *v.* hinder, stop up, choke, obstruct.

close 1. *adj.* mean, stingy *generous* 2. *adj.* adjacent, close by, near *distant* 3. *adj.* stuffy, uncomfortable, oppressive *fresh* 4. *v.* shut, fasten *open* 5. *v.* end, cease, finish.

cloth *n.* fabric, material.

clothe *v.* attire, dress, cover, wrap.

cloudy *adj.* dim, obscure, murky, blurred, overcast *fair*.

clown *n.* fool, jester, buffoon, dunce, dolt.

club *n.* 1. society, set, company, clique 2. stick, bludgeon, cudgel.

clue *n.* sign, suggestion, hint, guide, lead CLEW.

clumsy *adj.* blundering, ungainly, unwieldy, awkward *deft*, *graceful*, *skillful*.

cluster *n.* bunch, group, clump.

clutch *v.* clasp, grasp, clench, seize, grab.

clutter *n.* disorder, jumble, mess.

coach 1. *v.* instruct, train, drill 2. *n.* vehicle, carriage, bus.

coarse *adj.* 1. rude, vulgar, gross, indelicate 2. impure, crude, rough *dainty*, *elegant*, *fine* COURSE.

coast *n.* beach, seaside, shore.

coat *n.* jacket, wrap, overcoat, layer.

coax *v.* flatter, wheedle, cajole, persuade *bully*, *coerce* COKES.

cock *n.* 1. male bird, rooster, 2. tap, valve, faucet.

coddle *v.* pamper, indulge, fondle, caress, spoil.

coerce *v.* drive, force, compel *coax*.

coffer *n.* casket, box, chest, case.

coil *v.* twist, loop, wind.

coin 1. *v.* invent, devise, create *Shakespeare was a writer who coined many new expressions* 2. *n.* cash, money.

coincidence *n.* concurrence, consistency, correspondence, chance.

cold *adj.* icy, chill, wintry, frosty, bleak, raw *hot*, *warm*.

collapse 1. *n.* failure, breakdown, downfall 2. *v.* fall, drop, subside *recover*.

collar *v.* nab, seize, capture.

colleague *n.* partner, associate, ally, companion, workmate *opponent*.

collect *v.* assemble, accumulate, amass, gather *disperse*, *scatter*.

collection *n.* gathering, cluster, store, group, pile.

college *n.* university, academy, school, institute.

collide *v.* crash, smash, strike.

color *n.* tint, hue, shade, pigment.

colossal *adj.* huge, immense, enormous, gigantic, vast *tiny*, *insignificant*.

column *n.* 1. article, feature 2. post, pillar, row.

combat *v.* battle, resist, fight, oppose.

combine *v.* join, blend, mix, unite *separate*, *divide*.

come *v.* arrive, reach, get to *go*, *leave*, *depart*.

comedy *n.* burlesque, humor, wit, farce, slapstick *tragedy*.

comfort 1. *n.* ease, relief, rest, enjoyment *discomfort* 2. *v.* cheer, soothe, gladden, console.

comfortable *adj.* pleasant, grateful, snug, convenient *uneasy*, *uncomfortable*.

comical *adj.* funny, humorous, droll, laughable, amusing *sad*, *tragic*.

command 1. *n.* decree, order, direction 2. *v.* govern, control, rule *obey*, *entreat*.

A coughing coffer

25

commemorate *v.* celebrate, solemnize, observe, honor, remember.

commence *v.* begin, originate, start *end*, *stop*, *finish*.

commend *v.* applaud, praise, recommend *blame*, *censure*, *criticize*.

comment *n.* note, remark, observation.

commerce *n.* trade, exchange, business, dealing.

commission *n.* 1. committee, council, board 2. fee, compensation.

commit *v.* do, perform, promise, enact, entrust.

committee *n.* board, council, commission.

commodity *n.* goods, merchandise, product.

common 1. *n.* green, park, field 2. *adj.* vulgar, usual, customary, ordinary, habitual *unusual*, *genteel*, *scarce*.

commonplace *adj.* ordinary, hackneyed, stale *unusual*, *distinctive*.

commotion *n.* noise, turmoil, bustle, upheaval, fuss, rumpus, stir *calm*.

communicate *v.* give, bestow, disclose, reveal, impart *conceal*, *withhold*.

community *n.* society, group, district, association.

commuter *n.* traveler, passenger.

compact 1. *n.* agreement, pact, contract 2. *adj.* dense, firm, solid, compressed *loose*, *slack*.

companion *n.* fellow, partner, comrade, associate, colleague.

company *n.* party, society, group, firm, business.

comparable *adj.* like, relative, alike *incomparable*, *different*.

compare *v.* contrast, match, liken.

compartment *n.* division, section, part.

compassion *n.* tenderness, understanding, sympathy, kindness *harshness*.

compassionate *adj.* tender, kind, merciful, clement *harsh*.

compatible *adj.* consistent, accordant, harmonious *incompatible*.

compel *v.* coerce, force, oblige, impel *coax*, *wheedle*, *cajole*.

compensate *v.* recompense, make up for, reimburse, reward.

compete *v.* contend, contest, rival.

competent *adj.* capable, able, suitable, fit, qualified *inept*, *awkward*.

competition *n.* rivalry, tournament, contest.

compile *v.* compose, prepare, combine, gather.

complacent *adj.* contented, smug, satisfied, gratified *dissatisfied*.

complain *v.* protest, lament, grumble, moan *rejoice*.

complaint *n.* 1. disease, ailment, malady 2. accusation, murmur, lamentation.

complement *n.* quota, completeness, fulfillment COMPLIMENT.

complete 1. *adj.* total, full, whole *partial*, *incomplete* 2. *v.* perfect, execute, achieve, finish.

complex 1. *n.* organization, network *Outside the town a large complex of roads had grown up* 2. *adj.* tangled, complicated, intricate, involved *simple*.

complicate *v.* involve, confuse, entangle *simplify*.

complicated *adj.* complex, involved, intricate *simple*, *rudimentary*.

compliment *n.* congratulation, praise, approval, admiration *insult* COMPLEMENT.

complimentary *adj.* flattering, laudatory, commendatory *derogatory*.

comply with *v.* agree to, consent to, satisfy, observe, fulfill *refuse*.

compose *v.* 1. quell, pacify, quiet, calm 2. write, make up, invent.

composed *adj.* calm, quiet, unruffled, placid, sedate *frantic*, *agitated*.

composure *n.* quiet, calm, self-possession, calmness *embarrassment*.

compound 1. *n.* mixture, composition *Gunpowder is a compound of several different chemicals* 2. *v.* mingle, mix, blend, combine 3. *adj.* complex, complicated.

comprehend *v.* understand, perceive, grasp *misunderstand*.

comprehensive *adj.* complete, broad, full, extensive *partial*, *incomplete*.

compress *v.* condense, squeeze, press, abridge *expand*, *stretch*.

comprise *v.* include, embrace, contain, consist of, enclose *exclude*.

compromise *v.* 1. imperil, jeopardize, endanger 2. settle, agree, adjust *differ*.

compulsory *adj.* enforced, obligatory, necessary *optional*, *voluntary*.

compute *v.* calculate, estimate, reckon, count, figure.

computer *n.* calculator, word processor, microprocessor.

comrade *n.* colleague, companion, friend, fellow, pal *enemy*.

concave *adj.* hollow, hollowed, depressed *convex*.

conceal *v.* secrete, hide, bury, cover up, cover *reveal*, *display*.

concede *v.* yield, grant, surrender, admit *deny*, *dispute*.

conceit *n.* vanity, egotism, priggery, self-esteem *modesty*.

conceited *adj.* arrogant, vain, smug, proud, opinionated *modest*.

conceive *v.* create, invent, imagine, contrive, devise *misconceive*.

concentrate *v.* 1. focus, engross, centralize *distract* 2. reduce, condense, localize.

concept *n.* notion, idea, theory, opinion.

concern 1. *n.* matter, consequence, affair 2. *n.* business, company, firm *He was president of a large steel concern* 3. *v.* trouble, disturb, disquiet 4. *v.* interest, affect, touch.

concerning *prep.* about, regarding, respecting.

concert *n.* recital, performance, agreement.

concerted *adj.* together, united, joint.

conciliate *v.* appease, reconcile, restrain, pacify *estrange*.

concise *adj.* terse, pithy, brief, condensed, short *diffuse*, *rambling*.

A computer

27

conclude

conclude *v.* 1. determine, presume, understand, judge 2. finish, end, terminate, stop.

conclusion *n.* 1. end, termination, finish 2. judgment, completion, settlement.

concoct *v.* contrive, invent, devise, plan.

concord *n.* peace, harmony, agreement, friendship *discord*.

concrete *adj.* firm, real, solid, definite *abstract*.

concur *v.* agree, harmonize, combine, coincide *disagree*.

condone *v.* forgive, overlook, pardon *punish*.

conduct 1. *n.* behavior, actions, manner 2. *v.* direct, guide, manage, lead, escort.

confederation *n.* alliance, union, league, coalition.

confer *v.* 1. converse, discuss, consult 2. give, grant, bestow.

conference *n.* meeting, convention, consultation, interview, council.

confess *v.* own up, admit, concede, acknowledge *deny*.

confide *v.* entrust *mistrust*.

Concurring

Conquering

concussion *n.* clash, crash, shock, agitation, head injury.

condemn *v.* sentence, blame, disapprove, judge, convict *pardon*, *excuse*, *absolve*.

condense *v.* concentrate, compress, compact, reduce, abbreviate, abridge *expand*, *enlarge*, *increase*.

condition *n.* state, situation, predicament, case, plight.

confident *adj.* certain, positive, sure, assured *uncertain*, *shy*.

confidential *adj.* private, secret, intimate *open*, *public*.

confine *v.* shut up, restrict, keep in, imprison *release*, *free*, *liberate*.

confirm *v.* verify, assure, corroborate, strengthen *disclaim*, *deny*.

confiscate *v.* appropriate, seize, distrain, take.

conflict 1. *v.* interfere, oppose, clash, differ 2. *n.* fight, battle, struggle *agreement*, *harmony*.

conform *v.* comply, yield, submit, tally, agree, obey *rebel*, *disagree*.

confound *v.* bewilder, mystify, perplex, embarrass, puzzle.

confront *v.* oppose, face, challenge, threaten.

confuse *v.* perplex, mix up, mislead, disorder, bewilder, mystify, puzzle *clarify*, *enlighten*.

congeal *v.* thicken, clot, solidify, freeze *melt*, *soften*.

congenial *adj.* agreeable, suited, favorable, pleasant *disagreeable*.

congested *adj.* crowded, dense, blocked, full, thick *empty*.

congratulate *v.* compliment, acclaim, praise, flatter.

congregate *v.* meet, assemble, gather, convene *disperse*, *scatter*.

congress *n.* conference, convention, meeting, assembly, council.

conjecture *n.* guess, supposition, theory.

conjuror *n.* wizard, magician, sorcerer.

connect *v.* link, join, combine, couple *separate*.

connection *n.* union, alliance, communication, relationship.

conquer *v.* defeat, beat, overcome, overthrow, vanquish *surrender*.

conquest *n.* victory, triumph.

conscientious *adj.* scrupulous, honest, diligent, fair *careless*.

conscious *adj.* awake, alive, alert, aware *unaware*, *insensible*.

consecutive *adj.* successive, continuous, serial *irregular*, *random*.

consent 1. *n.* permission, approval, agreement 2. *v.* agree, assent, approve *disagreement*, *refusal*.

consequence *n.* result, effect, outcome.

conservative *adj.* careful, cautious, moderate *reckless*, *rash*.

conserve *v.* protect, maintain, preserve, save, keep *squander*.

consider *v.* contemplate, ponder, examine, study *ignore*.

considerable *adj.* worthwhile, respectable, a good deal of.

considerate *adj.* thoughtful, polite, patient, charitable *selfish*.

consist *v.* contain, comprise, compose, constitute.

consistent *adj.* suitable, compatible, harmonious *erratic*.

consolation *n.* sympathy, solace, comfort *burden*.

consolidate *v.* unite, combine.

consort *n.* partner, companion, associate, spouse.

conspicuous *adj.* outstanding, apparent, prominent, noticeable *inconspicuous*.

conspiracy *n.* intrigue, plot, scheme.

constant *adj.* 1. unchanging, permanent, stable *The factory received a constant supply of basic materials* **occasional** 2. true, loyal, faithful *fickle*.

consternation *n.* dismay, fright, alarm, terror, horror, dread *equanimity*.

constitute *v.* establish, compose, set up, form *dissolve*.

constitution *n.* 1. law, code, formation, organization *The new constitution of the country allowed the President to rule for five years* 2. health, temperament, spirit.

constrain *v.* 1. restrain, confine, curb 2. force, drive, compel, oblige, urge *release*.

constrict *v.* compress, cramp, contract, squeeze, crush.

construct *v.* erect, raise, build, fabricate *destroy*, *demolish*.

consult *v.* discuss, ask, confer, deliberate.

consume *v.* 1. destroy, exhaust, burn *The factory was entirely consumed by fire* 2. devour, eat.

contact *v.* touch, connect, join, reach, approach.

contagious *adj.* catching, infectious.

contain *v.* include, comprise, embody.

contaminate *v.* taint, infect, defile, pollute, corrupt.

contemplate *v.* ponder, study, survey, consider.

contempt *n.* disdain, derision, scorn, mockery *respect*, *awe*.

contend *v.* 1. maintain, claim, assert, affirm 2. fight, combat, dispute *disclaim*.

content 1. *n.* satisfaction 2. *v.* satisfy, appease 3. *adj.* happy, pleased, satisfied *discontented*.

contest 1. *v.* dispute, oppose, argue 2. *n.* controversy, dispute, debate, competition.

continual *adj.* perpetual, endless, incessant *intermittent*.

continue *v.* persist, carry on, proceed, endure, last *interrupt*.

contort *v.* distort, deform, twist, writhe *straighten*.

contract 1. *n.* agreement, bargain, treaty, pact 2. *v.* diminish, shrink, shorten, lessen *expand* 3. *v.* acquire, take, get.

contradict *v.* dispute, challenge, deny, oppose, disagree *agree*.

contrary *adj.* perverse, disagreeable, opposed, stubborn conflicting *agreeable*.

contrast 1. *v.* differ, distinguish, compare, match 2. *n.* difference, opposition *agreement*.

contribute *v.* donate, supply, give, grant, bestow *deny*.

contribution *n.* donation, offering.

contrite *adj.* humble, penitent, sorry, repentant.

contrive *v.* invent, devise, form, scheme, plot, plan.

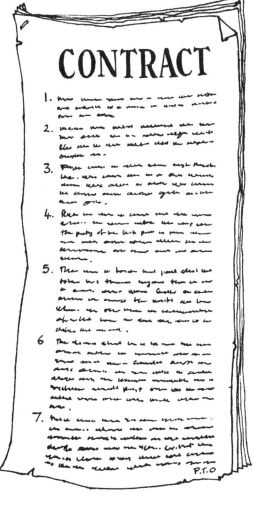

control 1. *n.* command, direction, mastery 2. *v.* manage, regulate, rule, direct.

controversy *n.* argument, dispute, debate, quarrel *agreement*.

convene *v.* muster, congregate, meet, assemble, gather *disband*, *disperse*.

convenience *n.* accessibility, suitability, advantage, benefit.

convenient *adj.* suited, appropriate, proper *awkward*.

convent *n.* nunnery, abbey, priory.

convention *n.* 1. custom, practice *It is a convention that men's suits have buttons on the right* 2. meeting, assembly, conference.

conventional *adj.* usual, customary, common, normal, regular *informal*.

converge *v.* meet, unite, join *diverge*.

converse *v.* talk, discuss, speak about, communicate.

convert *v.* transform, change, alter.

convex *adj.* protruberant *concave*.

convey *v.* bear, bring, transmit, transport, carry.

conveyance *n.* vehicle, carriage, transport.

convict 1. *n.* criminal, felon, prisoner 2. *v.* sentence, find guilty *acquit*.

convince *v.* prove, persuade, demonstrate.

convulse *v.* shake, disturb, agitate.

cook *v.* heat, grill, fry, boil, broil, stew, simmer, roast.

cool *adj.* 1. calm, quiet, composed, collected *fiery* 2. frigid, chilly, cold *hot*, *warm*.

cooperate *v.* collaborate, united, combine *oppose*.

coordinate *v.* arrange, harmonize, organize.

cope *v.* endure, manage.

copious *adj.* plentiful, ample, profuse, abundant *scanty*.

copse *n.* coppice, grove, thicket.

copy *v.* reproduce, duplicate, imitate.

cord *n.* line, rope, string, CHORD.

cordial 1. *n.* liqueur, juice, essence 2. *adj.* ardent, affectionate, earnest, sincere, hearty *hostile*.

core *n.* heart, kernel CORPS.

corn *n.* cereal, maize, grain.

corner *n.* bend, angle, nook, recess, niche.

corpse *n.* carcass, body.

corpulent *adj.* fat, fleshy, plump, rotund, portly *thin*.

correct 1. *v.* rectify, amend, put right 2. *adj.* precise, right, faultless, accurate, true *wrong*, *erroneous*.

correction *n.* amendment, improvement, redress *error*.

correspond *v.* 1. write, communicate 2. agree, suit, fit.

corridor *n.* hall, passage, gallery.

corroborate *v.* confirm, agree, support, strengthen, establish.

corrode *v.* erode, wear, rust.

corrupt 1. *v.* bribe, deprave, entice 2. *adj.* wicked, evil, dishonest, crooked *honest*, *upright*.

cost *n.* 1. damage, suffering, sacrifice *The army took the town at the cost of many men's lives* 2. price, expense, outlay, charge, value.

costly *adj.* dear, expensive, sumptuous, rich *cheap*.

costume *n.* uniform, dress.

cot *n.* bed.

couch *n.* sofa, settee, ottoman, chaise longue.

council *n.* committee, meeting, conference, assembly COUNSEL.

counsel *n.* 1. opinion, suggestion, advice 2. lawyer, advocate, attorney COUNCIL.

count *v.* reckon, estimate, calculate, add up.

counter 1. *n.* table, board, bench 2. *n.* token, chip, disk 3. *prep.* against, contrary, anti.

counteract *v.* oppose, resist, thwart, contravene *aid*.

counterfeit *adj.* fake, bogus, false, spurious, forged *genuine*, *authentic*.

countless *adj.* many, unlimited, innumerable, endless *few*, *limited*.

country 1. *n.* state, fatherland, nation 2. *adj.* rustic, rural *urban*.

couple *n.* brace, pair, two.

coupon *n.* slip, ticket, certificate.

courage *n.* valor, gallantry, fearlessness, bravery *cowardice*, *fear*.

courageous *adj.* fearless, gallant, brave, daring, valorous *cowardly*.

courier *n.* messenger, runner.

course *n.* 1. way, road, route, track 2. passage, advance, progress COARSE.

court 1. *v.* flatter, woo, make love to 2. *n.* tribunal, justice 3. *n.* courtyard, yard, square, plaza.

courteous *adj.* polite, affable, civil, respectful *rude*, *impolite*.

courtesy *n.* respect, politeness, civility *rudeness*, *discourtesy*.

covenant *n.* treaty, agreement, contract, pledge.

cover *v.* 1. hide, secrete, conceal, mask 2. comprise, include, embrace *The insurance policy covers all losses while you travel abroad* 3. disguise, cloak, screen *expose*, *reveal*.

covert *adj.* hidden, covered, secret, concealed *open*, *revealed*.

covet *v.* hanker after, long for, desire *despise*.

cow 1. *n.* female ox 2. *v.* overawe, frighten, intimidate, abash.

coward *n.* dastard, weakling, poltroon, milksop, shirker, sneak, faint heart *hero*, *champion*, *daredevil*, *desperado* COWERED.

cowardice *n.* fear, timidity *courage*, *pluck*, *valor*.

cowardly *adj.* fearful, timid, timorous, base, chicken-hearted, craven *brave*, *dauntless*, *heroic*, *plucky*, *valiant*.

cower *v.* cringe, crouch, stoop, flinch.

coy *adj.* bashful, modest, timid, shy *bold*, *brash*.

cozy *adj.* snug, warm, comfortable *unpleasant*.

crack 1. *n.* chink, crevice, fissure, cleft 2. *v.* split, snap, crack, break.

craft *n.* 1. guile, deceit, cunning *openness*, *frankness*, *artlessness* 2. art, trade, occupation, handicraft 3. ability, skill, expertise, expertness, talent.

cram *v.* fill, ram, press, stuff.

cramp 1. *v.* restrict, restrain 2. *n.* spasm, pain, crick.

crank *n.* fanatic, faddist *He is a food crank, and will only eat brown-colored eggs* 2. bend, turn, turning handle.

cranny *n.* nook, cleft, fissure, crack.

crash *v.* smash, splinter, shatter.

crass *adj.* raw, stupid, gross, coarse.

crate *n.* case, container, box, hamper.

crave *v.* desire, hunger for, beg, entreat *renounce*, *relinquish*.

crazy *adj.* mad, insane, lunatic *sane*, *rational*, *lucid*.

crease *n.* pleat, fold, furrow, wrinkle.

create *v.* make, originate, form, produce *destroy*, *obliterate*.

creation *n.* invention, origination *destruction*.

creature *n.* being, animal, brute, person.

credible *adj.* trustworthy, believable, reliable *incredible*.

credit 1. *n.* trust, faith, belief 2. *n.* esteem, reputation, regard 3. *n.* honor, praise, merit 4. *v.* believe, have faith in *discredit* 5. *v.* enter on credit side.

credulous *adj.* easily convinced, overtrustful *skeptical*.

creed *n.* faith, dogma, belief.

creek *n.* bay, bight, inlet, cove CREAK.

creep *v.* crawl, cringe, glide, fawn.

crestfallen *adj.* dejected, depressed, discouraged, downcast *elated*.

crevice *n.* cleft, crack, fissure, chink, gap.

crew *n.* crowd, party, band, company, staff.

crib 1. *n.* cot, manger, bin 2. *v.* purloin, steal, pilfer *During the tests, she was able to crib the answers from her partner.*

crime *n.* offense, felony, sin.

criminal 1. *n.* culprit, crook, convict, felon 2. *adj.* unlawful, illegal *honest*.

cringe *v.* fawn, sneak, crouch.

cripple 1. *n.* paraplegic, invalid, disabled person 2. *v.* disable, maim, make lame, injure.

crisis *n.* climax, emergency, acme, height.

criterion *n.* test, standard, basis.

critical *adj.* 1. hazardous, risky, dangerous *safe* 2. carping, disapproving, faultfinding *praising* 3. crucial, decisive, important. *The timing of the new state laws is critical trivial.*

criticism *n.* objection, faultfinding, objection *praise*.

criticize *v.* examine, estimate, scold, judge, censor *applaud*, *commend*.

crony *n.* friend, pal, partner, chum.

crooked *adj.* 1. curved, distorted, bent *straight* 2. dishonest, criminal, unfair *honest*, *upright*.

crop 1. *n.* harvest 2. *v.* pluck, gather, shear, cut.

cross *v.* 1. intersect, traverse, go over 2. thwart, obstruct, hinder 3. interbreed, mingle 4. *adj.* peevish, testy, fretful *amiable*.

crouch *v.* stoop, cower, cringe, squat *stand*.

crow *v.* brag, boast, bluster.

A crowing crow

crowd *n.* herd, horde, mob, throng, multitude, mass.

crown *n.* 1. coronet, garland, circlet, chaplet, tiara 2. skull, head 3. summit, crest, top, peak.

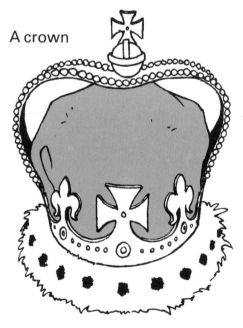

A crown

crucial *adj.* decisive, severe, searching, critical.

crude *adj.* coarse, immature, raw, uncooked, vulgar *elegant*.

cruel *adj.* savage, ferocious, brutal, inhuman, merciless *merciful*, *humane*, *compassionate*.

cruelty

cruelty *n.* inhumanity, barbarity, ferocity, brutality *mercy*, *pity*.

cruise *v.* voyage, sail, rove CREWS.

crumb *n.* fragment, morsel, particle, bit.

crumble *v.* disintegrate, crush, fall to pieces, perish, break up.

crumple *v.* crease, wrinkle, rumple.

crush *v.* squeeze, compress, squash, break, smash, conquer, subdue.

cry *v.* 1. weep, sob, shed tears *laugh* 2. call, shout, exclaim.

cuddle *v.* hug, fondle, embrace, snuggle, nestle.

cue *n.* intimation, suggestion, hint, lead 2. rod QUEUE.

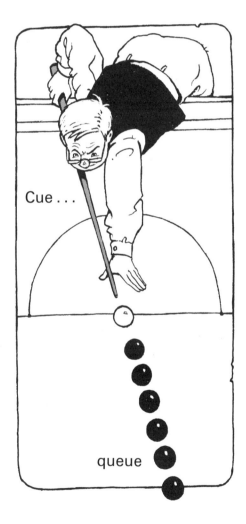

Cue . . .

queue

cull *v.* choose, pick, gather, select.

culminate *v.* terminate, end, reach highest point *defeat*.

culprit *n.* criminal, malefactor, offender, felon *hero*.

cult *n.* 1. fashion, fad, craze 2. homage, worship, sect.

cultivate *v.* 1. farm, till, work 2. improve, educate, train.

cultivated *adj.* educated, refined, cultured *savage*, *crude*, *primitive*.

culture *n.* breeding, refinement, civilization.

cumbersome *adj.* clumsy, awkward, troublesome, unwieldy *light*.

cunning *adj.* sly, wily, crafty, artful, shrewd *simple*, *naive*, *ingenuous*.

cup *n.* bowl, beaker, mug, vessel.

cupboard *n.* cabinet.

curb *v.* control, check, restrain, hold back *encourage*, *foster*.

cure 1. *v.* restore, heal, preserve 2. *n.* remedy, treatment, antidote.

curious *adj.* 1. inquisitive, prying, nosy 2. unusual, strange, odd, peculiar, unique.

curl *n.* twist, curve, coil.

current 1. *n.* course, stream, tide 2. *adj.* common, general, present *obsolete* CURRANT.

curse 1. *n.* malediction, oath 2. *v.* damn, condemn, denounce, swear *bless*.

cursed *adj.* blighted, banned, damned, detestable, hateful *fortunate*.

curt *adj.* terse, rude, tart, short, brief, off-hand.

curtail *v.* shorten, abridge, cut short, diminish, lessen.

curve *v. & n.* twist, turn, bend.

cushion *n.* support, bolster, bag, pillow.

custom *n.* fashion, practice, rule, usage, habit.

customary *adj.* usual, common, habitual, conventional **rare**, **unusual**.

customer *n.* client, purchaser, buyer, patron.

cut *v.* 1. slice, sever, cleave 2. wound, hurt, gash 3. chop, lop, crop 4. decrease, reduce.

cute *adj.* 1. clever, smart, shrewd 2. charming, appealing, delightful **dull**, **unattractive**.

cycle *n.* 1. circle, period, revolution 2. bike, bicycle.

Cycle

cynical *adj.* sarcastic, sneering, scornful, waspish, mocking.

dabble *v.* 1. meddle, trifle, tamper 2. spatter, wet, sprinkle.

dagger *n.* blade, knife, stiletto, dirk.

dainty *adj.* elegant, neat, delicate, small, pretty **clumsy**, **coarse**.

dally *v.* trifle, dawdle, idle, waste time, loiter **hustle**.

damage *n.* harm, mischief, loss, injury **reparation**.

dame *n.* mistress, lady, matron, madam.

damn *v.* curse, judge, condemn, doom **bless**.

damp 1. *v.* dampen, moisten 2. *adj.* moist, humid, wet, dank **dry**, **arid**.

dance *v. & n.* caper, hop, waltz, glide, jive.

dandy 1. *adj.* good, great, nifty 2. *n.* beau, swell, fop.

danger *n.* peril, jeopardy, risk, hazard **safety**.

dangerous *adj.* risky, perilous, unsafe, hazardous **safe**, **secure**, **harmless**.

dangle *v.* hang, sway, swing.

dank *adj.* damp, wet, moist.

dare *v.* risk, defy, brave, challenge **cower**.

daring *adj.* brave, fearless, bold, adventurous **afraid**.

dark *adj.* shadowy, murky, dusky, shady, overcast **light**, **bright**, **sunny**.

darken *v.* obscure, cloud, shade, blacken, dim **lighten**, **brighten**.

darling *n.* beloved, dear, precious, favorite, pet.

dart 1. *n.* arrow, missile 2. *v.* emit, shoot, hurl, throw, run, hurry.

dash *v.* 1. run, rush, dart 2. smash, break, strike.

date *n.* time, era, epoch, age.

dated *adj.* old, antiquated, veteran, vintage, archaic **recent**.

daub *v.* plaster, smear, cover, smirch.

daunt *v.* thwart, deter, tame, intimidate, frighten **encourage**.

dauntless *adj.* gallant, valiant, fearless, intrepid **timid**, **cowardly**, **fearful**.

dawdle

dawdle *v.* linger, idle, lag, dally, loiter *hurry*.

dawn *n.* sunrise, daybreak *sunset*, *nightfall*, *dusk*.

day *n.* daytime, sunshine, daylight *night*.

daze *v.* confuse, blind, bewilder, dazzle DAYS.

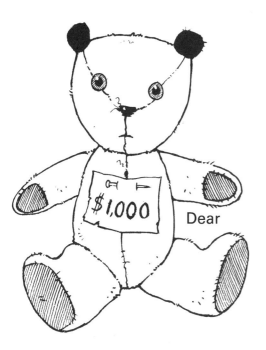

Dear

Deer

dazzle *v.* 1. glow, glare, shine 2. confound, surprise, daze, astonish.

dead *adj.* 1. inert, dull, flat 2. lifeless, deceased *alive*.

deadly *adj.* lethal, fatal, mortal, murderous *vital*.

deaf *adj.* unhearing, heedless, regardless *conscious*, *aware*.

deal *v.* 1. trade, traffic, have commerce 2. allot, divide, distribute, give.

dear *adj.* 1. expensive, high-priced, costly *cheap* 2. beloved, darling, precious *hateful* DEER.

death *n.* decease, demise, extinction *life*, *birth*.

debate *n.* dispute, argument, discussion *agreement*.

debt *n.* due, obligation, debit, liability.

decay *v.* decline, waste, perish, rot, spoil, decompose *flourish*.

deceive *v.* delude, dupe, trick, fool.

decelerate *v.* slow down, ease up, slacken, relax *accelerate*.

decent *adj.* fit, seemly, proper, respectable, becoming *improper*.

deception *n.* deceit, fraud, guile, trickery, treachery *honesty*.

decide *v.* determine, choose, settle, conclude, resolve *hesitate*.

decision *n.* settlement, conclusion, judgment, determination.

declare *v.* say, state, affirm, assert, aver *deny*.

decline 1. *n.* incline, slope, descent 2. *v.* reject, refuse, avoid, turn down, deteriorate *agree*, *accept*, *improve*, *prosper*.

decompose *v.* decay, rot, putrefy, corrupt, crumble.

decorate *v.* adorn, ornament, deck, paint, beautify *spoil*, *deface*.

decoy 1. *v.* entice, tempt, allure, lure *guide* 2. *n.* bait, lure.

decrease *v.* dwindle, diminish, lessen, wane *increase*, *expand*.

decree *n.* law, edict, regulation, order.

dedicate *v.* consecrate, devote, sanctify, hallow.

deduct *v.* subtract, remove, take away, withdraw *add*, *increase*.

deed *n.* 1. policy, indenture, title 2. action, performance, feat, act, achievement.

deep *adj.* 1. profound, bottom, low 2. wise, sagacious, shrewd *shallow*.

deface *v.* spoil, mar, soil, disfigure, deform *beautify*, *adorn*.

defeat *v.* conquer, overcome, beat, frustrate *submit*, *yield*.

defect 1. *v.* abandon, leave, desert 2. *n.* blemish, fault, weakness, flaw.

defective *adj.* deficient, inadequate, incomplete, imperfect *flawless*.

defend *v.* protect, shield, guard *attack*, *assault*.

defense *n.* guard, bulwark, protection.

defer *v.* delay, postpone, put off *hurry*, *hasten*, *rush*.

defiant *adj.* obstinate, bold, resistant, courageous, daring *submissive*.

deficient *adj.* defective, insufficient, incomplete *complete*.

deficit *n.* shortage, shortfall, omission, lack *glut*, *surplus*.

defile *v.* dirty, stain, tarnish, soil, debase *purify*, *cleanse*.

define *v.* clarify, explain, describe, interpret.

definite *adj.* exact, fixed, certain, precise *indefinite*, *random*.

deflate *v.* dwindle, shrink, diminish, *inflate*.

deform *v.* mar, distort, deface, disfigure *improve*, *adorn*.

defraud *v.* trick, dupe, cheat, gull, hoodwink.

deft *adj.* skillful, expert, clever, apt, dexterous *clumsy*.

defy *v.* disobey, disregard, resist, flout *yield*, *submit*.

degrade *v.* dishonor, demote, disgrace, humiliate.

degree *n.* 1. award, honor, grade 2. stage, step, standard *Today is warm; a few degrees higher than yesterday.*

deign *v.* descend, condescend, stoop, grant, vouchsafe.

dejected *adj.* discouraged, downcast, depressed, dispirited, blue *cheerful*.

delay *v.* postpone, put off, defer, tarry, linger *advance*, *forward*, *quicken*.

delegate 1. *v.* nominate, appoint, authorize 2. *n.* deputy, representative.

delete *v.* cancel, erase, remove, efface *include*, *add*.

deliberate 1. *v.* consider, ponder, reflect, think 2. *adj.* careful, wary, cautious, planned *accidental*, *haphazard*.

delicate *adj.* frail, tender, soft, dainty *robust*, *strong*.

delicious *adj.* tasty, delectable, luscious, palatable *loathsome*.

delight *n.* pleasure, gladness, joy, ecstasy *revulsion*, *disgust*.

delightful *adj.* enchanting, pleasant, charming, ravishing *nasty*, *horrid*.

deliver *v.* 1. release, set free *confine* 2. convey, hand over, transfer *withhold*.

delude *v.* mislead, deceive, dupe, cheat *guide*.

deluge *n.* downpour, flood, inundation, overflow, torrent, storm.

delusion *n.* deception, fancy, fallacy, hallucination, trick.

delve *v.* dig, search, hunt.

demand *v.* request, ask, want, *answer*, *entreat*.

demolish *v.* raze, destroy, overthrow *build*, *erect*.

demon

demon *n*. fiend, spirit, devil, goblin **angel**.

demonstrate *v*. show, exhibit, prove, establish.

demote *v*. degrade, reduce, downgrade, debase **promote**.

demur *v*. 1. stop, waver, hesitate, pause 2. object, scruple, take exception **consent**.

demure *adj*. bashful, modest, prim, coy **bold**.

den *n*. retreat, cave, haunt.

denial *n*. contradiction, disavowal, disclaimer **offer**.

denote *v*. mean, signify, indicate, imply.

denounce *v*. blame, censure, condemn, accuse **commend**, **praise**, **acclaim**.

dense *adj*. 1. dull, stupid, foolish **clever** 2. compact, close, thick, condensed **sparse** DENTS.

dent *n*. notch, depression, indent, nick.

deny *v*. dispute, refute, refuse, contradict, renounce **admit**, **allow**.

depart *v*. 1. go away, leave, set out, vanish **arrive**, **stay** 2. die, decease, pass on.

department *n*. section, portion, part, branch.

dependent *adj*. sustained by, contingent, conditioned **independent** DEPENDANT.

depend on *v*. rely on, trust to, confide in, count upon.

depict *v*. portray, describe, paint, sketch, illustrate.

deplorable *adj*. regrettable, distressing, pitiable, sad.

deposit 1. *n*. hoard, store 2. *n*. pledge, stake 3. *v*. put, place, lay, lay down **withdraw**.

depot *n*. store, storehouse, warehouse, railroad station.

deprave *v*. pollute, demoralize, corrupt **improve**.

deprecate *v*. reproach, reprove, censure, inveigh against **brag**.

depreciate *v*. devalue, undervalue, deflate, reduce, lessen **appreciate**.

depress *v*. 1. dishearten, deject, discourage, sadden **cheer**, **exalt** 2. press, press down, lower.

depressed *adj*. disheartened, unhappy, sad, melancholy **elated**, **overjoyed**.

depression *n*. 1. recession, hard times, inactivity 2. hollow, dent, cavity 3. sadness, gloom, dejection.

deprive *v*. deny, refuse, divest, rob **supply**, **provide**.

depth *n*. profundity, deepness, profoundness **height**, **tallness**.

deputy *n*. representative, agent, delegate, envoy.

derange *v*. disorder, disjoint, upset **adjust**.

derelict *adj*. abandoned, dilapidated, left, forsaken.

deride *v*. laugh at, mock, jeer, ridicule **respect**.

derive *v*. obtain, procure, get, receive, deduce.

derogatory *adj*. unfavorable, offensive, disparaging, insulting **complimentary**.

descend *v*. sink, fall, drop, subside **ascend**, **mount**.

descendant *n*. offspring, family, progeny **ancestor**, **forefather**.

descent *n*. fall, drop, plunge, decline **rise**.

describe *v*. define, picture, characterize, detail, specify, depict, tell.

description *n*. narrative, report, explanation, account.

desert 1. *v*. leave, forsake, quit, abandon **accompany** 2. *adj*. desolate, barren, wild 3. *n*. wilderness, wasteland, wild, DESSERT.

deserted *adj*. abandoned, neglected, shunned, uninhabited.

deserve *v.* merit, be entitled to, be worthy of, be qualified for *forfeit*.

design 1. *n.* drawing, sketch, outline, pattern 2. *v.* devise, plan, concoct.

desirable *adj.* pleasing, attractive, captivating, agreeable *undesirable*.

desire *v.* crave, lust after, wish for, fancy *abhor*, *detest*.

desist *v.* stop, cease, halt, hold, *persevere*, *persist*.

desolate *adj.* lonely, solitary, empty, deserted.

despair *v.* surrender, give up, lose hope *hope*.

despairing *adj.* disconsolate, suicidal, dejected, downcast *hopeful*.

desperate *adj.* reckless, despairing, hopeless, despondent *calm*, *collected*.

despicable *adj.* worthless, mean, base, contemptible *admirable*, *worthy*.

despise *v.* disdain, scorn, spurn, ridicule *admire*, *like*, *revere*.

despite *prep.* notwithstanding, regardless of, in spite of.

despondent *adj.* dejected, melancholy, dispirited, sad *happy*, *jubilant*.

despot *n.* tyrant, oppressor, autocrat, dictator.

destination *n.* objective, goal, end, terminal *beginning*.

destiny *n.* fate, fortune, lot, doom.

destitute *adj.* poor, needy, distressed, penniless *wealthy*.

destroy *v.* ruin, demolish, wipe out, raze, finish *create*, *repair*, *start*.

destruction *n.* ruin, havoc, demolition, wreckage *creation*.

detach *v.* separate, sever, divide, unfasten *attach*, *connect*.

detail *n.* portion, part, item, feature.

detain *v.* retain, stop, delay, stay, retard *hurry*, *rush*, *forward*.

detect *v.* ascertain, discover, expose, track down, find out *conceal*.

deter *v.* hinder, discourage, prevent, restrain *encourage*, *impel*.

deteriorate *v.* decline, degenerate, worse, weaken *develop*.

determine *v.* 1. check, certify, find out 2. decide, settle, adjust *waver*.

deterrent *n.* snag, drawback, hindrance, impediment *incentive*.

Desert

Dessert

detest

detest *v.* loathe, hate, abominate, *like*, *love*, *admire*.

devastate *v.* destroy, despoil, wreck, ravage, pillage, sack *reconstruct*.

develop *v.* 1. reveal, disclose 2. expand, grow, flourish, increase *deteriorate*.

deviate *v.* diverge, turn aside, digress, err *continue*.

device *n.* invention, contrivance, instrument, machine, plan.

devil *n.* fiend, imp, demon, goblin, Satan, Lucifer *angel*.

devious *adj.* 1. indirect, roundabout, evasive 2. cunning, tricky, crafty, sly, *candid*, *forthright*, *frank*.

devise *v.* create, contrive, plan, invent, make up.

devoid *adj.* destitute, empty, vacant, bare *full*.

devote *v.* apply, assign, dedicate, give *withdraw*, *ignore*.

devoted *adj.* affectionate, ardent, attached, loving, faithful *faithless*.

devour *v.* gulp, gorge, swallow, gobble.

devout *adj.* pious, saintly, holy, religious *profane*.

diagram *n.* design, plan, sketch, drawing.

dial *n.* face, clock.

dialect *n.* speech, accent, tongue, language, vernacular.

dictate *v.* order, decree, speak, utter, direct.

die *v.* depart, perish, expire, wither *flourish*, *live* DYE.

differ *v.* 1. contrast, diverge, vary 2. disagree, oppose, argue *agree*.

difference *n.* variation, disagreement, contrast, diversity *similarity*, *accord*.

different *adj.* unalike, unlike, distinct, contrary, separate *similar*.

difficult *adj.* laborious, complicated, hard, complex *easy*, *simple*.

diffuse *adj.* lengthy, long, repetitive, rambling, vague *concise*, *terse*.

dig *v.* burrow, excavate, shovel, plow, scoop, delve.

digest *v.* 1. absorb, assimilate, dissolve 2. summarize, condense, compress *expand*.

digit *n.* figure, number, numeral, symbol, finger, toe.

Digits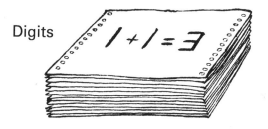

dignified *adj.* noble, majestic, grave, stately *lowly*.

dignity *n.* distinction, bearing, majesty, stateliness, presence *lowliness*.

dilapidated *adj.* shabby, decayed, ruined, battered, run down.

dilemma *n.* predicament, quandary, plight, uncertainty.

diligent *adj.* industrious, busy, active, hardworking, zealous *lazy*.

dilute *v.* weaken, thin, adulterate, reduce, water down.

dim *adj.* vague, pale, faint, weak, shadowy, unclear *bright*.

dimension *n.* measure, size, extent, proportions, gauge.

diminish *v.* reduce, shrink, lessen, decrease, condense *enlarge*, *increase*, *magnify*.

diminutive *adj.* small, tiny, little, puny *large*, *gigantic*.

din *n.* noise, sound, clamor, racket, uproar *quiet*.

dingy *adj.* dull, dusky, sullied, soiled, drab *bright*.

dip *v.* immerse, douse, plunge, dunk, wet.

diplomat *n.* envoy, ambassador, emissary, consul, attaché.

dire *adj.* dismal, dreadful, shocking, fearful, grim *harmless* DYER.

direct 1. *v.* aim, point, show 2. *v.* order, command, instruct 3. *adj.* plain, frank, straight, candid *dishonest*, *crooked*.

direction *n.* 1. guidance, control 2. course, way, bearing.

director *n.* controller, leader, manager, superintendent, guide.

dirt *n.* grime, soil, filth, muck, squalor *cleanliness*.

dirty *adj.* foul, filthy, soiled, unclean, grimy *clean*, *pure*.

disable *v.* cripple, paralyze, weaken, incapacitate, lame.

disadvantage *n.* handicap, drawback, defect, liability, inconvenience *advantage*.

disagree *v.* dispute, argue, oppose, differ, quarrel *agree*.

disagreeable *adj.* unpleasant, offensive, distasteful, unsavory *pleasant*.

disagreement *n.* misunderstanding, discord, conflict, opposition *accord*.

disappear *v.* dissolve, vanish, cease, fade *appear*.

disappoint *v.* foil, dissatisfy, frustrate, fail, let down, displease *please*.

disappointment *n.* failure, frustration, dissatisfaction, chagrin *satisfaction*.

disapproval *n.* dislike, displeasure, reproof, criticism *praise*.

disapprove *v.* remonstrate, censure, condemn, dislike, reject *praise*.

disarm *v.* 1. weaken, divest, disable, disband 2. calm, appease, reconcile.

disaster *n.* mishap, misfortune, catastrophe, calamity *blessing*.

disbelief *n.* distrust, doubt, skepticism, scorn *faith*.

discard *v.* scrap, throw away, reject, get rid of *keep*, *employ*.

discern *v.* perceive, see, discover, distinguish, behold *ignore*.

discharge *v.* 1. dismiss, oust, fire *employ* 2. emit, eject, expel 3. fulfill, perform, accomplish 4. unload, remove, free.

disciple *n.* supporter, follower, student, pupil *leader*.

discipline *n.* training, regime, coaching, practice, routine.

disclaim *v.* renounce, reject, forswear, disown, disinherit *confirm*.

disclose *v.* reveal, betray, uncover, show, expose *hide*, *conceal*.

discomfort *n.* nuisance, pest, trial, tribulation, handicap *comfort*, *pleasure*.

disconcert *v.* defeat, balk, frustrate, upset *compose*, *calm*.

disconnect *v.* disjoin, sever, separate, detach *connect*, *attach*.

disconsolate *adj.* desolate, cheerless, melancholy, forlorn *joyous*, *cheerful*.

discontent *n.* uneasiness, restlessness, dissatisfaction *satisfaction*.

discontinue *v.* cease, interrupt, stop *begin*, *start*, *launch*.

discord *n.* conflict, disagreement, strife *accord*, *agreement*, *harmony*.

discordant *adj.* tuneless, harsh, strident, shrill, opposed *harmonious*, *melodious*.

discount *n.* rebate, reduction, allowance *premium*.

discourage *v.* depress, deject, dishearten, daunt *encourage*, *inspire*.

discourteous *adj.* impolite, rude, ill-bred, uncivil *courteous*, *gracious*.

discover *v.* learn, find, find out, reveal *conceal*, *hide*, *mislay*.

discreet

discreet *adj.* wise, cautious, prudent, tactful *careless*, *rash* DISCRETE.

discriminate *v.* discern, distinguish, judge, segregate.

discuss *v.* consider, debate, deliberate.

discussion *n.* dispute, debate, conference, talk.

disdain *n.* arrogance, scorn, contempt *admiration*, *honor*.

disease *n.* sickness, malady, ailment, illness.

disfigure *v.* deface, blemish, deform, injure, scar *adorn*.

disgrace *n.* shame, dishonor, disfavor, infamy, scandal *honor*, *esteem*.

disguise *v.* hide, camouflage, conceal, mask, *display*, *show*.

disgust 1. *v.* displease, offend, revolt *delight* 2. *n.* distaste, nausea, loathing *liking*, *admiration*.

dish *n.* 1. food, course, meal 2. plate, bowl, container, platter.

dislike *v.* hate, loathe, disapprove, disfavor *like*.

disloyal *adj.* faithless, false, treacherous *loyal*.

dismal *adj.* gloomy, cheerless, dark, dull *cheerful*, *glad*.

dismantle *v.* strip, take apart, demolish, raze *equip*.

dismay *n.* fright, terror, dread, fear *assurance*.

dismiss *v.* discharge, release, discard, send away *engage*, *hire*.

disobey *v.* defy, ignore, disregard, neglect *keep*, *obey*.

disorder *n.* turmoil, confusion, disarray, disturbance *order*.

dispense *v.* distribute, deal out, administer, allot.

disperse *v.* separate, diffuse, scatter *collect*, *assemble*.

display 1. *n.* exhibition, show, parade, pageant 2. *v.* show, parade, exhibit *disguise*, *conceal*, *hide*.

A dish

A dish

dishearten *v.* dismay, unnerve, discourage, dispirit *gladden*.

disheveled *adj.* muddled, untidy, disordered, loose *tidy*, *neat*.

dishonest *adj.* crooked, false, corrupt, fraudulent *honest*, *frank*.

disintegrate *v.* decay, crumble, separate.

disk *n.* counter, coin, token, plate.

dispose *v.* order, array, arrange, regulate.

dispose of *v.* sell, get rid of, discard.

disposition *n.* nature, temperament, character, temper.

disprove *v.* deny, refute, discredit, rebut *prove*, *witness*.

dispute 1. *v.* discuss, bicker, argue *concede* 2. *n.* argument, debate, quarrel *agreement*.

dodge

disregard *v.* ignore, neglect, overlook, disobey *heed, consider*.

disreputable *adj.* low, base, vulgar, mean, discreditable *respectable*.

dissect *v.* dismember, cut, examine, lay open, analyze, scrutinize.

dissent *v.* differ, disagree *agree*.

dissipate *v.* scatter, waste.

dissolve *v.* 1. liquefy, melt 2. end, break up, terminate, fade away, disappear.

distance *n.* length, extend, space, remoteness *nearness, vicinity*.

distinct *adj.* different, definite, clear, separate *vague, obscure*.

distinguish *v.* perceive, discern, detect, divine *confuse*.

distinguished *adj.* noted, eminent, celebrated, famous *obscure, unknown*.

distort *v.* deform, falsify, twist, misrepresent *straighten*.

distract *v.* divert, sidetrack, perplex, bewilder *concentrate*.

distress *n.* agony, anguish, trouble, danger, pain *tranquility, relief*.

distribute *v.* dispense, divide, allocate, apportion *collect, gather*.

district *n.* area, region, section, quarter, territory.

distrust *v.* suspect, doubt, disbelieve *trust, confide*.

disturb *v.* 1. disorder, disarrange 2. vex, annoy, trouble, ruffle *calm, pacify*.

disturbance *n.* commotion, disorder, tumult, riot *calm, serenity*.

dive *v.* jump, plunge, drop, fall.

diverge *v.* spread, deflect, digress, deviate *converge, meet*.

diverse *adj.* different, miscellaneous, assorted *similar*.

divert *v.* 1. entertain, amuse, please 2. distract, deflect, turn away.

divide *v.* separate, sever, share, disunite *gather, collect, join*.

A divine divining

divine *adj.* 1. delightful, excellent, superlative. 2. holy, heavenly, godlike, sacred *earthly*.

division *n.* portion, compartment, partition, section.

divorce *v.* disunite, separate, disjoin, part, annul *join, wed*.

divulge *v.* reveal, disclose, expose, release *conceal, hide*.

dizzy *adj.* unsteady, giddy, fickle, flighty *steady*.

do *v.* 1. perform, execute, act 2. finish, accomplish, complete *neglect, undo*.

docile *adj.* mild, tame, meek, obedient, willing *obstinate*.

dock 1. *v.* clip, shorten, cut 2. *n.* quay, wharf, pier.

doctor *n.* physician, medical man, healer.

doctrine *n.* dogma, principle, creed, tenet.

document *n.* record, writ, paper, certificate.

dodge *v.* elude, avoid, quibble, evade, duck.

dogged

A dogged dog

dogged *adj.* stubborn, obstinate, perverse, willful, plucky.

dole *n.* grant, share, allotment.

doleful *adj.* woeful, sad, sorrowful, dismal *cheerful*, *merry*.

domestic *adj.* household, home-loving, tame, native *foreign*, *wild*.

dominant *adj.* commanding, ruling, predominating.

dominate *v.* command, lead, rule, control, oversee *liberate*.

donation *n.* gift, present, grant, gratuity, dole.

doom *n.* destiny, lot, fate, death, damnation.

door *n.* opening, portal, entrance, gateway.

dose *n.* portion, quantity, amount.

dot *n.* speck, spot, point, mark.

double *adj.* twice, twofold, coupled, duplicate, paired.

doubt *v.* suspect, mistrust, question *trust*, *believe*.

doubtful *adj.* dubious, uncertain, undecided *certain*, *sure*.

dowdy *adj.* shabby, slovenly, awkward, frumpish *smart*.

downcast *adj.* dejected, unhappy, sad, crestfallen *cheerful*, *jubilant*.

downfall *n.* defeat, destruction, ruin, failure, collapse *rise*.

downhearted *adj.* sad, dejected, glum, gloomy, downcast, melancholy *happy*, *cheerful*.

downright *adj.* candid, frank, plain, simple, thorough.

doze *v.* nap, slumber, sleep, drowse *wake*.

drab *adj.* dingy, dull, dreary, flat, dismal *bright*.

draft *n.* plan, drawing, sketch, diagram, outline.

drag *v.* tug, tow, pull, haul, draw.

drain 1. *n.* duct, channel, sewer 2. *v.* exhaust, draw off, empty *fill*, *absorb*.

drastic *adj.* powerful, extreme, severe, harsh, acute *moderate*.

draw *v.* 1. sketch, trace. 2. pull, drag, haul, tug *push*, *propel* 3. attract, entice 4. inhale, suck in.

drawback *n.* fault, defect, disadvantage *advantage*.

drawing *n.* sketch, picture, plan, outline.

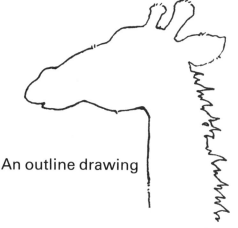

An outline drawing

dread *n.* terror, fear, apprehension, awe, *confidence*, *security*.

dreadful *adj.* dire, awful, terrible, horrible *splendid*, *hopeful*.

dream *n.* reverie, vision, fantasy, nightmare *reality*.

dreary *adj.* dismal, cheerless, gloomy, dark, somber *cheerful*.

drench *v.* wet, soak, saturate, steep, flood.

dress 1. *v.* clothe, attire, don, fit out 2. *n.* skirt, frock, robe, gown 3. *n.* costume, habit, clothes.

drift *v.* wander, float, stray, cruise.

drill *v.* 1. exercise, train, teach 2. pierce, perforate.

drink *v.* quaff, swallow, sip, imbibe.

drip *v.* dribble, trickle, drop, leak.

drive *v.* 1. control, operate, steer, direct 2. impel, hurl, propel, send.

drivel 1. *v.* slaver, dribble 2. *n.* nonsense, twaddle, rubbish.

drizzle *n.* rain, shower, spray.

droll *adj.* amusing, funny, comic, laughable, ludicrous ***sad***.

drone 1. *v.* hum, buzz 2. *n.* male bee 3. *n.* idler, sluggard, loafer.

droop *v.* wither, wilt, fade, hang, sag ***straighten***, ***rise***.

drop 1. *n.* globule, droplet 2. *v.* lower, let fall 3. *n.* fall, tumble.

drown *v.* submerge, sink, immerse, engulf, perish.

drowsy *adj.* sleepy, tired.

drudge *n.* servant, slave, plodder, toiler.

drug 1. *v.* deaden, stupefy, medicate 2. *n.* narcotic 3. *n.* potion, remedy, medicine.

drunk *adj.* intoxicated, inebriated, besotted, tipsy ***sober***.

dry *adj.* 1. boring, tedious, uninteresting 2. parched, thirsty, arid, waterless ***wet***, ***humid***.

dubious *adj.* uncertain, suspect, doubtful ***certain***.

duck 1. *v.* dive, plunge, immerse 2. *n.* bird 3. *v.* avoid.

due *adj.* 1. expected, scheduled 2. proper, fit, suitable 3. owed, owing, payable, outstanding DEW.

dull *adj.* 1. unsharp 2. slow, stupid, obtuse 3. boring, tedious, dry, uninteresting ***keen***, ***sharp***, ***bright***.

dumb *adj.* 1. speechless, mute, silent 2. silly, stupid, dense ***clever***, ***bright***.

dummy *n.* doll, puppet, figure, form, model.

dump *n.* heap, pile, tip.

dunce *n.* ignoramus, blockhead, dullard, simpleton, fool ***genius***.

dungeon *n.* prison, jail, cell, keep, vault.

duplicate *n.* copy, replica, double, repeat.

durable *adj.* lasting, permanent, stable, firm, sturdy ***perishable***.

duration *n.* span, period, term, time.

dusk *n.* sunset, twilight, evening, nightfall ***dawn***.

duty *n.* 1. tax, toll, custom, tariff 2. task, obligation, responsibility.

dwarf *n.* midget, pigmy, runt ***giant***.

dwell *v.* reside, inhabit, stay, live.

dwindle *v.* lessen, wane, diminish, decrease ***increase***, ***gain***.

dye *n.* color, tint, hue, stain, tinge DIE.

A duck ducking

A duck

eager

eager *adj.* keen, fervent, willing, avid, desirous, enthusiastic, intent *listless*, *indifferent*, *reluctant*.

early *adj.* soon, recent, forward, premature, first *late*, *tardy*.

earn *v.* acquire, gain, win, merit, deserve, get *forfeit*, *spend* URN.

earnest *adj.* ardent, eager, serious, determined *frivolous*, *flippant*.

earth *n.* 1. soil, dirt, ground, land 2. world, planet, globe.

ease *n.* 1. readiness, facility 2. rest, repose, contentment.

easy *adj.* comfortable, satisfied, quiet 2. simple, effortless, obvious *difficult*, *irksome*.

eat *v.* 1. masticate, chew, consume, devour, gobble, gorge 2. wear, corrode *The locks on the casket had been eaten away with rust.*

ebb *v.* decrease, wane, recede, retreat, decline *flow*, *wax*.

eccentric *adj.* whimsical, peculiar, abnormal, odd, quirkish *normal*.

echo *v.* reverberate, resound, imitate, repeat.

eclipse *v.* obscure, darken, dim, blot out, overcast *brighten*.

economical *adj.* thrifty, sparing, saving, frugal *extravagant*.

ecstasy *n.* joy, pleasure, delight, rapture, elation *misery*.

edge *n.* brim, border, brink, margin, rim, verge.

edible *adj.* eatable, comestible, wholesome *uneatable*.

edict *n.* order, decree, command, law.

edit *v.* revise, amend, correct, alter, rewrite, check.

educate *v.* teach, instruct, train, tutor, enlighten.

eerie *adj.* weird, strange, fearful.

effect 1. *n.* consequence, outcome, result 2. *v.* produce, realize, cause.

efficient *adj.* clever, useful, skillful, competent, able *weak*.

effort *n.* endeavor, struggle, strain, attempt *ease*.

eject *v.* discharge, expel, throw out, discard, emit, oust *retain*.

elaborate *adj.* decorated, ornate, complicated, intricate *simple*.

elapse *v.* expire, slip by, pass, go *remain*.

elastic *adj.* flexible, pliable, springy *rigid*, *stiff*.

Elastic

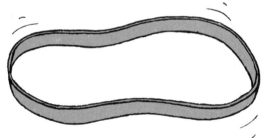

elated *adj.* excited, jubilant, exultant, cheered, proud *depressed*, *crestfallen*.

elect *v.* select, pick, choose, vote *reject*.

electrify *v.* excite, astonish, rouse, thrill.

elegant *adj.* refined, graceful, superior, fine *vulgar*, *crude*.

elementary *adj.* simple, basic, primary, fundamental *advanced*.

elevate *v.* lift, raise, exalt *drop*, *lower*.

eligible *adj.* qualified, fit, desirable, preferable, suitable.

eliminate *v.* exclude, expel, remove, omit *include*.

elongate *v.* extend, stretch, lengthen **shorten**.

elope *v.* abscond, sneak off, run away, leave.

eloquent *adj.* expressive, fluent, articulate, impassioned **halting**.

elude *v.* escape, avoid, evade, shun, dodge **encounter**.

embarrass *v.* harass, distress, humiliate, shame.

emblem *n.* sign, badge, symbol, mark, device.

embody *v.* comprise, include, contain, embrace.

embrace *v.* 1. include, contain, enclose 2. clasp, hug, kiss.

embroider *v.* stitch, embellish, decorate, ornament, adorn.

emerge *v.* appear, issue, come out **recede**.

emergency *n.* crisis, urgency, dilemma, predicament.

empty 1. *v.* exhaust, drain, clear, discharge **fill** 2. *adj.* void, unoccupied, vacant, unfilled **full**.

enable *v.* sanction, allow, empower, qualify **prevent**.

enchant *v.* captivate, fascinate, charm, bewitch **bore**.

enclose *v.* wrap, cover, envelop, surround, fence **exclude**.

encounter 1. *v.* face, confront, meet **avoid** 2. *n.* clash, meeting, collision.

encourage *v.* inspire, support, hearten, urge, foster **discourage**.

encroach *v.* intrude, infringe, trespass.

end 1. *v.* finish, conclude, terminate, stop, close **start** 2. *n.* purpose, object, aim 3. *n.* extremity, boundary, limit.

endanger *v.* imperil, jeopardize, risk **protect**.

Elongated

emigrate *v.* depart, leave, migrate, remove **immigrate**.

eminent *adj.* distinguished, high, celebrated, lofty, elevated **ordinary**.

emit *v.* discharge, expel, eject, exhale **inhale**.

emotion *n.* passion, sentiment, feeling.

emphasis *n.* importance, stress, accent **insignificance**.

emphatic *adj.* definite, decided, positive, strong, forceful **lax**.

employ *v.* 1. engage, hire, contract, enlist **dismiss** 2. apply, use.

employee *n.* worker, hand, servant, wage earner **employer, boss**.

endear *v.* captivate, charm, win **estrange**.

endeavor *v.* attempt, strive, try, aim.

endless *adj.* infinite, everlasting, boundless, continuous **limited**.

endorse *v.* confirm, approve, confirm, guarantee, sanction, ratify **oppose**.

endow *v.* bestow, confer, enrich, give, invest **deprive**.

endure *v.* 1. remain, persist, continue **perish** 2. support, tolerate, bear, sustain, suffer, undergo **flinch**.

enemy *n.* opponent, foe, adversary, antagonist **friend, ally**.

energetic

energetic *adj.* active, strong, effective, vigorous **indolent, languid**.

energy *n.* power, force, might, efficiency, strength **lethargy**.

enforce *v.* force, make, require, compel, urge **persuade**.

engage *v.* 1. pledge, espouse, betroth 2. occupy, busy, involve 3. hire, employ *I shall engage you for a job in my office* **dismiss**.

engaging *adj.* captivating, charming, attractive **boring**.

engine *n.* machine, motor, locomotive, instrument, device.

engrave *v.* cut, chisel, carve.

engross *v.* absorb, preoccupy, engage, occupy.

engulf *v.* absorb, gulp, consume, swallow up.

enhance *v.* increase, improve, enrich, augment **diminish**.

enigma *n.* riddle, mystery, puzzle, problem.

enjoy *v.* relish, appreciate, delight in, like **dislike**.

enjoyment *n.* delight, pleasure, satisfaction, gratification **displeasure**.

enlarge *v.* expand, increase, broaden, magnify, extend, amplify **shrink, condense**.

enlighten *v.* educate, instruct, teach, inform **mystify, perplex**.

enlist *v.* register, enroll, enter, volunteer, join up **quit**.

enmity *n.* hatred, hostility, rancor, animosity, antagonism **amity**.

enormous *adj.* huge, immense, vast, gigantic, monstrous **tiny**.

enough *adj.* ample, adequate, sufficient, abundant **inadequate**.

enrage *v.* infuriate, inflame, madden, anger **appease, calm**.

enrich *v.* ornament, embellish, adorn, endow **impoverish**.

enroll *v.* register, join, engage, enlist **quit**.

enslave *v.* dominate, overpower, master **emancipate, free**.

ensue *v.* result, succeed, follow, come after **precede**.

ensure *v.* determine, secure, assure, guarantee, make certain **imperil**.

entangle *v.* tangle, perplex, bewilder, entrap, catch **extricate**.

enter *v.* invade, penetrate, go into **leave**.

enterprise *n.* 1. courage, energy, boldness **caution** 2. adventure, undertaking, venture, project.

The entrance to the toyshop

essential

entertain *v.* amuse, divert, cheer, please, delight *bore*.

enthusiasm *n.* eagerness, zeal, ardor *coolness*.

enthusiast *n.* zealot, fan, fanatic, devotee, supporter.

entice *v.* tempt, coax, cajole, lure, attract *deter*, *repel*.

entire *adj.* complete, intact, full, whole *partial*.

entitle *v.* 1. empower, authorize, sanction *disqualify* 2. christen, call, dub, style, name.

entrance 1. *n.* access, entry, way in, door *exit* 2. *v.* enchant, delight, fascinate, charm *repel*.

Entranced

entreat *v.* beseech, beg, crave, implore, plead *demand*.

entry *n.* access, passage, entrance, record, note *exit*.

envelop *v.* surround, encircle, wrap, fold, enfold, cover *expose*.

environment *n.* neighborhood, setting, surroundings.

envoy *n.* ambassador, diplomat, minister, agent.

envy *n.* jealousy, covetousness, malice, grudge *disdain*.

episode *n.* incident, happening, event, occurrence.

equal *adj.* 1. even, regular *unequal* 2. equivalent, same, like, alike 3. fit, sufficient, adequate *You may be keen, but are you equal to such a task?*.

equip *v.* provide, supply, furnish, arm, fit *divest*.

equipment *n.* apparatus, gear, outfit, baggage, furniture.

equivalent *adj.* same, equal, tantamount, interchangeable *unequal*.

era *n.* period, epoch, date, age, time.

eradicate *v.* exterminate, remove, annihilate, destroy *instill*.

erase *v.* cancel, remove, expunge, obliterate, rub out *restore*.

erect 1. *adj.* standing, vertical, upright 2. *v.* construct, build, raise, build *demolish*.

erode *v.* corrode, destroy, consume, wear away *restore*.

err *v.* blunder, misjudge, lapse, mistake *rectify*.

errand *n.* task, job, message, mission, chore.

erratic *adj.* eccentric, changeable, irregular *constant*, *reliable*.

erroneous *adj.* inexact, wrong, false, incorrect *correct*.

error *n.* blunder, mistake, fallacy, offense, sin *correction*, *accuracy*, *soundness*.

erupt *v.* eject, emit, explode, expel.

escape *v.* elude, abscond, evade, avoid *confront*.

escort 1. *v.* accompany, attend, lead 2. *n.* guard, guide, convoy.

especially *adv.* principally, peculiarly, unusually, particularly *ordinarily*.

essay *n.* theme, article, paper, commentary, study.

essence *n.* 1. odor, perfume, extract 2. substance, character, nature.

essential *adj.* necessary, required, indispensable, important, vital, basic *superfluous*, *incidental*.

establish *v.* originate, fix, found, settle, set up *discontinue*, *abolish*.

estate *n.* property, fortune, land, residence.

esteem 1. *n.* respect, regard, reverence 2. *v.* value, prize, admire, like *disdain*, *scorn*.

estimate 1. *n.* valuation, calculation 2. *v.* appraise, value, reckon, gauge, *miscalculate*.

estrange *v.* alienate, separate, antagonize *endear*.

etch *v.* engrave, scrape, incise, corrode.

eternal *adj.* endless, always, everlasting *temporary*.

etiquette *n.* decorum, manners, politeness, breeding, form.

evacuate *v.* empty, abandon, quit, leave *fill*, *occupy*.

evade *v.* elude, dodge, escape, shun, bypass *face*.

evaporate *v.* vaporize, vanish, fade, disappear *appear*.

even 1. *adj.* equal, calm, steady 2. *adj.* level, flat, smooth 3. *adv.* still, yet.

evening *n.* dusk, nightfall, twilight, sunset *dawn*.

event *n.* incident, happening, occurrence, episode.

eventually *adv.* finally, ultimately, in the end, at last.

ever *adv.* always, forever, evermore *never*.

everlasting *adj.* perpetual, ceaseless, eternal, endless *temporary*.

everyday *adj.* customary, usual, common *unusual*, *rare*.

evict *v.* dispossess, dismiss, expel, dislodge, turn out.

evidence *n.* testimony, witness, facts, proof, grounds.

evident *adj.* obvious, apparent, plain, clear *doubtful*, *inexplicable*.

evil *adj.* wicked, sinful, harmful, bad, unhappy, wrong *good*.

evolve *v.* expand, develop, grow, open.

exact *adj.* accurate, precise, correct *faulty*, *inexact*.

exaggerate *v.* overstate, enlarge, embroider, amplify, magnify *understate*.

exalt *v.* dignify, glorify, adore, worship *humiliate*.

examination *n.* inquiry, scrutiny, inspection, test.

examine *v.* scrutinize, inspect, investigate, check.

example *n.* instance, pattern, sample, model.

exasperate *v.* aggravate, annoy, provoke, irritate *calm*.

excavate *v.* burrow, dig, scoop, hollow, unearth.

exceed *v.* surpass, excel, beat, outdo.

excel *v.* better, surpass, outdo.

excellent *adj.* admirable, superior, choice, fine *poor*.

except *prep.* excluding, but, excepting, barring.

exceptional *adj.* unusual, extraordinary, remarkable, rare *commonplace*.

excess *adj.* 1. abundant, extravagant, intemperate 2. surplus, remaining, spare *sparse*.

excessive *adj.* 1. intemperate, immoderate *moderate* 2. enormous, superfluous, extravagant.

exchange 1. *n.* dealing, trade, interchange 2. *v.* trade, swap.

excite *v.* provoke, stimulate, arouse, awaken *soothe*, *pacify*.

exciting *adj.* thrilling, startling, astonishing, stimulating *tedious*.

exclaim *v.* cry out, call, shout, declare.

exclude *v.* debar, forbid, shut out, prohibit *include*.

exclusive *adj*. restricted, choice, limited **common**.

excursion *n*. expedition, trip, outing, journey, pilgrimage.

excuse 1. *n*. plea, apology, reason 2. *v*. exempt, release, free 3. *v*. forgive, pardon **condemn**.

execute *v*. 1. accomplish, perform, do, carry out 2. put to death, kill.

executive 1. *n*. manager, director, official 2. *adj*. managerial, directorial, legislative.

exempt 1. *adj*. immune, free, released, excused 2. *v*. free, release, let off.

exercise 1. *v*. train, practice, drill, work out 2. *n*. training, practice.

exit *n*. door, gate, way out **entrance**.

exorbitant *adj*. overpriced, excessive, unreasonable **cheap**.

expand *v*. enlarge, increase, swell, extend, stretch **contract**.

expect *v*. await, hope, anticipate, contemplate.

expediency *n*. advantage, interest.

expedition *n*. 1. trip, journey, voyage, undertaking 2. speed, haste, quickness **delay**.

expel *v*. exile, banish, eject, remove, drive out, discharge.

expend *v*. consume, exhaust, waste, use **conserve**.

expensive *adj*. costly, dear, exorbitant **cheap**.

Exercise   Exert

Exhaust   Expire

exert *v*. strive, strain, struggle, utilize.

exhale *v*. emit, breathe out **inhale**.

exhaust *v*. 1. tire, wear out, weaken **refresh** 2. expend, drain, use up.

exhibit 1. *n*. exhibition, display, show 2. *v*. show, display, present, flaunt **hide**.

exhilarate *v*. gladden, cheer, invigorate, inspire **depress**.

exile *v*. expel, banish, deport, drive out.

exist *v*. subsist, survive, live, be **cease**.

experience 1. *n*. sensation, adventure, feeling 2. *n*. practice, skill, knowledge 3. *v*. suffer, endure, feel *I experienced several unpleasant diseases while I was in the tropics*.

experiment 1. *v*. test, try, examine, observe 2. *n*. examination, trial, test, research.

expert 1. *adj*. experienced, clever, skillful, proficient 2. *n*. authority, specialist, master.

expire *v*. cease, come to an end, stop, fail, die, perish **begin**.

explain

explain *v.* clarify, simplify, define, interpret, answer, show.

explicit *adj.* specific, express, positive, definite, exact ***unclear***.

explode *v.* detonate, blow up, burst, fulminate, discharge.

exploit 1. *v.* utilize, profit from, make the most of 2. *n.* deed, feat, achievement, act.

explore *v.* investigate, search, reconnoiter, prospect, examine, scrutinize, probe, hunt.

export *v.* send abroad, ship overseas, send out ***import***.

expose *v.* reveal, uncover, disclose, bare ***conceal***.

express 1. *adj.* speedy, nonstop, fast, quick 2. *v.* press out, squeeze out 3. *v.* speak, utter, state, say.

expression *n.* 1. look, aspect, mien, air *The expression on your face made me laugh!* 2. term, statement, phrase.

exquisite *adj.* delicate, precious.

extend *v.* expand, lengthen, stretch, reach out ***shorten***.

extensive *adj.* broad, vast, wide, large, spacious, considerable ***restricted***.

exterior 1. *adj.* external, outer, outward 2. *n.* outside, aspect, demeanor ***interior***.

exterminate *v.* annihilate, kill, eliminate, abolish, destroy ***originate***.

external *adj.* outside, outer, outward, exterior ***internal***.

extinct *adj.* finished, defunct, dead, vanished ***extant***.

extinguish *v.* quench, smother, suppress, put out ***ignite***.

extra *adj.* supplementary, spare, additional, more.

extract 1. *n.* essence, distillation *One of the ingredients was extract of a rare palm oil* 2. *n.* quotation, passage 3. *v.* withdraw, remove, pull out ***insert***, ***inject***.

extraordinary *adj.* remarkable, uncommon, rare, unusual ***commonplace***.

extravagant *adj.* lavish, wasteful, spendthrift, excessive ***frugal***.

extreme 1. *n.* extremity, limit, end 2. *adj.* utmost, farthest, radical, outermost ***moderate***.

fable *n.* myth, legend, parable, story, tale.

fabric *n.* textile, cloth, stuff, material.

fabulous *adj.* remarkable, incredible, legendary, amazing ***ordinary***.

face 1. *v.* confront, encounter, meet ***avoid***, ***shun*** 2. *n.* visage, countenance, front 3. *n.* appearance, look, expression.

Face

facetious *adj.* humorous, jocular, comical, witty.

facility *n.* 1. appliance, resource, convenience 2. ease, expertness, knack, ability ***difficulty, clumsiness***.

fact *n.* certainty, truth, reality, data, deed ***fiction, fallacy***.

faction *n.* party, combination, clique, gang.

factor *n.* element, part, ingredient, constituent, cause.

factory *n.* works, plant, workshop.

factual *adj.* accurate, exact, precise, realistic, correct ***legendary***.

faculty *n.* 1. facility, ability, power, capability, cleverness 2. staff, teacher, profession.

fad *n.* craze, rage, vogue, fashion ***convention***.

fade *v.* pale, bleach, weaken, discolor, wither.

fag 1. *n.* drudge, menial, slave 2. *v.* droop, weary, tire.

fail *v.* 1. cease, weaken, disappear 2. miss, miscarry, falter, lapse ***succeed, triumph***.

failing *n.* shortcoming, error, defect, fault ***success***.

failure *n.* default, collapse, breakdown, bankruptcy ***success***.

faint 1. *adj.* dim, feeble, weak, indistinct ***sharp, clear*** 2. *v.* collapse, swoon, pass out FEINT.

fair 1. *adj.* bright, sunny, ***cloudy, stormy*** 2. *adj.* mediocre, average, 3. *adj.* reasonable, frank, just, unbiased ***biased, unfair*** 4. *adj* beautiful, attractive 5. *adj.* blond, light, white ***dark*** 6. *n.* carnival, festival, market, exhibition FARE.

fairy *n.* pixie, sprite, elf, fay.

faith *n.* 1. trust, confidence, belief ***mistrust*** 2. religion, creed, doctrine, belief.

faithful *adj.* 1. loyal, true, devoted, trustworthy, ***false*** 2. strict, accurate, exact ***inaccurate***.

fake 1. *n.* forgery, fraud, imitation 2. *adj.* counterfeit, false ***authentic, genuine***.

fall 1. *n.* waterfall 2. *n.* descent, collapse, decline 3. *n.* autumn 4. *v.* die, perish 5. *v.* drop, descend, plunge, sink ***rise, ascend*** 6. *v.* diminish, decrease ***increase***.

fallible *adj.* imperfect, frail, weak, erring ***infallible***.

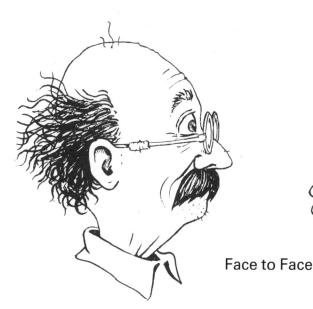

Face to Face

fallow

fallow *adj*. untilled, neglected, uncultivated, unproductive.

false *adj*. 1. dishonest, treacherous, disloyal, deceitful **faithful** 2. incorrect, untrue 3. fake, counterfeit, artificial, imitation **genuine**, **real**.

falsehood *n*. lie, fib, untruth **truth**.

falter *v*. waver, stammer, hesitate, be undecided, hover.

fame *n*. repute, glory, reputation, honor, notoriety **dishonor**.

familiar *adj*. 1. well-acquainted, conversant 2. common, well-known 3. close, friendly, intimate **strange**.

family *n*. ancestry, clan, tribe, heritage, relatives.

famine *n*. scarcity, starvation, lack, want **plenty**, **glut**.

famished *adj*. starving, hungry, ravenous **well-fed**.

famous *adj*. distinguished, eminent, celebrated, renowned **unknown**, **obscure**.

fan 1. *v*. cool, refresh, ventilate 2. *v*. rouse, agitate, excite 3. *n*. enthusiast, follower, admirer.

fanatic *n*. devotee, enthusiast, zealot.

fancy 1. *v*. wish, desire, like 2. *v*. suppose, imagine 3. *n*. idea, notion, imagination 4. *adj*. nice, ornate, elegant **plain**.

fang *n*. tooth, tusk.

fantastic *adj*. incredible, unreal, imaginary, bizarre **realistic**.

far *adj*. remote, distant, inaccessible **near**, **close**.

farce *n*. burlesque, skit, comedy, parody **tragedy**.

fare *n*. 1. rations, food, provisions, nourishment 2. fee, price, charge FAIR.

farewell *inter*. adieu, good-bye, Godspeed..

farm *v*. cultivate, till, grow, plow, dig.

fascinate *v*. enrapture, attract, charm, enchant **repel**.

fascinating *adj*. enchanting, absorbing, attractive, bewitched **monotonous**.

fashion 1. *v*. shape, make, form *The local people fashioned wooden dolls from waste timber* 2. *n*. way, manner 3. *n*. style, custom, vogue, mode.

fashionable *adj*. stylish, smart, customary, modish **dowdy**, **obsolete**.

fast 1. *adj*. immovable, fixed, firm *Pull though they might, the sword was held fast in the stone* **loose** 2. *adj*. quick, swift **slow** 3. constant, steadfast 4. *v*. starve, go hungry **feast** 5. *adv*. quickly, swiftly.

fasten *v*. bind, tie, attach, fix, secure **free**, **loosen**, **release**.

fat 1. *n*. oil, grease 2. *adj*. thick, broad 3. *adj*. plump, stout, obese, fleshy **thin**, **lean**, **slender**.

fatal *adj*. lethal, mortal, deadly, disastrous, killing.

fate *n*. fortune, luck, destiny, doom FÊTE.

fatherly *adj*. tender, protective, paternal.

fathom *v*. penetrate, reach, understand, grasp.

fatigue *n*. weariness, tiredness, lassitude, exhaustion.

fatuous *adj*. silly, absurd, foolish, idiotic **sensible**.

fault *n*. 1. blame, offense, error, misdeed **merit** 2. defect, flaw.

faulty *adj*. defective, damaged, imperfect, deficient **perfect**.

favor 1. *v*. prefer, approve, **disapprove** 2. *n*. benefit, good deed, kindness.

favorite 1. *adj*. choice, preferred, liked, esteemed 2. *n*. darling, dear.

fawn *v*. kneel, cringe, cower, crouch, stoop, flatter FAUN.

fear 1. *v.* dread, be afraid, distrust 2. *n.* terror, fright, dread, alarm **courage**.

fearful *adj.* nervous, timid, cowardly, afraid, apprehensive **fearless**, **courageous**.

fearless *adj.* intrepid, bold, brave, courageous **fearful**.

feast 1. *v.* wine, dine, regale, revel, make merry 2. *n.* banquet, treat, meal, party, entertainment **fast**.

feat *n.* deed, trick, exploit, achievement, act FEET.

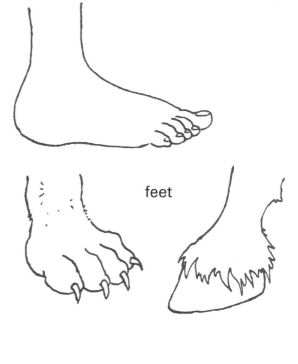

feet

A remarkable feat

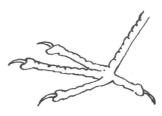

feature 1. *v.* headline, star, promote, highlight, emphasize *The local newspaper always featured sports personalities* 2. *n.* characteristic, trait, outline.

fee *n.* fare, payment, reward, charge, cost, compensation.

feeble *adj.* frail, infirm, powerless, weak, dim **strong**, **robust**.

feed 1. *n.* fodder, provender, pasture, food 2. *v.* sustain, nurture, nourish, satisfy **starve**.

feel *v.* handle, grasp, touch, sense, experience, suffer.

feeling *n.* emotion, sentiment, sensation, sympathy, passion.

feign *v.* sham, bluff, simulate, pretend FAIN.

feint *n.* trick, dodge, pretense, wile, ruse FAINT.

felicity *n.* blessedness, joy, bliss, happiness **misfortune**.

fell *v.* hew, knock down, cut down, level, raze.

fellow *n.* comrade, chap, mate, guy, companion **stranger**.

fellowship *n.* partnership, communion **animosity**.

felon

felon *n.* criminal, convict, culprit, lawbreaker.

female *adj.* feminine, ladylike, womanly *male*, *masculine*.

feminine *adj.* female, gentle *masculine*.

fence 1. *v.* duel, defend with a sword 2. *v.* shuffle, evade *He's a tricky prisoner; he fences all our questions* 3. *n.* rail, paling, barrier, hedge.

fend *v.* 1. protect, cope, look after 2. deflect, deter, repel.

ferocious *adj.* fierce, savage, wild, cruel, barbarous *harmless*.

ferret *v.* hunt, unearth, dig up, find out, fathom.

fertile *adj.* abundant, fruitful, fecund, prolific, plentiful *sterile*.

fervent *adj.* eager, zealous, earnest, ardent, enthusiastic *apathetic*.

festival *n.* anniversary, holiday, feast, celebration.

festive *adj.* gay, merry, joyous, jovial *mournful*.

fetch *v.* carry, convey, bring, go for, get.

fetching *adj.* pleasing, charming, attractive, fascinating.

fête *n.* carnival, festival, holiday, gala, party FATE.

fetish *n.* talisman, charm, superstition, amulet.

fetter *v. & n.* chain, shackle, manacle, tie.

feud *n.* fight, squabble, quarrel, dispute *concord*.

fever *n.* illness, excitement, heat, flush, sickness.

few *adj.* very little, not many, rare, scanty *many*, *countless*.

fiasco *n.* failure, farce, disaster, calamity.

fib *n.* falsehood, untruth, lie *truth*.

fickle *adj.* capricious, unstable, flighty, changeable *constant*.

fiction *n.* story, fable, novel, fantasy, invention *fact*.

fiddle *n.* violin, viol, viola, cello.

fidelity *n.* 1. accuracy, preciseness 2. devotion, loyalty, faithfulness *disloyalty*.

fidget *v.* twitch, worry, chafe, fret, fuss, squirm.

field *n.* ground, plot, tract, glebe, meadow, pasture.

fiend *n.* devil, monster, ogre, demon *angel*.

fiendish *adj.* devilish, diabolical, cruel, infernal *angelic*.

fierce *adj.* ferocious, furious, wild, savage, raging *tame*.

fiery *adj.* fervent, passionate, hot, heated, burning *cool*.

fight 1. *v.* combat, struggle, strive, battle, quarrel *submit* 2. *n.* battle, combat, conflict, war.

figure 1. *n.* number, digit, cipher, emblem 2. *n.* outline, pattern, shape, form 3. *v.* compute, calculate, reckon.

filch *v.* purloin, steal, crib, pilfer, thieve.

file 1. *n.* index, list, dossier 2. *n.* column, line, row 3. *n.* rasp, abrasive, grinder 4. *v.* classify, arrange, sort, document.

fill *v.* replenish, stuff, load, pack, cram *empty*, *drain*.

film *n.* 1. skin, membrane, coating, layer, veil 2. movie, motion picture, picture.

filter *v.* percolate, ooze, strain, sift, separate PHILTER.

filth *n.* muck, dirt, trash, refuse, dregs, slime *cleanliness*.

filthy *adj.* nasty, dirty, foul, vile, unclean *clean*.

final *adj.* latest, ultimate, closing, terminal, last *first*, *initial*.

find *v.* discover, locate, perceive, come upon, meet with *lose* FINED.

fine 1. *n.* forfeit, penalty, confiscation 2. *adj.* thin, minute, little *coarse* 3. admirable, good, excellent, select *inferior*.

finery *n.* trinkets, trappings, frippery, glad rags, ornaments.

finger 1. *v.* touch, handle, point 2. *n.* digit, arrow, pointer.

finish 1. *n.* polish, gloss, refinement 2. *v.* end, terminate, close, accomplish *start*, *begin*.

fire *n.* combustion, burning, blaze.

firm 1. *adj.* steadfast, robust, strong *lax* 2. *adj.* fast, rigid, fixed, stiff *flabby*, *limp* 3. *n.* business company, concern, enterprise.

first *adj.* chief, leading, principal, foremost, earliest *last*, *ultimate*.

fissure *n.* crevice, chink, cleft, crack, cranny FISHER.

fit 1. *adj.* well, healthy, sturdy, hardy *unfit* 2. *adj.* right, suitable, competent *incompetent* 3. *v.* adjust, suit, adapt 4. *v.* supply, equip, provide 5. *n.* paroxysm, stroke, spasm.

fix 1. *n.* predicament, plight, dilemma 2. *v.* mend, repair 3. *v.* connect, tie, fasten, attach *detach* 4. *v.* settle, establish, stabilize.

fixed *adj.* secured, fastened, firm, settled, rigid *temporary*.

flabbergasted *adj.* astounded, surprised, dumbfounded.

flabby *adj.* limp, lax, soft, yielding *firm*.

flag 1. *v.* tire, languish, droop 2. *n.* banner, standard, pennant.

flake *n.* chip, sliver, slice, scale, splinter.

flame *n.* fire, blaze, passion.

flap *v.* flutter, vibrate, wave.

flare *v.* blaze, glow, flame, flash FLAIR.

flash 1. *n.* instant, second 2. *v.* gleam, glare, spark, glitter.

flat 1. *adj.* dull, lifeless *She spoke in a flat, boring monotone interesting* 2. *adj.* horizontal, even, level, smooth *rough* 3. *n.* apartment, tenement, room, studio.

flatter *v.* praise, compliment, cajole, humor *insult*, *slight*.

flavor *n.* relish, taste, savor, tang, seasoning.

flaw *n.* spot, defect, blemish, imperfection, fault.

flawless *adj.* perfect, complete, whole, unblemished *defective*, *faulty*.

fleck *n.* speck, speckle, spot, streak.

flee *v.* escape, fly, run, abscond *advance*, *charge* FLEA.

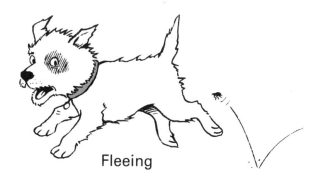

Fleeing

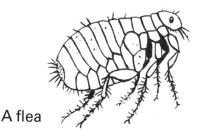

A flea

fleece *v.* 1. rob, plunder, strip 2. shear, clip.

fleet 1. *adj.* rapid, quick, nimble, swift *slow* 2. *n.* navy, flotilla, squadron, armada.

fleeting *adj.* temporary, passing, brief *lasting*.

flexible *adj.* pliant, elastic, pliable, supple *rigid*.

flicker *v.* fluster, twinkle, waver.

flight *n.* 1. departure, leaving, exodus 2. soaring, flying.

flimsy *adj.* weak, feeble, fragile, frail *substantial*, *sturdy*.

flinch

flinch v. withdraw, wince, shrink, cower, cringe *endure*.

fling v. hurl, pitch, throw, toss.

flippant adj. frivolous, pert, impertinent, forward, bold, saucy *serious*.

flit v. skim, flutter, fly, glide.

float v. swim, waft, drift, sail *sink*.

flock 1. v. crowd, gather, herd *scatter* 2. n. herd, fold, pack, drove, group, gathering, collection.

flog v. beat, whip, lash, thrash.

flood 1. v. flow, overflow, drench 2. n. inundation, overflow, deluge *drought*, *ebb*.

floor 1. n. ground, deck, pavement, story 2. v. defeat, overcome, crush.

flop v. 1. lose, fail, flounder 2. fall, droop, sag, slump, drop.

flounce 1. v. jerk, toss, fling 2. n. frill, trimming, ruffle.

flounder 1. v. struggle, tumble, wallow 2. n. flatfish.

flourish v. 1. brandish, flaunt, wave 2. succeed, grow, develop, prosper *decline*, *fade*.

flout v. ridicule, taunt, insult, scorn, disdain *respect*.

flow v. run, pour, glide, gush, stream *ebb* FLOE.

flower v. & n. bloom, blossom FLOUR.

fluent adj. 1. eloquent, voluble, articulate *terse* 2. liquid, flowing, gliding.

fluid n. watery, liquid.

flush 1. adj. even, level, flat 2. v. color, blush, redden, blush.

fluster v. agitate, bustle, confuse, excite.

flutter 1. n. confusion, agitation 2. v. flap, quiver, hover, ruffle.

fly v. 1. flee, run away, abscond 2. soar, hover, float, sail, glide.

foam n. froth, lather, bubble.

foe n. enemy, opponent, adversary *friend*, *ally*.

fog n. mist, cloud, haze, vapor, smog.

foil 1. n. sword, rapier 2. n. flake, metal, film, leaf 3. v. defeat, outwit, thwart, baffle *aid*.

fold 1. n. pen, enclosure 2. v. double, crease, bend FOALED.

follow v. 1. obey, heed 2. succeed, ensue, come next 3. chase, pursue *lead*.

folly n. stupidity, absurdity, foolishness, nonsense *wisdom*.

fond adj. liking, loving, affectionate, tender.

fondle v. coddle, caress, cuddle, pet *whack*.

food n. nutriment, nourishment, provisions, fare, rations.

fool 1. n. jester, buffoon, clown 2. n. dunce, scatterbrain, idiot *sage* 3. v. cheat, deceive, trick, dupe.

foolhardy adj. reckless, daring, rash, bold *cautious*.

Flying

A fly

foolish *adj.* silly, stupid, daft, senseless *sensible*, *prudent*.

foray *v.* raid, plunder, pillage.

forbid *v.* ban, disallow, prohibit, hinder, veto *allow*.

forbidding *adj.* grim, hostile, harsh, surly, stern *inviting*.

force 1. *n.* army, troop, squadron 2. *n.* strength, might, power, energy, vigor 3. *v.* coerce, push, compel *induce*.

fore *adj.* leading, first, front, face *aft*, *rear* FOR FOUR.

forecast *v.* foresee, predict, foretell.

forefather *n.* forebear, ancestor, predecessor *descendant*.

forehead *n.* brow, front.

foreign *adj.* strange, exotic, outlandish, alien *native*.

foremost *adj.* advanced, principal, first, leading *hindmost*.

foresight *n.* prudence, precaution, caution, forethought *imprudence*.

forest *n.* woodland, wood, grove.

foretell *v.* forecast, predict, prophesy.

forfeit 1. *n.* penalty, loss, fine 2. *v.* renounce, relinquish, lose *gain*.

forge *v.* 1. invent, make, construct 2. falsify, fake, counterfeit.

forget *v.* overlook, neglect, disregard, ignore, lose sight of *remember*, *recall*.

forgive *v.* excuse, absolve, pardon *censure*, *avenge*.

forgo *v.* give up, sacrifice *keep*.

forlorn *adj.* desolate, hopeless, wretched, miserable *cheerful*.

form 1. *v.* shape, contrive, mold 2. *n.* manner, method, mode 3. *n.* figure, mold, shape 4. *n.* system, style, kind, sort.

formal *adj.* 1. precise, dignified, punctilious 2. conventional, regular, orderly *informal*, *casual*, *unassuming*.

former *adj.* prior, previous, past, earlier *latter*.

formidable *adj.* fearful, alarming, dangerous, appalling, difficult *easy*, *simple*.

forsake *v.* quit, desert, abandon, leave, give up *retain*.

fort *n.* citadel, fortress, stronghold, castle.

forth *adv.* ahead, onward, forward, out.

forthright *adj.* direct, candid, frank, outspoken *devious*.

fortify *v.* brace, reinforce, strengthen.

fortitude *n.* courage, strength, stamina, endurance *weakness*.

fortunate *adj.* favorable, happy, advantageous, successful, lucky *cursed*, *wretched*.

fortune *n.* 1. wealth, affluence, prosperity, riches 2. fate, chance, luck *misfortune*.

forward 1. *adj.* bold, arrogant, brazen 2. *adv.* ahead, onward, in advance *rear* FOREWARD.

foster *v.* favor, cherish, support, promote, nurse, nourish, patronize.

foul *adj.* 1. base, scandalous, wicked, vile 2. dirty, nasty, impure, filthy *pure* 3. rainy, cloudy, stormy *sunny* FOWL.

A fowl

found

found *v.* originate, set up, establish.

foundation *n.* establishment, ground, base.

foundry *n.* forge, smelter, crucible.

fountain *n.* well, spring, stream, source.

foxy *adj.* cunning, crafty, artful, sly, canny ***artless***.

fraternity *n.* society, brotherhood, company, circle.

fraud *n.* trickery, swindle, deception, deceit ***honesty***.

fraudulent *adj.* false, cheating, dishonest ***honest***.

fray 1. *v.* chafe, tatter, rub, wear 2. *n.* fight, conflict, battle.

Foxy

fraction *n.* portion, part, fragment, piece ***whole***.

fracture *n.* crack, cleft, break, rupture.

fragile *adj.* weak, delicate, brittle, frail ***sturdy***, ***strong***.

fragment *n.* piece, remnant, segment, chip, scrap ***whole***.

fragrant *adj.* aromatic, spicy, perfumed, scented ***noxious***.

frail *adj.* feeble, delicate, fragile, brittle, weak ***strong***, ***burly***.

frame *n.* 1. surround, edging, mount, border 2. form, carcass, skeleton, framework.

frank *adj.* honest, sincere, direct, open, candid ***devious***.

frantic *adj.* frenzied, raving, furious, wild, hysterical ***tranquil***.

freak *adj.* grotesque, bizarre.

free 1. *adj.* gratis, gratuitous, complimentary, without charge 2. *adj.* liberated, independent, unrestricted 3. *adj.* loose, lax, untied 4. *v.* dismiss, release, acquit ***enslave***.

freedom *n.* independence, emancipation, liberty ***bondage***.

freeze *v.* refrigerate, chill, congeal ***melt***, ***thaw*** FREES, FRIEZE.

freight *n.* goods, cargo, shipment, load, burden.

frenzy *n.* fury, rage, madness, lunacy, mania, insanity ***sanity***.

frequent 1. *v.* resort, haunt 2. *adj.* often, common, customary ***rare***.

fresh *adj.* 1. vigorous, healthy 2. sweet, new, unused ***stale***.

future

fret *v.* grieve, fume, fuss, worry.

friction *n.* 1. disagreement, tension, wrangling *agreement* 2. abrasion, grating, rubbing.

friend *n.* companion, comrade, ally, colleague, associate, chum, pal, mate *enemy*, *foe*.

friendly *adj.* affectionate, amicable, amiable *hostile*.

fright *n.* terror, dismay, alarm, fear, panic, dread.

frighten *v.* scare, shock, alarm, terrify *reassure*.

frightful *adj.* awful, dire, dreadful, fearful, alarming *pleasing*.

frigid *adj.* stiff, aloof, icy, cold, cool *warm*, *genial*.

frill *n.* edging, gathering, border, ruffle, flounce.

fringe *n.* border, hem, trimming, edge.

frisky *adj.* lively, sportive, frolicsome, playful.

frivolous *adj.* silly, trivial, foolish, trifling, facetious *serious*.

frolic *v.* play, frisk, gambol, romp.

front *n.* brow, face, façade, forehead *rear*, *back*.

frontier *n.* boundary, limit, border.

frosty *adj.* frigid, chilly, freezing, wintry, cold, cool *warm*.

froth *n.* lather, foam, spume, spray, scum.

frown *v.* pout, scowl, glower, glare *smile*.

frugal *adj.* sparing, careful, stingy, thrifty, prudent *extravagant*.

fruitful *adj.* fertile, plentiful, abundant, prolific *barren*.

fruitless *adj.* futile, useless, unavailing, barren, sterile *fruitful*.

frustrate *v.* balk, foil, baffle, discourage, defeat *encourage*.

fugitive *n.* refugee, escaper, deserter, runaway.

fulfill *v.* realize, accomplish, perform, finish, complete *fail*.

full *adj.* complete, filled, entire, stuffed *empty*.

fumble *v.* feel, grope, mishandle, blunder.

fume 1. *v.* rave, rage, storm 2. *n.* vapor, steam, gas, smoke.

fun *n.* pleasure, sport, amusement, merriment, gaiety.

function 1. *v.* operate, act, work 2. *n.* purpose, use, exercise 3. *n.* business, performance, ceremony *Granting house loans is a main function of this bank.*

fund *n.* capital, money, assets, supply.

fundamental *adj.* primary, basic, radical, essential *incidental*.

funeral *n.* burial, interment, cremation, mourning.

funny *adj.* 1. strange, curious, odd 2. amusing, humorous, comical, laughable *serious*, *sad*.

furious *adj.* angry, stormy, frantic, raging, infuriated *calm*.

furnish *v.* 1. equip, fit out 2. provide, give, supply *The children were furnished with colors for their painting class.*

furrow *n.* groove, trench, channel, seam, wrinkle.

further *adj.* 1. farther, more remote 2. more, additional.

furthermore *adv.* besides, also, too.

furtive *adj.* secret, sly, stealthy, surreptitious, sneaky.

fury *n.* frenzy, madness, wrath, fierceness, rage, anger, ferocity *calm*.

fuse *v.* liquefy, blend, join, melt, weld, intermingle.

fuss 1. *v.* pester, bother, fret 2. *n.* bustle, worry, flurry, ado.

fussy *adj.* choosy, finicky, fidgety.

futile *adj.* pointless, useless, vain, worthless, profitless, idle, frivolous *worthwhile*.

future *adj.* tomorrow, hereafter, imminent, prospective, coming.

gabble

G

Gamble

Gamboling

gabble *v.* prattle, jabber, chatter.

gadget *n.* contraption, appliance, instrument, device.

gag 1. *n.* joke, jest 2. *v.* stifle, silence, muzzle.

gain 1. *n.* increase, profit, addition *loss* 2. *v.* get, acquire, obtain, earn, win *lose*.

gale *n.* wind, storm, hurricane, tempest.

gallant *adj.* 1. courageous, brave, valiant *cowardly* 2. noble, courteous, chivalrous.

gallery *n.* balcony, corridor, passage, arcade.

gallop *v.* ride, scamper, run, hurry.

gamble *v.* wager, bet, risk, game, chance GAMBOL.

gambol *v.* frolic, frisk, dance, caper, play GAMBLE.

game 1. *n.* contest, match, competition, sport, play, amusement 2. *adj.* brave, fearless, courageous.

gang *n.* band, crew, clique, ring, party.

gap *n.* ravine, cleft, crevice, opening, space, interval.

gape *v.* stare, yawn, open, gaze.

garb *n.* dress, clothes, costume, attire.

garbage *n.* rubbish, offal, remains, refuse, waste, trash, debris.

garish *adj.* gaudy, showy, flashy, tawdry, loud.

garland *n.* wreath, crown, chaplet.

garment *n.* dress, coat, frock, robe.

garnish *v.* decorate, beautify, adorn, trim, embellish.

gash *v.* cut, slash, wound.

gasp *v.* choke, pant, wheeze, puff, blow.

gate *n.* entrance, door, portico GAIT.

gather *v.* 1. muster, accumulate, collect, assemble *scatter* 2. deduce, infer, conclude.

gathering *n.* assembly, company, meeting, collection.

gaudy *adj.* flashy, garish, tawdry, vulgar *quiet, chaste*.

gauge 1. *n.* meter, measure, instrument 2. *v.* appraise, judge, estimate GAGE.

gaunt *adj.* thin, skinny, haggard, scrawny, lean, spare.

gay *adj.* merry, bright, lively, jolly, joyous, cheerful *grave*.

gaze *v.* regard, stare, gape, look intently.

gear *n.* 1. cog, mechanism, rigging, harness, accessories 2. (slang) clothes.

gem *n.* jewel, treasure, precious stone.

general 1. *n.* commander-in-chief 2. *adj.* common, usual, universal 3. *adj.* indefinite, vague, inexact *exact*.

generally *adv.* usually, commonly, ordinarily.

generation *n.* 1. breed, offspring, family 2. production, creation.

generous *adj.* liberal, kind, unselfish, charitable *miserly*.

genial *adj.* cheerful, hearty, merry, agreeable *morose*.

genius *n.* 1. ability, talent, sagacity 2. master, sage, prodigy *dunce*.

gentle *adj.* mild, kind, bland, tender, moderate *rough*.

gentleman *n.* man of breeding, man of polish *boor*.

genuine *adj.* 1. real, true, actual, authentic *fraudulent* 2. frank, sincere, unaffected.

germ *n.* seed, nucleus, embryo, microbe, origin.

A germ

A ghost

gesture *n.* sign, movement, signal, action.

get *v.* 1. obtain, earn, win, gain, procure 2. carry, fetch, bring 3. prepare 4. become, go 5. reach, attain, arrive.

ghastly *adj.* hideous, grisly, horrible, dismal.

ghost *n.* spook, specter, phantom, spirit, shade.

ghostly *adj.* spooky, spectral, spine-chilling.

giant 1. *n.* colossus, ogre, monster 2. *adj.* gigantic, huge, enormous, vast *midget*.

gibe *v.* sneer, jeer, scoff, taunt *compliment*.

giddy

giddy *adj.* dizzy, reeling, careless, unsteady, flighty **steady**.

gift *n.* 1. present, donation, offering, contribution 2. talent, genius, ability.

gigantic *adj.* huge, enormous, giant **tiny**.

giggle *v. & n.* laugh, cackle, snigger, titter.

gingerly *adv.* daintily, cautiously, carefully, tenderly.

girl *n.* lass, damsel, female, maiden **boy**.

girlish *adj.* feminine, youthful **boyish**.

gist *n.* kernel, essence, pith, substance, point.

give *v.* 1. provide, grant, present, bestow **take** 2. issue, utter, communicate, emit *I give a good imitation of an old-time performer* 3. yield, produce *This soil will give the best wheat crop* 4. give way, recede 5. sacrifice, surrender **receive**.

glad *adj.* delighted, happy, pleased, cheerful, joyful **miserable**.

gladden *v.* make glad, elate, delight, cheer.

glamour *n.* allure, enchantment, charm, attraction.

glance *v. & n.* look, glimpse, peep.

glare 1. *n.* shine, glow, dazzle, glitter 2. *v.* scowl, stare, glower.

glass *n.* tumbler, beaker, goblet.

glaze *v. & n.* polish, gloss, burnish, shine, varnish.

gleam *v. & n.* sparkle, flash, glow, beam, glimmer.

glee *n.* merriment, mirth, jollity, cheer, fun **gloom**.

glen *n.* vale, dale, valley, dell.

glib *adj.* smooth, slick, fluent, talkative, voluble.

glide *v.* slide, skim, flow, soar.

glimmer 1. *n.* inkling, hint 2. *n.* gleam, beam 3. *v.* shine, glitter, shimmer.

glimpse *n.* look, view, glance, sight **scrutinize**.

glitter *v.* glisten, sparkle, flash, scintillate.

gloat *v.* glory, exult, revel, triumph.

global *adj.* worldwide, international.

globe *n.* ball, sphere, orb, world.

gloom *n.* 1. cloud, shadow, darkness, dullness **brightness** 2. dejection, depression, sadness **glee**.

gloomy *adj.* 1. unhappy, depressed, sad, dismal, cheerless, melancholy, glum **cheerful** 2. dark, dim, dusky, dreary **bright**.

glorify *v.* worship, praise, exalt, adore, bless, celebrate.

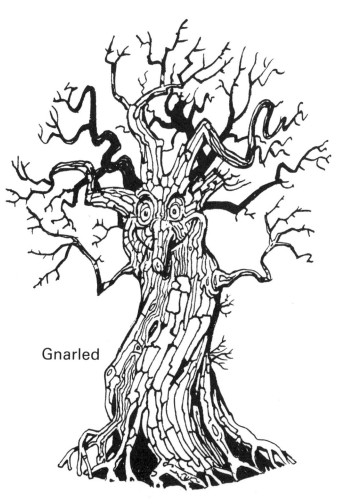

Gnarled

glorious *adj.* 1. distinguished, renowned, famous, celebrated *inglorious* 2. grand, magnificent, splendid, supreme.

glory *n.* renown, honor, praise, fame, splendor, grandeur *obscurity*, *dishonor*, *degradation*.

glossy *adj.* shiny, glazed, lustrous, smooth.

glow *v. & n.* gleam, shine, glimmer.

glower *v.* glare, stare, scowl, frown.

glue *v.* stick, cement, paste, bind.

glum *adj.* morose, moody, sullen, gloomy, sour *cheerful*.

glut *n.* excess, surplus, surfeit *famine*.

glutton *n.* gourmand, gobbler.

gnarled *adj.* twisted, contorted, knotty.

gnash *v.* grind, crunch.

gnaw *v.* grind, chew, nibble, bite.

go 1. *v.* proceed, travel, pass, advance, depart, walk *come* 2. *v.* become 3. *v.* work, function, operate *This clock goes by electricity* 4. *n.* turn, move *It's my go next!*

goal *n.* aim, purpose, end, object, destination, target.

gobble *v.* eat, devour, gulp, gorge, bolt.

God *n.* Lord, Deity, the Creator, Jehovah, the Father, the Almighty.

golden *adj.* yellow, shining, bright, favorable, splendid.

good 1. *adj.* kind, friendly, generous 2. *adj.* fine, excellent, admirable *poor* 3. *adj.* well-behaved, obedient, virtuous *bad* 4. *adj.* fit, proper, suitable, able *These scissors are good for cutting cloth* 5. *adj.* generous, kind, benevolent, friendly 6. *adj.* genuine, authentic, real *A good watch will last for years* 7. *n.* advantage, profit, benefit *It's no good telling me lies* *disadvantage*.

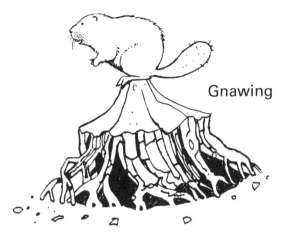

Gnawing

good-bye *n. or interj.* farewell, cheerio, adieu, so long.

goodness *n.* honesty, morality, virtue, excellence, value, benevolence.

goods *n.* property, wares, belongings, merchandise.

gorge 1. *n.* ravine, pass, defile 2. *v.* gulp, devour, stuff, swallow *fast*.

gorgeous *adj.* ravishing, beautiful, splendid, magnificent, superb, dazzling *ugly*.

gossip 1. *n.* hearsay, scandal, chitchat 2. *v.* chatter, tattle.

govern *v.* manage, regulate, rule, control, direct, supervise.

government *n.* administration, parliament, council, state, command, control, authority.

gown *n.* robe, garment, frock, dress.

grab *v.* seize, grip, grasp, snatch, clutch.

grace *n.* 1. refinement, elegance, polish, beauty, symmetry 2. mercy, forgiveness, pardon, clemency.

gracious *adj.* benevolent, courteous, friendly, polite, kindly *boorish*.

grade *n.* 1. class, category, brand, degree, stage 2. gradient, incline, slope.

gradual *adj.* slow, continuous, little by little *abrupt*.

graft

graft 1. *n.* corruption, bribery 2. *v.* join, splice, transplant GRAPHED.

grain *n.* 1. speck, atom, particle, bit, scrap 2. cereal, seed, corn.

grand *adj.* majestic, royal, stately, lordly, magnificent **mediocre**.

grant 1. *n.* allowance, allotment, award 2. *v.* award, allow, convey, bestow 3. *v.* consent, let, permit **refuse**.

graphic *adj.* lifelike, vivid, descriptive, pictorial.

grapple *v.* clutch, clasp, catch, seize.

grasp 1. *n.* comprehension, understanding 2. *v.* catch, clutch, clasp, grip.

grasping *adj.* miserly, avaricious, greedy.

grate 1. *n.* fireplace 2. *v.* scrape, grind, rub, scratch 3. *v.* irritate, annoy GREAT.

grateful *adj.* thankful, obliged, gratified, indebted **ungrateful**, **obnoxious**.

gratify *v.* please, satisfy, fulfill, delight **disappoint**.

gratitude *n.* appreciation, thankfulness, indebtedness.

grave 1. *n.* tomb, vault 2. *adj.* serious, sober, thoughtful, solemn 3. *adj.* important, essential **trivial**.

gravity *n.* 1. importance, seriousness 2. force, gravitation.

graze *v.* pasture, feed, eat grass 2. rub, contact, brush, scrape GRAYS.

grease *n.* oil, fat, lubrication.

great *adj.* 1. large, vast, big, huge, immense 2. leading, main 3. considerable, remarkable, important GRATE.

greatest *adj.* supreme, most, biggest, chief.

greedy *adj.* grasping, ravenous, selfish, avaricious.

green *adj.* 1. fresh, unripe, blooming, verdant 2. untrained, inexperienced, new.

greet *v.* accost, welcome, meet, hail address.

grief *n.* sadness, regret, distress, sorrow **happiness**.

grievance *n.* wrong, objection, complaint, injustice.

grieve *v.* mourn, lament, sorrow, suffer, distress, sadden, agonize, hurt **rejoice**.

grievous *adj.* severe, terrible, dreadful, atrocious, distressing, deplorable.

grim *adj.* 1. harsh, stern, severe 2. grisly, frightful, appalling, horrible.

grime *n.* dirt, filth, smut, soot.

grin *v.* smirk, smile, beam.

grind *v.* 1. grate, crush, crumble 2. whet, sharpen, file.

grip *v.* clasp, clutch, hold, grasp.

grisly *adj.* hideous, grim, dreadful, frightful, horrid GRIZZLY.

grit *n.* 1. sand, gravel 2. pluck, courage, perseverance.

groan *v.* howl, wail, whine, moan, complain GROWN.

groom 1. *n.* servant, valet, ostler, bridegroom 2. *v.* clean, preen, tend, tidy.

groove *n.* furrow, trench, channel, rut.

grope *v.* fumble, touch, feel.

gross *adj.* 1. vulgar, coarse, crude **delicate** 2. shameful, outrageous **honorable** 3. thick, dense.

grotesque *adj.* bizarre, fantastic, queer, odd, fanciful.

ground *n.* 1. soil, earth, dirt, turf 2. base, foundation.

grounds *n.* 1. cause, reasons, basis 2. estate, garden 3. dregs, sediment.

group *n.* cluster, collection, set, bunch.

grovel *v.* cringe, creep, crawl, cower, fawn.

grow *v.* 1. enlarge, expand, develop **shrink** 2. sprout, germinate.

growl *v.* snarl, complain, grumble, grouch.

growth *n.* increase, extension, expansion.

grudge 1. *n.* dislike, malice, spite, ill will 2. *v.* envy, begrudge, complain.

grudging *adj.* reluctant, unwilling, disinclined **willing**.

gruff *adj.* bluff, brusque, blunt, churlish, grumpy.

grumble *v.* protest, complain, growl, mutter.

grunt *v.* groan, rasp, snort.

guarantee *n.* warranty, pledge, assurance, surety.

guard 1. *n.* sentry, watchman, sentinel, conductor 2. *v.* defend, watch, protect, shield.

guess 1. *n.* conjecture, surmise, assumption 2. *v.* conjecture, reckon, assume, surmise **investigate**, **prove**.

guest *n.* visitor, caller **host** GUESSED.

guide 1. *n.* leader, director, pilot 2. *v.* lead, conduct, steer, pilot **mislead** GUYED.

guild *n.* association, society, union, fellowship GILD.

guilty *adj.* responsible, criminal, wrong, wicked **innocent**.

guise *n.* appearance, dress, aspect, form GUYS.

gulf *n.* 1. inlet, bay 2. chasm, abyss, opening.

gullible *adj.* naive, easily fooled.

gully *n.* valley, ditch, gorge, ravine.

gulp *v.* devour, bolt, swallow.

gun *n.* weapon, pistol, revolver, firearm, rifle, cannon.

gurgle *v.* burble, babble, chuckle, chortle.

gush *v.* spout, spurt, flow, rush.

gust *n.* squall, blast, wind.

gutter *n.* groove, channel, conduit, drain, sewer.

gutteral *adj.* throaty, hoarse, gruff, deep.

A growling dog

habit *n.* 1. practice, custom, usage 2. trait, mannerism, addiction 3. clothes, apparel.

habitation *n.* dwelling, lodging, residence, abode, quarters.

hack 1. *n.* hireling, mercenary 2. *v.* chop, hew, cut, split.

hackneyed *adj.* stale, common, threadbare.

hag *n.* virago, vixen, shrew, crone, witch, fury.

haggard *adj.* gaunt, lean, spare, drawn, raw.

haggle *v.* argue, bargain, worry.

hail 1. *n.* sleet, storm, rain 2. *v.* greet, salute, accost, welcome, call HALE.

hairy

hairy *adj.* shaggy, woolly, hirsute, bristly, bushy ***bald***.

A hairy dog

hale *adj.* robust, healthy, strong, sound, well ***infirm*** HAIL.

halfhearted *adj.* 1. lukewarm, indifferent, unconcerned ***enthusiastic*** 2. undecided, uncertain, irresolute.

half-witted *adj.* stupid, silly, foolish, dull.

hall *n.* entrance, vestibule, passage, chamber, corridor HAUL.

hallow *v.* consecrate, sanctify, dedicate, make holy.

hallucination *n.* illusion, delusion, vision, dream.

halo *n.* ring, circle, aureole.

halt 1. *n.* stop, end 2. *v.* stop, cease, pull up.

halting *adj.* hesitant, reluctant, indecisive ***fluent, ready***.

halve *v.* dissect, divide, split, share.

hammer 1. *n.* striker, mallet 2. *v.* drive, beat, forge, pound.

hamper 1. *n.* basket, box, crate, creel 2. *v.* restrain, thwart, obstruct, impede, hinder ***help***.

hand 1. *n.* fist, palm 2. *n.* employee, laborer, craftsman, helper 3. *n.* share, support, participation *Do you want a hand with that boat?* 4. *v.* pass, transmit, give, present *Hand me a chisel, please.*

handicap 1. *n.* burden, hindrance, impediment, disadvantage ***advantage*** 2. *v.* hinder, hamper, disable ***aid***.

handicraft *n.* pastime, trade, craft, art, occupation.

handle 1. *n.* stock, hilt, haft, knob 2. *v.* manage, manipulate, wield 3. *v.* feel, touch.

handsome *adj.* 1. attractive, good-looking, elegant, graceful ***ugly*** 2. ample, generous, considerable *After selling their business, they made a handsome profit* HANSOM.

handy *adj.* 1. clever, dexterous, adroit, skillful, helpful ***clumsy*** 2. nearby, close, convenient.

hang *v.* 1. dangle, suspend, droop, depend, sag 2. execute.

hanker *v.* covet, desire, yearn, crave.

haphazard *adj.* random, chance, accidental, aimless ***deliberate***.

hapless *adj.* unlucky, ill-fated, wretched, unfortunate ***lucky***.

happen *v.* occur, befall, take place, chance.

happiness *n.* joy, delight, enjoyment, pleasure, bliss ***misery***.

happy *adj.* pleased, joyful, glad, cheerful, blissful ***miserable***.

harass *v.* molest, harry, worry, disturb, torment, plague ***comfort***.

harbor 1. *n.* port, haven, dock, anchorage 2. *v.* protect, shield, shelter.

hard *adj.* 1. difficult, intricate, puzzling ***easy*** 2. solid, compact, firm, rigid ***soft*** 3. laborious, arduous, tiring, 4. stern, cruel, unkind, unfeeling ***lenient***.

harden *v.* solidify, fortify, become hard ***soften***.

hard-hearted *adj.* merciless, pitiless, cruel, unfeeling, hard ***tender***.

hardly *adv.* barely, scarcely, just, narrowly, not quite.

hardship *n.* trouble, difficulty, toil, fatigue, suffering, weariness, privation.

hardy *adj.* robust, strong, healthy, intrepid, brave, bold *feeble*.

hark *v.* listen, heed, harken.

harm 1. *n.* hurt, damage, injury 2. *n.* wrong, evil, wickedness 3. *v.* mistreat, hurt, injure *benefit*.

harmed *adj.* hurt, injured, maimed *unhurt*.

harmful *adj.* hurtful, injurious, noxious, mischievous *harmless*.

harmless *adj.* gentle, innocent, innocuous, inoffensive *harmful*.

harmonious *adj.* 1. cordial, agreeable, friendly *disagreeable* 2. tuneful, musical, melodious *discordant*.

harmony *n.* agreement, concord, accord *discord*.

harness 1. *n.* bridle, yoke, tackle, equipment 2. *v.* control.

harp 1. *n.* lyre 2. *v.* repeat, dwell on, reiterate.

harrow 1. *n.* plow, rake 2. *v.* torture, distress, wound, torment *soothe*.

harry *v.* 1. worry, annoy, harass, vex 2. plunder, raid, rob, pillage.

harsh *adj.* stern, severe, rude, churlish, coarse, rough, discordant, grating *gentle*.

harshness *n.* severity, ill-temper, rigor, austerity *compassion*.

harvest 1. *n.* crop, yield, produce 2. *v.* reap, gather, pick.

haste *n.* rush, hurry, speed.

hasty *adj.* 1. touchy, testy, rash, irritable *calm* 2. fleet, fast, quick, swift, rapid *slow*.

hat *n.* headgear, cap, bonnet, helmet, hood, millinery.

hatch 1. *n.* door, trap, hatchway, opening 2. *v.* incubate, breed 3. *v.* scheme, devise, concoct.

hatchet *n.* ax, tomahawk.

hate *v.* detest, loathe, dislike, despise, abhor *love*.

hateful *adj.* horrid, detestable, vile, disgusting, malevolent, malign *lovable*.

hatred *n.* hate, hostility, animosity, enmity, loathing *love*.

haughty *adj.* disdainful, supercilious, proud, arrogant *humble*.

haul *v.* tug, pull, draw, drag, tow *push* HALL.

haunt 1. *n.* resort, retreat, den 2. *v.* inhabit, frequent.

have *v.* 1. possess, hold, own, keep 2. gain, get, obtain, acquire *lose*.

haven *n.* harbor, port, refuge, shelter, sanctuary.

havoc *n.* damage, destruction, ruin, devastation.

hawk 1. *n.* falcon, kestrel 2. *v.* vend, sell, peddle.

hay *n.* fodder, grass, silage HEY.

hazard 1. *n.* risk, chance, peril, jeopardy 2. *v.* gamble, venture, offer.

haze *n.* fog, mist, dimness, murk HAYS.

hazy *adj.* 1. foggy, misty, cloudy 2. vague, unsure.

Hatch

head

head *n.* 1. skull, brain, crown 2. summit, top, acme, peak 3. chief, principal, director, leader.

headquarters *n.* base, main center, HQ.

headstrong *adj.* stubborn, dogged, obstinate, willful *docile*.

headway *n.* progress, improvement, leeway, advance, room.

heady *adj.* exciting, strong, impetuous, rash.

heal *v.* cure, restore, remedy *injure* HEEL, HE'LL.

healthy *adj.* well, robust, hale, hearty, wholesome *ill*.

heap *n.* pile, stack, load, mass, collection.

hear *v.* listen, hearken, heed HERE.

hearsay *n.* rumor, gossip, chatter.

heart *n.* 1. courage, spirit 2. core, center, interior 3. kindness, warmth, sympathy HART.

hearten *v.* comfort, cheer, stimulate, encourage, inspire *discourage*.

hearth *n.* fireside, fireplace, hearthstone.

heartless *adj.* pitiless, merciless, cruel, unfeeling *humane*.

hearty *adj.* eager, strong, sound, sincere, true *insincere*.

heat 1. *n.* warmth, fervor, fever, excitement *coldness* 2. *v.* warm, make hot, cook *cool*.

heathen *n.* pagan, unbeliever, infidel, idol worshiper.

heave *v.* hoist, raise, lift, pull, push.

heaven *n.* paradise, bliss, sky *hell*.

heavenly *adj.* blissful, wonderful, divine, angelic, rapturous, ecstatic *hellish*.

heavy *adj.* weighty, ponderous, hefty, bulky, laden *light*.

heckle *v.* interrupt with questions or abuse .

hectic *adj.* active, excited, heated, hot, feverish *calm*.

hedge 1. *n.* fence, border, barrier 2. *v.* evade, dodge, avoid, obstruct.

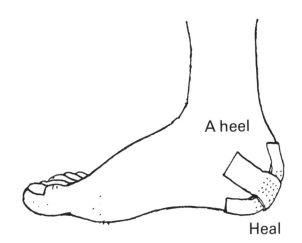

A heel

Heal

heed *v.* obey, listen to, regard, notice *ignore*.

heedful *adj.* observant, watchful, mindful, cautious *oblivious*.

heedless *adj.* unobservant, negligent, rash, headlong, reckless *cautious*.

height *n.* 1. altitude, hill, mountain, elevation *valley* 2. stature, tallness.

hell *n.* hades, inferno *heaven*.

hellish *adj.* fiendish, devilish, diabolical *heavenly*.

hello *interj.* salutations, greetings *good-bye*.

helmet *n.* helm, headpiece, casque.

help 1. *n.* assistance, aid, succor, relief 2. *v.* aid, assist, serve *hinder* 3. *v.* save, succor 4. *v.* prevent, avoid, deter *I can't help being clever*.

helpful *adj.* useful, profitable, beneficial, serviceable *useless, unavailing*.

helpless *adj.* feeble, weak, disabled, powerless *powerful*.

hem *n.* edge, margin, border, rim.

hence *adv.* therefore, consequently, accordingly.

herald *n.* messenger, harbinger, forerunner, crier.

herb *n.* plant, spice, flavoring, seasoning.

herd *n.* crowd, flock, collection, drove HEARD.

here *adv.* at present, in this place, present *absent* HEAR.

heresy *n.* error, misbelief, dissent, unorthodoxy.

heritage *n.* legacy, portion, bequest, inheritance.

hermit *n.* recluse, solitary.

hero *n.* champion, idol, favorite, celebrity, stalwart *coward*.

heroic *adj.* brave, bold, daring, gallant, valiant *cowardly*.

hesitate *v.* pause, falter, waver, doubt, delay *resolve*.

hesitating *adj.* halting, reluctant, uncertain, faltering *certain*.

hew *v.* chop, cleave, cut, hack, split HUE.

hidden *adj.* secret, concealed, mysterious, unknown *open*.

hide *v.* cover, conceal, screen, mask, cloak *discover* HIED.

hideous *adj.* frightful, ugly, appalling, dreadful, ghastly, repulsive *lovely*.

high *adj.* 1. tall, lofty, elevated *low* 2. superior, eminent, great, prominent 3. shrill, acute, sharp 4. expensive, dear HIE.

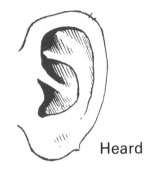

Heard

higher *adj.* 1. superior, greater, better 2. upper, uppermost, above HIRE.

highly *adj.* extremely, very, exceedingly.

highway *n.* road, thoroughfare, street, freeway.

hike *v.* 1. tramp, walk, ramble, trek 2. lift, raise, increase.

hilarious *adj.* mirthful, cheerful, merry, happy, jovial.

hill *n.* height, knoll, mound, elevation, hillock *vale*.

hilly *adj.* mountainous, undulating *flat*.

hind 1. *n.* female deer 2. *adj.* rear, back, posterior *fore*.

hinder *v.* impede, hamper, thwart, stop, prevent, obstruct *help*.

Herd

hindrance

hindrance *n.* obstruction, obstacle, restraint, stop **help**.

hint *v.* suggest, mention, intimate, insinuate.

hire *v.* rent, lease, charter, employ, let HIGHER.

hiss *v.* 1. whistle, fizz, buzz, spit 2. scorn, ridicule, boo, disapprove, deride.

historical *adj.* chronological, ancient **legendary**.

history *n.* record, story, chronicle, memoir, account.

hit 1. *n.* blow, stroke 2. *n.* chance, venture, success 3. *v.* beat, smite, knock, punch, strike, collide 4. *v.* win, attain, accomplish, discover **fail**.

hitch 1. *n.* impediment, obstacle, snag 2. *v.* tie, fasten, attach.

hoard *v.* amass, store, accumulate, save **spend** HORDE.

hoarse *adj.* harsh, raucous, husky, rough, grating, **clear** HORSE.

A hoarse horse

hoax *n.* trick, cheat, deception, joke, fraud.

hobble *v.* stagger, falter, limp, totter.

hobby *n.* pastime, recreation, pursuit, amusement.

hog 1. *n.* swine, pig 2. *v.* monopolize.

hoist 1. *n.* crane, derrick, lift 2. *v.* raise, lift, heave.

hold 1. *n.* cargo area 2. *n.* castle, fort 3. *v.* clutch, grasp, grip **release** 4. *v.* have, possess, retain, keep 5. *v.* admit, contain *The box holds a dozen pencils* 6. *v.* think, believe, judge *I hold to the beliefs of our forefathers* 7. *v.* stick, adhere *This glue will hold for many years* HOLED.

hole *n.* opening, aperture, hollow, cavity WHOLE.

Hole

Half

holiday *n.* vacation, leave, anniversary, festival.

hollow 1. *n.* hole, depression 2. *adj.* vacant, empty **full**, **solid** 3. *adj.* insincere, false 4. *v.* scoop, dig.

holy *adj.* blessed, hallowed, sacred, consecrated, devout, pious WHOLLY.

homage *n.* fidelity, respect, honor, loyalty, deference.

home *n.* 1. house, dwelling, residence 2. hearth, fireside 3. hospice, institution, asylum.

homely *adj.* 1. plain, unattractive, ugly 2. simple, comfortable, domestic.

honest *adj.* virtuous, genuine, reputable, upright, moral, frank, sincere **dishonest**.

honesty *n.* integrity, frankness, uprightness, fairness **dishonesty**.

honor 1. *n.* regard, esteem, distinction, respect 2. *n.* fame, repute, glory, reputation **shame** 3. *v.* respect, revere **abuse**.

honorable *adj*. 1. famed, illustrious
2. just, honest, fair *infamous*.

hood *n*. cowl, cover, veil.

hook *n*. hasp, fastener, crook, catch,
clasp, hanger.

hoop *n*. band, circle, circlet, ring
WHOOP.

hoot *v*. howl, screech, cry, yell,
shout.

hop *v. & n*. skip, caper, jump, leap,
spring.

hope 1. *n*. longing, yearning,
expectancy 2. *v*. desire, anticipate,
wish *despair*.

hopeful *adj*. expectant, optimistic,
confident *pessimistic*.

hopeless *adj*. downcast, forlorn,
helpless, despairing, *hopeful*.

hopelessness *n*. despair,
despondency *optimism*.

horde *n*. mob, multitude, crowd,
troop, gang, throng HOARD.

horizontal *adj*. level, flat, straight,
even *vertical*.

horn *n*. 1. antler, prong, bone
2. trumpet.

horrible *adj*. frightful, dreadful,
horrid, terrible *wonderful*.

horrid *adj*. alarming, horrifying,
frightful, fearful, hideous
delightful.

horror *n*. terror, awe, dread, dismay,
disgust.

horse *n*. steed, stallion, mare, filly,
colt, pony, charger HOARSE.

hose *n*. 1. pipe, tube 2. socks,
stocking HOES.

hospitable *adj*. generous, friendly,
welcoming, open, bountiful,
cordial *unfriendly*.

hospital *n*. sanatorium, clinic,
infirmary.

host *n*. 1. landlord, receptionist,
entertainer, innkeeper *guest*
2. swarm, army, legion, throng,
multitude.

hostel *n*. inn, hotel, boardinghouse
HOSTILE.

hostile *adj*. opposed, antagonistic,
unfriendly, adverse *friendly*
HOSTEL.

hot *adj*. 1. fiery, scorching, blazing,
burning *cold* 2. piquant, pungent,
sharp, peppery 3. passionate,
voilent, excitable.

hotel *n*. tavern, inn, hostel, guest
house, motel, public house, pub,
hostelry.

hound 1. *n*. dog, canine 2. *v*. urge,
spur, incite 3. *v*. harry, pursue,
persecute *Counsel is not allowed to
hound the witness*.

house 1. *n*. home, dwelling,
building, residence, habitation
2. *v*. protect, lodge, shelter.

household 1. *n*. family, brood,
belongings 2. *adj*. domestic,
home-loving.

housing *n*. 1. residential area,
bricks and mortar 2. casing,
structure, frame.

hovel *n*. shanty, shack, cabin, hut
palace.

hover *v*. flutter, float, fly, drift.

how *adv*. in what way, in what
manner.

however 1. *conj*. still, yet,
nevertheless, but, though,
notwithstanding 2. *adv*. in what
manner.

howl *v. & n*. yell, wail, lament, cry,
roar, screech.

hub *n*. center, core, middle, nave.

hubbub *n*. din, racket, tumult,
clamor, uproar, disorder *quiet*.

huddle *v*. cluster, bunch, crowd,
gather, throng *separate*.

hue *n*. color, tinge, tint, tone, shade,
complexion HEW.

huff *n*. rage, passion, tiff, anger,
temper.

hug *v*. embrace, enfold, squeeze,
clasp.

huge *adj*. big, large, vast, enormous,
immense, gigantic, colossal *small*.

hum *v. & n*. drone, murmur, buzz.

human

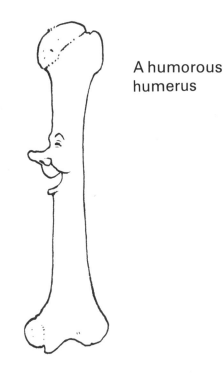

A humorous humerus

human *adj.* of mankind, mortal sympathetic ***inhuman***.

humane *adj.* kind, thoughtful, tender, sympathetic, benevolent, good ***cruel***.

humble *adj.* meek, lowly, modest, simple, unassuming, unpretentious ***pretentious***.

humbug *n.* hypocrisy, quackery, trickery, cant, imposture, swindle.

humdrum *adj.* boring, dull, tiresome, monotonous ***interesting***.

humid *adj.* moist, damp, dank, muggy, wet ***dry***.

humiliate *v.* embarrass, mortify, degrade, shame, insult, dishonor ***honor, dignify***.

humility *n.* humbleness, meekness, poorness, modesty ***pride***.

humor 1. *n.* temper, mood, nature 2. *n.* fun, wit, comedy, amusement 3. *v.* indulge, pamper, gratify *When the king is angry, we must humor him.*

humorous *adj.* funny, witty, comic, amusing, facetious ***serious*** HUMERUS.

hump *n.* bump, bulge, mound, ridge.

hunch *n.* feeling, impression, notion, suspicion.

hungry *adj.* starving, famishing ***satiated***.

hunt *v.* 1. chase, track, pursue 2. seek, look, probe, search.

hurdle *n.* 1. picket, barrier, fence 2. hazard, barrier, handicap.

hurl *v.* cast, fling, pitch, throw, toss, chuck.

hurricane *n.* cyclone, tornado, typhoon, gale, storm.

hurry 1. *n.* haste, quickness, dispatch 2. *v.* run, hasten, speed, race, rush, race ***dawdle*** 3. *v.* drive, urge, push.

hurt 1. *n.* damage, injury, mischief 2. *v.* injure, harm, mar, damage, wound, impair ***benefit*** 3. *v.* upset, grieve, distress.

hurtle *n.* clash, collide, jostle.

husband 1. *n.* spouse, partner 2. *v.* save, store, hoard, economize, preserve, keep.

hush *v. & n.* quiet, mute, still, silence.

husk *n.* rind, bark, covering, hull.

husky 1. *n.* Eskimo dog 2. *adj.* rough, harsh, hoarse, grating 3. *adj.* powerful, sturdy, rugged.

hustle *v.* 1. push, elbow, jostle 2. hasten, urge, speed ***dally***.

hut *n.* shanty, shack, shed, cabin, cottage.

hybrid *n.* mongrel, crossbreed.

hymn *n.* song, psalm HIM.

hypnotize *v.* mesmerize, fascinate, charm, entrance.

hypocrite *n.* impostor, pretender, cheat, deceiver, humbug.

hypocritical *adj.* insincere, false, hollow, deceitful.

hysterical *adj.* frenzied, delirious, wild, raging, uncontrollable.

I

ice 1. *n.* frost, sleet, icicle, frozen water 2. *v.* freeze, chill, frost, refrigerate, frost.

icy *adj.* cold, frosty, frozen, slippery **hot**.

idea *n.* thought, notion, fancy, opinion, judgment.

ideal 1. *n.* model, example, standard, aim, goal 2. adj. perfect, complete, model, supreme.

identical *adj.* same, like, indistinguishable, duplicate **different**.

identify *v.* recognize, distinguish, know, tell, name.

identity *n.* sameness, oneness, personality, individuality, character.

idiot *n.* fool, moron, imbecile, simpleton **genius**.

idiotic *adj.* foolish, silly, stupid, insane, fatuous **sensible**.

idle *adj.* 1. unoccupied, inactive, unemployed 2. indolent, sluggish, lazy **active** IDOL, IDYLL.

idol *n.* 1. favorite, darling, pet, hero, heroine 2. god, image, statue, deity IDLE, IDYLL.

ignite *v.* burn, fire, light, kindle, set fire to **extinguish**.

ignominious *adj.* shameful, infamous, scandalous **honorable**, **reputable**.

ignoramus *n.* blockhead, fool, dunce, dumbbell, dolt, simpleton **genius**.

ignorant *adj.* 1. unaware, uninformed 2. illiterate, uneducated, unlettered, untrained **educated**, **learned**.

ignore *v.* disregard, overlook, snub, neglect **heed**, **consider**.

ill *adj.* 1. evil, naughty, surly, bad 2. ailing, sick, unwell **healthy**, **well**.

illegal *adj.* illicit, unlawful, unlicensed, forbidden **legal**.

illegible *adj.* unintelligible, unreadable, indecipherable, obscure **readable**.

illegitimate *adj.* illegal, unlawful, illicit, improper, spurious **legitimate**.

illiterate *adj.* unlearned, ignorant, unlettered, uneducated **learned**.

illness *n.* ailment, sickness, complaint, disease.

illogical *adj.* irrational, absurd, preposterous, unreasonable **logical**.

illuminate *v.* 1. explain, enlighten, clarify 2. illumine, brighten, light **darken**.

Illumination

illusion

illusion *n.* fallacy, fantasy, vision, delusion *reality*.

illustrate *v.* 1. demonstrate, show, explain 2. portray, depict, picture, embellish.

illustration *n.* picture, drawing, sketch, diagram, photograph, example.

image *n.* 1. statue, idol 2. figure, picture, resemblance, likeness.

imaginary *adj.* unreal, illusory, hypothetical, fanciful, supposed *real*.

imagination *n.* thought, impression, supposition, conception, vision, fancy, idea *reality*.

imagine *v.* 1. suppose, assume, believe 2. fancy, dream, picture, conceive, envisage.

imbecile *n.* idiot, moron, fool, half-wit, *genius*.

imitate *v.* mimic, mock, parody, copy, ape.

immaculate *adj.* pure, stainless, spotless, clean *dirty*, *untidy*.

immature *adj.* 1. youthful, simple, inexperienced *adult*, *mellow* 2. unripe, unformed, green, raw, undeveloped *mature*, *ripe*.

immediate *adj.* 1. near, close, proximate 2. instantaneous, prompt, present.

immediately *adv.* instantly, now, forthwith, at once *later*.

immense *adj.* enormous, gigantic, stupendous, colossal, huge, vast *tiny*, *small*, *minute*.

immerse *v.* plunge, submerge, dunk, douse, dip.

imminent *adj.* approaching, forthcoming, close, impending *remote*.

immobile *adj.* motionless, immovable, stationary, fixed *mobile*.

immoderate *adj.* excessive, unreasonable, extravagant *reasonable*.

immodest *adj.* coarse, indelicate, shameless, gross *modest*, *meek*.

immoral *adj.* sinful, wicked, corrupt, wrong, bad *good*, *moral*, *righteous*.

immortal *adj.* eternal, endless, everliving, undying *mortal*.

immune *adj.* invulnerable, protected, exempt, spared.

immunity *n.* liberty, exemption, protection, freedom, privilege *liability*.

imp *n.* elf, pixie, goblin *angel*.

impact *n.* shock, impulse, contact, collision, impression.

impair *v.* weaken, harm, injure, damage *improve*.

impartial *adj.* unbiased, candid, neutral, indifferent, fair, just *prejudiced*, *biased*.

impassive *adj.* indifferent, insusceptible, unmoved, insensible *emotional*, *susceptible*.

impatience *n.* testiness, shortness, brusqueness, intolerance *patience*.

impatient *adj.* impetuous, hasty, testy, restless *patient*.

impede *v.* stop, obstruct, restrain, thwart, hinder *help*.

impel *v.* urge, push, compel, incite, drive *restrain*.

impend *v.* loom, menace, threaten, lurk, hang over.

imperative *adj.* obligatory, commanding, compulsory, binding *optional*.

imperceptible *adj.* invisible, faint, minute, vague, obscure *visible*.

imperfect *adj.* incomplete, faulty, blemished, defective *perfect*.

imperial *adj.* majestic, regal, grand, royal.

imperil *v.* endanger, jeopardize, hazard, risk *rescue*.

imperious *adj.* lordly, haughty, tyrannical, arrogant, dictatorial *docile*.

impersonate *v.* mimic, imitate, ape.

impertinent *adj.* 1. inapplicable, inappropriate, irrelevant 2. impudent, rude, insolent, saucy, cheeky.

impetuous *adj.* passionate, rash, hasty, impulsive *prudent*.

implement 1. *v.* execute, fulfill, complete 2. *n.* tool, utensil, instrument.

implicate *v.* entangle, include, involve *extricate*.

implicit *adj.* understood, tacit, implied, unspoken *explicit*.

implore *v.* beg, crave, beseech, entreat.

imply *v.* suggest, hint, signify, indicate, mean *declare*.

impolite *adj.* uncivil, boorish, rude, discourteous *courteous*, *gracious*.

import 1. *v.* introduce, admit, bring in 2. *n.* drift, sense, meaning, essence, spirit, intention *After the broadcast, the people realized the full import of the President's message.*

important *adj.* serious, influential, significant, weighty, critical *trivial*, *insignificant*, *petty*.

impose *v.* appoint, put, set, place, prescribe, burden with.

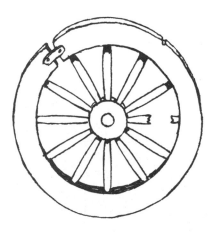

Imperfect

imposing *adj.* majestic, impressive, grand, stately *unimpressive*.

impossible *adj.* unthinkable, unattainable, unworkable, inconceivable *possible*.

impostor *n.* pretender, charlatan, deceiver, impersonator, fraud.

impoverish *v.* ruin, bankrupt, pauperize, weaken, enfeeble *enrich*.

impractical *adj.* unworkable, unrealistic, unfeasible *viable*, *practical*.

impregnable *adj.* unassailable, invulnerable, unconquerable *vulnerable*.

impress *v.* 1. fix, influence, affect 2. imprint, emboss, stamp, print.

impression *n.* 1. stamp, brand, dent, mark 2. influence, sensation.

impressive *adj.* affecting, overpowering, moving, striking *tedious*.

imprison *v.* jail, incarcerate, lock up, confine *release*, *liberate*.

improbable *adj.* doubtful, uncertain, unlikely, questionable, *probable*, *likely*.

impromptu *adj.* improvised, spontaneous, unrehearsed, impulsive *prepared*.

improper *adj.* 1. indecent, unseemly 2. unfit, inappropriate, unsuitable *suitable*, *correct*, *proper*.

improve *v.* amend, correct, rectify, better, perfect *impair*, *relapse*.

improvident *adj.* imprudent, thoughtless, prodigal, thriftless, wasteful *thrifty*.

improvise *v.* extemporize, devise, make up, invent.

imprudent *adj.* injudicious, ill-advised, indiscreet, rash, careless, unwise *cautious*, *prudent*, *wary*.

impudent *adj.* impertinent, pert, insolent, rude, brazen, forward *polite*, *courteous*.

impulse

impulse *n.* 1. whim, fancy, notion, caprice 2. urge, force, impetus, thrust, push.

impulsive *adj.* quick, impetuous, emotional, rash, hasty *deliberate*.

impure *adj.* foul, contaminated, polluted, unclean *pure*, *clean*, *chaste*.

inability *n.* impotence, incompetence, incapacity, ineptitude *ability*, *power*.

inaccessible *adj.* unapproachable, unreachable, remote, unattainable *accessible*.

inaccurate *adj.* inexact, erroneous, wrong, incorrect *accurate*, *faithful*.

inactive *adj.* immobile, indolent, idle, dormant, inert *active*, *diligent*, *busy*.

inadequate *adj.* unequal, incomplete, defective, insufficient *enough*, *adequate*.

inadvertent *adj.* neglectful, careless, negligent, accidental, inconsiderate *careful*.

inane *adj.* puerile, vain, frivolous, empty, void *sensible*.

inanimate *adj.* dead, inert, defunct, extinct, lifeless *alive*.

inappropriate *adj.* unfitting, unsuitable, improper, *appropriate*, *suitable*.

inattentive *adj.* heedless, thoughtless, unobservant, negligent *attentive*.

inaudible *adj.* indistinct, faint, noiseless, muffled *loud*.

inaugurate *v.* begin, start, originate, install, launch, initiate *terminate*.

incapable *adj.* incompetent, weak, unable, unqualified *capable*, *qualified*, *able*.

incense 1. *n.* fragrance, perfume, aroma, scent 2. *v.* inflame, anger, enrage, exasperate, vex.

incentive *n.* stimulus, spur, encouragement, motive, inducement *deterrent*.

incessant *adj.* perpetual, constant, ceaseless, continual *spasmodic*.

incident *n.* event, happening, occurrence, experience.

incidental *adj.* casual, accidental, subordinate, minor *essential*.

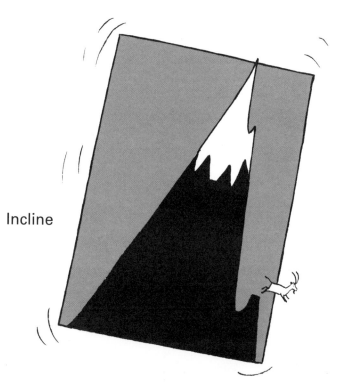

Incline

incisive *adj.* acute, sarcastic, satirical, biting, sharp *mild*.

incite *v.* spur, urge, provoke, arouse *dissuade*.

inclement *adj.* harsh, rigorous, severe, rough *mild*.

inclination *n.* bias, tendency, leaning, dispostion *reluctance*.

incline 1. *v.* slant, slope, tilt, lean 2. *v.* be willing, be disposed, tend 3. *n.* hill, gradient, slope.

include *v.* hold, embrace, involve, comprise *exclude*, *omit*.

incognito *adj. & adv.* unknown, concealed, disguised.

incoherent *adj.* confused, rambling, inarticulate, unintelligible *coherent*.

income *n.* revenue, gains, earnings, salary, wages, profit *expenditure*, *outlay*.

incomparable *adj.* unequaled, unique, matchless, unrivaled *ordinary*.

incompatible *adj.* inconsistent, unadapted, unsuited, contrary *compatible*.

incompetent *adj.* unfit, incapable, disqualified, unable *fit*, *able*.

incomplete *adj.* deficient, imperfect, faulty, unfinished, lacking *complete*, *perfect*.

incomprehensible *adj.* unthinkable, perplexing, puzzling, inconceivable, obscure *comprehensible*, *intelligible*.

inconceivable *adj.* unthinkable, incredible, unimaginable *believable*.

inconsiderate *adj.* heedless, thoughtless, careless, selfish *considerate*.

inconsistent *adj.* contradictory, illogical, variable, contrary *consistent*.

inconvenient *adj.* 1. annoying, untimely, troublesome 2. awkward, cumbersome, inappropriate *convenient*.

incorrect *adj.* inaccurate, false, wrong, untrue, erroneous *correct*, *precise*.

increase 1. *n.* growth, expansion, enlargement 2. *v.* expand, enlarge, extend, grow, prolong *diminish*, *decrease*, *lessen*.

incredible *adj.* doubtful, preposterous, unbelievable, fabulous *credible*, *plausible*, *believable*.

incriminate *v.* involve, prejudice, accuse, implicate, charge *clear*.

incur *v.* bring, contract, become liable, acquire.

incurable *adj.* hopeless, terminal, not curable *curable*.

indebted *adj.* beholden, involved, obliged, owing.

indecent *adj.* immodest, impure, improper, immoral, outrageous *decent*.

indeed *adv.* really, certainly, surely, truly, in fact.

indefinite *adj.* obscure, confused, vague, uncertain, doubtful *definite*, *explicit*.

indelicate *adj.* coarse, rude, immodest, unseemly *modest*.

independent *adj.* free, sovereign, unrestricted, separate, self-reliant *dependent*.

index *n.* catalog, list, register, contents, file.

indicate *v.* denote, designate, show, point out, exhibit.

indifferent *adj.* 1. unconcerned, heedless, unmoved *concerned* 2. neutral, impartial, unbiased 3. ordinary, mediocre, middling.

indignant *adj.* incensed, irate, angry, wrathful *serene*.

indirect *adj.* devious, tortuous, winding, roundabout *direct*.

indiscreet *adj.* rash, reckless, imprudent, unwise, foolish, ill advised *cautious*.

indispensable

indispensable *adj.* essential, needed, required, necessary, vital **unnecessary**.

indisposed *adj.* 1. unwell, ill, sick 2. reluctant, unwilling, averse **well**.

indistinct *adj.* obscure, vague, faint, dim, indefinite **clear**.

individual 1. *n.* person, character, somebody, human 2. *adj.* special, separate, particular **general**.

indolence *n.* sloth, laziness, idleness **diligence**.

indolent *adj.* idle, lazy, laggard, sluggardly, apathetic **energetic**.

induce *v.* impel, urge, incite, move, influence, persuade **dissuade**.

indulge *v.* satisfy, humor, gratify, pamper **deny**, **abstain**.

industrious *adj.* hardworking, busy, diligent, brisk **lazy**.

ineffectual *adj.* fruitless, powerless, weak, useless **effective**.

inefficient *adj.* incapable, wasteful, incompetent **efficient**.

inept *adj.* foolish, silly, useless, stupid **competent**, **capable**.

inert *adj.* passive, motionless, inactive, dull, lifeless, sluggish, idle **active**, **brisk**.

inevitable *adj.* unavoidable, doomed, destined, inescapable **uncertain**, **avoidable**.

inexact *adj.* incorrect, inaccurate, faulty, wrong, erroneous **accurate**, **exact**.

inexcusable *adj.* indefensible, unpardonable, unforgivable **pardonable**.

inexpensive *adj.* reasonable, cheap, low-priced, economical **expensive**, **dear**, **costly**.

inexperienced *adj.* fresh, raw, unskilled, immature, untrained **skilled**, **expert**, **proficient**.

inexplicable *adj.* mysterious, incomprehensible, unexplainable, strange **obvious**, **evident**.

infallible *adj.* certain, sure, unfailing, unerring **unreliable**.

infamous *adj.* shameful, wicked, base, disreputable, scandalous **moral**, **honorable**.

infatuated *adj.* smitten, enamored, charmed, fascinated, besotted.

infect *v.* pollute, corrupt, affect, contaminate **purify**, **disinfect**.

infectious *adj.* contagious, contaminating, catching, polluting **harmless**.

infer *v.* gather, presume, deduce, conclude, suppose **know**.

inferior *adj.* subordinate, lower, secondary, poor, mean **superior**, **superb**, **fine**, **select**.

infernal *adj.* fiendish, damnable, diabolical, hellish **heavenly**.

infest *v.* plague, molest, worry, throng, overrun, permeate.

infinite *adj.* immense, enormous, absolute, boundless, limitless **finite**, **limited**.

infirm *adj.* frail, sickly, ill, feeble, weak **strong**, **healthy**.

inflame *v.* animate, incite, provoke, excite, arouse **soothe**, **pacify**.

inflate *v.* swell, distend, expand, blow up **deflate**.

Inflate

inflexible *adj.* rigid, firm, dogged, stubborn, unbending **flexible**, **pliable**, **supple**.

inflict *v.* impose, apply, deal, give.

influence 1. *v.* direct, persuade, control, modify **dissuade** 2. *n.* sway, control, authority, power **weakness**.

inform *v.* acquaint, relate, advise, enlighten, tell, notify **conceal**.

informal *adj.* unceremonious, free, easy, unconventional **formal**, **conventional**, **official**, **precise**, **prim**.

information *n.* knowledge, news, instruction, facts, intelligence.

infrequent *adj.* rare, uncommon, seldom, occasional, unusual **common**, **plentiful**, **frequent**, **prevalent**.

infringe *v.* disobey, encroach, violate, break **obey**, **observe**.

infuriate *v.* anger, enrage, annoy, madden **calm**, **soothe**.

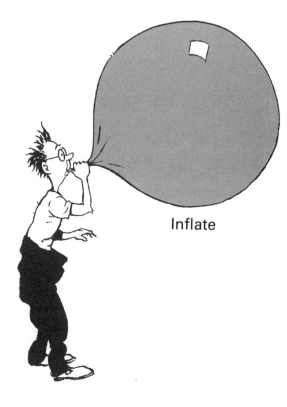

Inflate

ingenious *adj.* skillful, clever, inventive, creative **unskillful**.

ingenuous *adj.* naïve, innocent, candid, artless, unsophisticated **sophisticated**, **cunning**.

ingredient *n.* element, particle, component, part, member, unit.

inhabit *v.* dwell, reside, occupy, abide, live in, lodge.

inhale *v.* breathe in, inspire, draw in, sniff, gasp **exhale**, **emit**.

inheritance *n.* legacy, patrimony, heritage, bequest.

inhuman *adj.* savage, merciless, brutal, barbarous, cruel **merciful**.

iniquity *n.* crime, offense, wickedness, injustice, sin **justice**, **righteousness**.

initial *adj.* beginning, commencing, primary, first **last**, **final**, **terminal**.

initiate *v.* 1. teach, instruct, educate 2. commence, start, begin, open, inaugurate **close**, **end**.

inject *v.* inoculate, vaccinate, insert, fill **extract**.

injure *v.* hurt, damage, impair, harm, maltreat, wound **right**, **heal**, **benefit**.

injurious *adj.* hurtful, harmful, pernicious, damaging **harmless**.

injustice *n.* unfairness, inequity.

inkling *n.* intimation, whisper, suggestion, hint.

inlet *n.* bay, fjord, cove, nook **outlet**.

inmate *n.* dweller, denizen, occupant, tenant, resident.

inn *n.* tavern, hostelry, hotel, pub IN.

innate *adj.* natural, native, inbred, inborn **acquired**.

innocent *adj.* 1. inoffensive, naïve, harmless 2. sinless, blameless, guiltless **guilty**, **sophisticated**, **mature**.

innocuous *adj.* harmless, safe, mild, innocent **harmful**.

innumerable *adj.* infinite, many, unlimited, countless **few**.

inoffensive

inoffensive *adj.* innocuous, innocent, harmless **offensive**.

inquisitive *adj.* inquiring, questioning, snooping, curious, prying **uninterested**.

insane *adj.* mad, lunatic, demented, unbalanced **sane**, **rational**.

inscribe *v.* imprint, write, engrave, address **erase**.

insecure *adj.* uncertain, unsure, unsafe, dangerous **secure**, **safe**.

insensible *adj.* 1. unconscious, numb **conscious** 2. stupid, dull, apathetic, unfeeling.

inseparable *adj.* intimate, solid indivisible, joined **separate**.

insert *v.* inject, introduce, inset, inlay, place, put in **extract**.

inside 1. *adj.* inner, internal, interior 2. *n.* inner part, interior **outside**.

insidious *adj.* wily, sly, crafty.

insight *n.* penetration, judgment, perception, discernment, vision.

insignificant *adj.* petty, trifling, paltry, unimportant, trivial **important**, **prominent**.

insincere *adj.* faithless, dishonest, false, hypocritical, untrue **sincere**, **earnest**, **frank**.

insinuate *v.* intimate, hint, suggest, imply.

insipid *adj.* tasteless, flavorless, dull, flat, stale, lifeless **tasty**, **lively**.

insist *v.* demand, contend, stress, urge, press **yield**, **waive**.

insolent *adj.* impudent, impertinent, saucy, pert, disrespectful, insulting, rude, defiant, bold **polite**, **courteous**, **respectful**.

insoluble *adj.* 1. inexplicable, unexplainable, insolvable, enigmatic 2. indissolvable, not to be melted **soluble**.

inspect *v.* scrutinize, study, investigate, examine, observe.

inspector *n.* overseer, superintendent, examiner.

inspiration *n.* 1. breathing, inhalation, respiration 2. insight, enthusiasm, stimulus, spur, idea.

inspire *v.* 1. respire, breathe, inhale **exhale** 2. enliven, cheer, stimulate, encourage **discourage**.

install *v.* establish, set up, inaugurate, introduce.

instant 1. *adj.* quick, urgent, prompt, immediate 2. *n.* second, moment, minute, flash, jiffy, twinkling.

instantly *adv.* now, immediately, forthwith, at once **later**.

instead *prep.* rather than, in lieu of, in place of.

instill *v.* introduce, impress, implant, insinuate **eradicate**.

instinct *n.* intuition, impulse, tendency, leaning, propensity **reason**.

institute 1. *v.* found, originate, start, establish 2. *n.* school, academy, college, institution, establishment.

instruct *v.* 1. educate, train, teach, inform, enlighten **learn** 2. direct, order, command *I have instructed my men to put up road blocks around the town.*

instrument *n.* implement, tool, utensil, device.

insufferable *adj.* unbearable, intolerable, detestable, outrageous **tolerable**.

insufficient *adj.* lacking, inadequate, meager, deficient **enough**, **ample**, **sufficient**, **abundant**.

insulate *v.* disconnect, line, cover, envelop, separate, isolate.

insult 1. *n.* offense, slander, insolence, outrage 2. *v.* abuse, offend, affront, humiliate **compliment**, **respect**, **flatter**.

insure *v.* guarantee, underwrite, indemnify, warrant.

intact *adj.* complete, whole, unbroken, entire, unharmed, untouched **broken**.

integrity *n.* goodness, uprightness, honesty, virtue **disrepute**.

intellect *n.* judgment, sense, brains, intelligence, reason, understanding.

intellectual *adj.* thoughtful, learned, intelligent, scholarly.

intelligent *adj.* clever, shrewd, bright, astute, quick, alert **stupid**, **dull**, **vacant**, **half-witted**.

intelligible *adj.* clear, distinct, plain, comprehensible **incoherent**.

intend *v.* contemplate, propose, mean, expect, plan.

intense *adj.* 1. eager, earnest, ardent 2. extreme, severe **moderate** INTENTS.

intent 1. *adj.* eager, earnest, resolute, bent **irresolute** 2. *n.* intention, object, aim, design.

intention *n.* purpose, aim, design, object.

intentional *adj.* designed, intended, deliberate, willful, planned **accidental**.

inter *v.* entomb, bury **exhume**.

intercept *v.* obstruct, seize, deflect, interrupt, arrest, hold up.

intercourse *n.* connection, communication, correspondence, commerce.

interest 1. *n.* advantage, portion, share, profit *My bank offers the highest rate of interest in town* 2. *n.* sympathy, attention, regard **apathy**, **disinterest** 3. *v.* attract, concern, engage **bore**, **weary**.

interesting *adj.* engaging, absorbing, entertaining, fascinating, gripping **boring**, **tedious**, **monotonous**.

interfere *v.* intervene, interpose, meddle, intrude.

interior *v.* & *n.* inside, inland, middle, nucleus **exterior**.

intermediate *adj.* interposed, halfway, temporary, intervening.

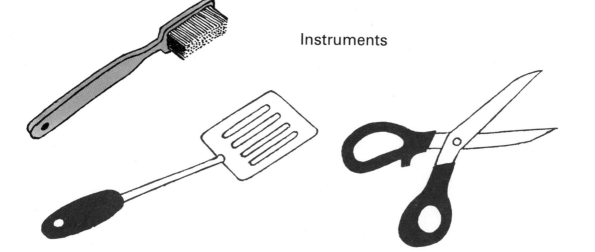

Instruments

interminable

interminable *adj.* unending, boundless, endless, infinite, unlimited ***brief***, ***limited***.

intermittent *adj.* spasmodic, recurrent, periodic, irregular ***regular***, ***continual***, ***perpetual***, ***incessant***.

internal *adj.* inner, inside, inward, interior ***external***.

international *adj.* universal, cosmopolitan, global, worldwide ***domestic***.

interpret *v.* define, translate, explain, construe, decipher, clarify, decode.

interrogate *v.* examine, ask, inquire, question, cross-examine, quiz.

interrupt *v.* disturb, cut, sever, hinder, interfere, intrude, stop ***resume***, ***continue***.

interval *n.* interlude, break, gap, interruption, pause, period.

intervene *v.* come between, interrupt, mediate, interfere.

interview *n.* conference, talk, consultation, meeting.

intimate 1. *v.* hint, insinuate, suggest, allude *Paula intimated that she would like to be invited to the party* 2. *adj.* confidential, familiar, close, personal, friendly ***distant***.

intimidate *v.* scare, daunt, dismay, frighten, alarm, threaten, cow ***encourage***, ***reassure***.

intolerable *adj.* insufferable, unendurable, unbearable ***bearable***, ***endurable***, ***tolerable***.

intolerant *adj.* bigoted, arrogant, overbearing, dictatorial ***tolerant***, ***fair***, ***broad-minded***, ***sympathetic***.

intoxicated *adj.* drunk, tipsy, inebriated ***sober***.

intrepid *adj.* dauntless, bold, heroic, fearless, valiant ***cowardly***.

intricate *adj.* complex, perplexing, complicated, involved ***simple***.

intrigue 1. *v.* fascinate, beguile, charm, enthrall 2. *n.* conspiracy, ruse, scheme, plot.

intriguing *adj.* 1. tantalizing, absorbing, fascinating 2. crafty, sly, wily, cunning.

introduce *v.* 1. commence, start, inaugurate ***withdraw*** 2. acquaint, present.

introduction *n.* preface, foreward, preamble, presentation ***finale***.

intrude *v.* trespass, encroach, infringe, interfere.

inundate *v.* deluge, flood, submerge, overflow, drown, drench.

invade *v.* assault, overrun, encroach, attack, raid INVEIGHED.

invalid 1. *adj.* void, null, without value, quashed ***valid*** 2. *n.* sick person, patient, sufferer, victim.

invaluable *adj.* precious, costly, very valuable, priceless ***worthless***.

invasion *n.* attack, raid, aggression, assault.

invent *v.* conceive, create, devise, originate, concoct, make up, develop.

invention *n.* design, gadget, contrivance, fabrication, device, contraption.

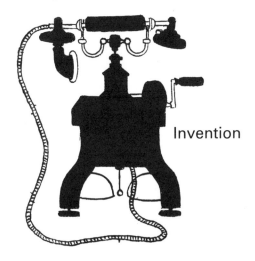

Invention

invert *v.* reverse, overturn, upset, transpose, capsize, spill.

invest *v.* venture, lay out, endow, capitalize, donate.

investigate *v.* scrutinize, inspect, examine, study, probe.

invigorate *v.* fortify, strengthen, animate, stimulate, vitalize *tire*.

invisible *adj.* imperceptible, hidden, unseen, undiscernible *visible*.

invite *v.* ask, prevail upon, request, entice, summon *repel*.

inviting *adj.* attractive, pleasing, alluring, engaging *repellent*.

invoice *n.* statement, bill, check, charge, manifest, account, reckoning.

invoke *v.* entreat, plead, beg, implore.

involuntary *adj.* 1. reluctant, unwilling, forced *willful*, *voluntary* 2. automatic, spontaneous, unintentional, instinctive.

involve *v.* 1. complicate, entangle, confound, confuse 2. concern, affect, implicate, include.

inward *adj.* inner, inside, interior, internal *outward*.

irate *adj.* angry, enraged, exasperated, annoyed *pleased*.

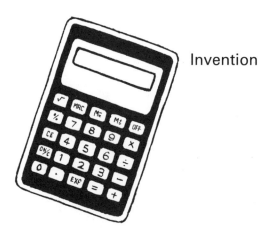

Invention

irksome *adj.* annoying, boring, tedious, tiresome *agreeable*.

irony *n.* satire, sarcasm, banter, mockery.

irrational *adj.* meaningless, illogical, absurd, silly, ridiculous, foolish *rational*, *reasonable*, *logical*.

irregular *adj.* 1. unequal, uneven, unsymmetrical *uniform*, *even* 2. unnatural, unusual, exceptional, abnormal *regular*, *constant*.

irrelevant *adj.* unfitting, inapplicable, inappropriate, unimportant *relevant*, *appropriate*.

irresistible *adj.* compelling, overwhelming, overpowering.

irresolute *adj.* wavering, hesitant, weak, undetermined, unsure *resolute*, *intent*.

irresponsible *adj.* untrustworthy, unreliable, lawless, reckless, rash *responsible*, *conscientious*.

irreverent *adj.* profane, impious, disrespectful, impudent, impolite, sacrilegious *reverent*, *respectful*.

irritable *adj.* testy, snappish, peevish, peppery, touchy, cross, irascible *agreeable*, *good-tempered*.

irritate *v.* 1. provoke, exasperate, enrage, vex 2. pain, chafe, stimulate, make sore *soothe*, *appease*.

isolate *v.* detach, insulate, seclude, separate, set apart *unite*.

issue 1. *n.* question, problem, matter *Our debating society is considering the issue of taxing food* 2. *n.* copy, number, edition, publication 3. *v.* send out, publish, distribute, deliver 4. *v.* come out, appear, flow, emerge.

itch *n.* 1. craving, desire, hankering 2. irritation, sensation, tingle.

item *n.* entry, detail, part.

jab

jab *v.* push, prod, poke, thrust.
jacket *n.* jerkin, covering, coat.
jade *v.* tire, weary, fag, fatigue.
jagged *adj.* uneven, ragged, notched, indented **even**.
jail *n.* prison, lockup, jailhouse, calaboose.
jam 1. *n.* conserve, preserve 2. *v.* press, squeeze, ram, crowd JAMB.

Jam in a jar

jar 1. *v.* bicker, clash, quarrel, argue 2. *v.* jolt, shake, agitate, vibrate 3. *n.* urn, pot, crock, vase, bottle.
jaunt *n.* ramble, trip, tour, excursion, outing, expedition, journey.
jealous *adj.* resentful, envious, covetous.

jealousy *n.* resentment, ill will, grudge, spite, distrust.
jeer *v.* sneer, mock, gibe, taunt, scoff.
jerk *v. & n.* pull, yank, flip, shake, jolt.
jest *v. & n.* jape, joke, quip.
jetty *n.* pier, breakwater, wharf, dock, landing.
jewel *n.* ornament, gem.
jiffy *n.* twinkling, flash, instant, moment.
jingle 1. *v.* jangle, clink, tinkle, chime, ring 2. *n.* chorus, chant, song, tune, melody.
job *n.* employment, profession, calling, task, work.
jockey 1. *v.* twist, maneuver, turn 2. *n.* rider, horseman, equestrian.

A door ajar on a jamb

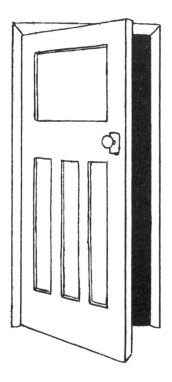

jocular *adj.* facetious, droll, witty, joking, funny **serious**.
jog *v.* trot, sprint, run.

join *v.* couple, unite, assemble, fasten, connect, link *split*, *separate*, *divide*, *sever*.

joint 1. *adj.* combined, united, concerted *separate*, *divided* 2. *n.* juncture, connection, union.

joke *n.* jest, anecdote, prank, quirk, witticism, crack.

joker *n.* clown, jester, humorist, wag, comic, comedian.

jolly *adj.* cheerful, merry, jovial, funny, joyous, glad *gloomy*, *melancholy*, *somber*, *glum*.

jolt *v. & n.* jar, jerk, shock, bump, shake.

jostle *v.* hustle, press, push, crowd, jolt, shove.

jot 1. *n.* particle, atom, scrap, grain, tittle 2. *v.* scribble, note, record, write down.

journal *n.* 1. register, diary, log, account 2. periodical, newspaper.

journey *n.* trip, voyage, expedition, tour, excursion.

jovial *adj.* joyful, joyous, jolly, merry *sad*, *glum*, *solemn*.

joy *n.* glee, ecstasy, pleasure, happiness *gloom*, *misery*, *sadness*, *pain*, *worry*, *grief*.

joyful *adj.* delighted, glad, gratified, jubilant, cheerful *miserable*, *melancholy*, *despondent*, *sad*.

joyous *adj.* exulting, triumphant, overjoyed, rejoicing *downcast*, *despondent*.

judge 1. *n.* referee, adjudicator, umpire 2. *n.* magistrate, justice 3. *n.* critic, connoisseur, expert 4. *v.* regard, appreciate, consider 5. *v.* condemn, pass sentence, try.

judgment *n.* 1. understanding, intelligence, discernment 2. opinion, estimate, conclusion, decision.

jug *n.* ewer, flagon, pitcher, flask, jar.

juggle *v.* conjure, maneuver, manipulate, fake, alter.

juice *n.* liquid, moisture, sap, fluid.

jumble *n.* disorder, muddle, mixture, confusion.

jump *v.* leap, bound, skip, spring, hop, vault.

junction *n.* 1. crossover, rail center, crossroads 2. joint, connection.

jungle *n.* forest, bush, thicket, timberland, wilderness.

junk *n.* rubbish, trash, salvage, scrap, garbage, litter.

just 1. *adj.* impartial, right, fair *partial*, *biased* 2. *adj.* lawful, reasonable *unjust*.

justice *n.* equity, impartiality, fairness.

justify *v.* defend, absolve, exonerate, acquit, vindicate.

jut *v.* protrude, project, stick out.

juvenile *adj.* childish, young, puerile, youthful, minor, teenaged.

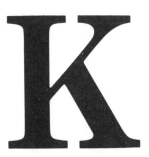

keen *adj.* 1. sharp, acute 2. ardent, zealous, earnest, eager, clever, enthusiastic *dull*, *stupid*, *obtuse*.

keep 1. *v.* support, sustain *Mary and Tom have a family of four children to keep* 2. *v.* detain, hold, maintain, retain *yield* 3. *v.* preserve, save *Joe keeps all kinds of old magazines* *discard* 4. *v.* obey, observe *Religious people keep all the festivals of the church* 5. *v.* continue *Henry keeps asking me to marry him* *abolish* 6. *n.* dungeon, cell, stronghold, vault.

key

A knight

A knight at night

key *n*. 1. opener, latchkey 2. pitch, tone, note 3. guide, clue, lead, solution QUAY.

kick *v*. push, shove, hit, tap (with foot), boot.

kidnap *v*. carry off, abduct, rape, capture, steal, seize.

kill *v*. execute, destroy, annihilate, slay, murder, slaughter.

kin *n*. kinsfolk, family, relatives, relations, kith, kindred, folks.

kind 1. *n*. manner, description, type, sort 2. *adj*. amiable, gentle, generous, warm, friendly *unkind*, *mean*, *heartless*, *pitiless*.

kindle *v*. 1. arouse, excite, incite, provoke 2. ignite, fire, light *extinguish*.

king *n*. monarch, ruler, sovereign, emperor, tsar, caesar.

kingdom *n*. empire, monarchy, realm, dominion.

kiss *v*. embrace, buss, greet, salute, osculate.

kit *n*. outfit, set, equipment, apparatus, tools.

knack *n*. skill, dexterity, adroitness, talent.

knave *n*. scoundrel, rogue, rascal, villain NAVE.

knead *v*. pulverize, mold, pound, massage, work NEED.

knife *n*. blade, cutter, edge.

knight *n*. champion, cavalier, partisan, equestrian, nobleman, gentleman NIGHT.

knob *n*. handle, stud, boss, lump, chunk.

knock *v*. & *n*. hit, strike, thump, tap, rap, pound, beat.

knot *v*. tie, join, connect, splice NOT.

know *v*. perceive, recognize, comprehend, understand, discriminate NO.

knowing *adj*. shrewd, astute.

knowledge *n*. wisdom, judgment, education, information, learning, understanding, sapience.

L

label *n.* tag, ticket, sticker, mark, stamp.

labor 1. *v.* work, toil, strive *rest*, *laze* 2. *n.* work, toil, effort, exertion.

laborious *adj.* arduous, tiresome, difficult, irksome *simple*, *easy*.

lack 1. *n.* shortage, scarcity, need, dearth *plenty*, *abundance* 2. *v.* need, require, want.

lad *n.* youth, boy, stripling, youngster *lass*.

laden *adj.* weighed down, hampered, loaded, charged.

ladle *n.* scoop, spoon, dipper.

lady *n.* woman, gentlewoman, dowager, matron, dame *gentleman*.

lag *v.* linger, dawdle, loiter, tarry, fall behind *hurry*.

lair *n.* burrow, den, hole, nest.

lame *adj.* limping, hobbling, crippled, disabled.

lament *v.* grieve, weep, sorrow, bewail, mourn *rejoice*.

lamp *n.* lantern, torch, light.

lance 1. *v.* pierce, cut, perforate, puncture 2. *n.* javelin, spear, pike, knife, scalpel, lancet.

land 1. *v.* alight, disembark, arrive, go ashore, touch down *embark* 2. *n.* ground, earth, soil.

landlord *n.* proprietor, host, innkeeper, owner.

landscape *n.* scene, prospect, view.

lane *n.* passage, court, alley, LAIN.

language *n.* tongue, talk, speech, dialect, jargon, vernacular *gibberish*, *babel*.

languid *adj.* drooping, languishing, inactive, weak, feeble, slow *energetic*, *vigorous*, *thriving*.

lank *adj.* lean, slender, skinny, thin, gaunt *stocky*, *plump*.

lap 1. *n.* orbit, circuit, round 2. *n.* seat, knees 3. *v.* lick, drink, lick up 4. wrap, cover, fold, turn.

lapse *v.* fail, end, sink, weaken, decline *persevere* LAPS.

lard *n.* fat, grease, blubber, tallow, oil.

large *adj.* bulky, broad, massive, big, great, huge, vast, immense *little*, *small*, *tiny*, *diminutive*, *minute*, *wee*.

lash 1. *v.* whip, strike, scourge, flog 2. *n.* cane, scourge, thong, whip.

lass *n.* damsel, maiden, girl, miss *lad*.

last 1. *v.* remain, continue, endure, go on *fade*, *vanish*, *fleet* 2. *adj.* hindmost, final, ultimate, latest, ultimate *first*, *initial*, *beginning*.

lasting *adj.* enduring, persisting, permanent, continuing *fleeting*.

late *adj.* tardy, slow, delayed, behind *early*, *prompt*, *premature*.

lately *adv.* latterly, recently, previously, formerly.

lather *n.* froth, suds, foam, bubbles.

latitude *n.* 1. freedom. laxity, liberty 2. scope, extent, range.

latter *adj.* recent, last, latest *former*.

laugh *v. & n.* giggle, chuckle, guffaw, titter *cry*.

launch 1. *n.* tender, boat, tug 2. *v.* inaugurate, start, begin, despatch.

lavatory *n.* washroom, toilet, cloakroom, privy, latrine.

lavish 1. *v.* squander, bestow, waste 2. *adj.* liberal, extravagant, generous, plentiful *stingy*, *scanty*, *mean*, *economical*.

law

A leak

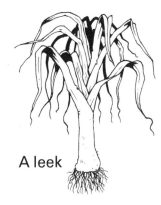

A leek

law *n*. regulation, statute, decree, edict, rule, order.

lawful *adj*. legal, proper, legitimate ***illegal***.

lawyer *n*. attorney, counsel, advocate, barrister, solicitor.

lax *adj*. slack, negligent, lenient, loose, relaxed ***firm***, ***rigid*** LACKS.

lay 1. *n*. ballad, poem, song 2. *adj*. non-clerical, worldly, common, ordinary, amateur *Although only a lay teacher at the school, she was very successful* 3. *v*. charge, impute, attribute, deposit, place, put *The police will lay charges against him.*

layer *n*. row, stratum, seam, bed, coating.

lazy *adj*. slothful, inactive, idle, slack, indolent ***active***, ***industrious***, ***diligent***, ***busy***, ***energetic***.

lead *v*. direct, command, guide, conduct ***follow***.

leader *n*. chief, head, commander, ruler, director, guide ***follower***, ***disciple***.

leaf *n*. foliage, frond, flag, blade, sheet LIEF.

league *n*. union, alliance, combination, society, covenant.

leak *v*. dribble, drip, ooze, percolate LEEK.

lean 1. *adj*. gaunt, slim, skinny, thin ***fat*** 2. *v*. tilt, incline, slope, recline, slant LIEN.

leap *v. & n*. spring, bound, vault, hop, caper, jump.

learn *v*. ascertain, master, find out, memorize, acquire, discover ***forget***.

learned *adj*. erudite, literate, educated, scholarly, knowledgeable ***ignorant***, ***illiterate***.

least *adj*. 1. slightest, feeblest 2. tiniest, smallest, fewest ***greatest***, ***most*** LEASED.

leave 1. *n*. permission, consent 2. *n*. vacation, holiday, liberty *The soldiers had seven days' leave to visit their families* 3. *v*. bequeath, promise, will 4. *v*. vacate, depart, desert, abandon, quit ***arrive***, ***come***, ***stay***, ***remain***.

lecture 1. *v*. speak, address, teach, talk 2. *n*. talk, lesson, address, speech, sermon.

ledge *n*. ridge, edge, shelf.

legacy *n*. gift, bequest.

legal *adj*. proper, allowable, lawful, legitimate, honest ***illegal***.

legend *n*. myth, fable, tale, story, fiction ***fact***, ***history***.

legendary *adj*. fabulous, romantic, mythical, fictitious, celebrated ***historical***, ***factual***.

legible *adj*. clear, apparent, decipherable, readable, plain ***obscure***, ***illegible***, ***unclear***.

legion *n*. 1. brigade, army, regiment, squadron, corps, battalion 2. host, crowd, throng, flock, rabble.

legitimate *adj*. legal, lawful, rightful, genuine, allowable *illegitimate*.

leisure *n*. liberty, freedom, spare time, ease, rest, comfort.

lend *v*. give, advance, loan, grant *borrow*.

length *n*. measure, reach, span, extent, distance *breadth*.

lengthen *v*. extend, stretch, prolong, elongate, *shorten*, *shrink*, *contract*, *abbreviate*.

lenient *adj*. tolerant, lax, gentle, merciful, mild *strict*, *austere*, *hard*, *severe*, *rigorous*, *stern*.

less *adj*. inferior, minor, fewer, smaller *more*.

lessen *v*. decrease, reduce, diminish, shrink *expand*, *swell*, *increase*, *multiply* LESSON.

lesson *n*. lecture, teaching, example, instruction, exercise LESSEN.

let *v*. 1. hire, rent, lease 2. permit, consent, grant, allow *deny*, *hinder*.

lethargic *adj*. sluggish, sleepy, slow, dull, heavy *alert*.

letter *n*. 1. character, type, initial, sign 2. note, message, note, communication, epistle.

level 1. *n*. grade, step, degree 2. *adj*. flat, even, smooth, horizontal *uneven* 3. *v*. point, aim 4. *v*. demolish, destroy, raze 5. *v*. flatten, smoothe.

lever *n*. bar, crow, crowbar, jimmy.

liability *n*. debt, indebtedness, obligation, responsibility *immunity*.

liable *adj*. accountable, responsible, answerable.

liar *n*. fibber, perjurer, fraud, cheat LYRE.

libel *v*. defame, slander, impugn, vilify, criticize.

liberal *adj*. bountiful, kind, lavish, generous, unselfish, tolerant, broad-minded *mean*, *stingy*, *selfish*.

liberate *v*. free, release, discharge *imprison*, *jail*, *confine*, *capture*, *suppress*.

liberty *n*. independence, freedom, autonomy, *bondage*, *slavery*, *servitude*.

license *v*. allow, consent, authorize, permit, sanction *forbid*, *prohibit*.

lick *v*. taste, lap, wash.

lid *n*. cap, stopper, cover, top.

lie 1. *n*. fib, falsehood, untruth, prevarication 2. *v*. lie down, recline, remain, repose, couch *stand* 3. *v*. tell a lie, fib, 4. *v*. be located, be situated LYE.

life *n*. being, animation, energy, existence, spirit *death*.

lift 1. *v*. elevate, raise, rise, mount, hoist *lower* 2. *n*. elevator.

light 1. *adj*. buoyant, airy, flimsy *heavy* 2. *v*. ignite, burn, kindle *extinguish* 3. *n*. candle, taper, match, torch, lamp 4. *n*. illumination, radiance, brilliance *dark*, *shade*.

like 1. *v*. admire, approve, love, enjoy, admire, esteem *dislike*, *hate* 2. *adj*. similar, resembling, equal, alike *different*.

likely *adj*. credible, possible, probable, suitable *improbable*, *unlikely*, *impossible*.

likeness *n*. copy, image, picture, portrait, similarity, resemblance.

limit 1. *v*. restrain, hinder, confine, restrict 2. *n*. restraint, hindrance, check 3. *n*. frontier, boundary, end.

limited *adj*. restricted, confined, cramped, restrained, bound *endless*, *infinite*, *interminable*.

limp 1. *adj*. sagging, flimsy, flexible, floppy, drooping, supple *firm*, *stiff* 2. *v*. stagger, hobble, totter, dodder.

line

line *n*. 1. row, file, sequence, rank, queue 2. stroke, mark, strip, stripe 3. cord, string, rope, cable, thread.

linger *v*. delay, tarry, stay, lag, loiter **hurry**, **race**, **rush**.

link 1. *n*. bond, tie, connection 2. *v*. join, unite, connect, fasten **sever**.

lip *n*. border, rim, brim, edge.

liquefy *v*. dissolve, fuse, melt **solidify**.

liquid *n*. fluid, beverage, juice, sap **solid**.

list *n*. roll, register, inventory, series, catalog.

listen *v*. attend, heed, hear, hark **disregard**.

listless *adj*. heedless, inattentive, languid, apathetic, indifferent **attentive**, **active**, **alert**.

literally *adv*. actually, exactly, really, precisely.

literate *adj*. scholarly, cultured, educated, learned, lettered **illiterate**, **ignorant**.

literature *n*. writings, letters, works, books, plays, printed matter.

lithe *adj*. pliant, supple, bending, elastic, flexible **rigid**.

litter *n*. 1. bedding, couch 2. refuse, garbage, waste, rubbish.

little *adj*. minute, tiny, small, short, slight, diminutive, brief **big**, **large**, **huge**, **long**, **massive**, **much**.

live 1. *adj*. alive, living, breathing, active **dead** 2. *v*. dwell, reside, abide 3. *v*. be, exist, continue, endure **die**.

lively *adj*. agile, nimble, supple, brisk, alert, active, vigorous, energetic **slow**, **sluggish**.

livid *adj*. 1. furious, enraged, angry 2. pale, purple, grayish.

living *n*. maintenance, support, livelihood.

load *n*. weight, cargo, burden, freight LODE, LOWED.

loaf 1. *v*. idle, lounge, loiter, laze 2. *n*. cake, chunk, piece, slab.

loan *v*. advance, lend, entrust **borrow** LONE.

loathe *v*. detest, hate, abhor, abominate **love**, **admire**, **adore**.

loathesome *adj*. repulsive, repellent, offensive, revolting, atrocious.

lobby *n*. vestibule, entrance, foyer, passage, hall.

local *adj*. district, provincial, regional **widespread**, **international**, **universal**.

locate *v*. 1. discover, find 2. situate, fix, place.

lock 1. *v*. latch, bolt, fasten **open**, **unlock** 2. *n*. sluice, weir, floodgate 3. *n*. padlock, bolt, latch, fastening 4. *n*. tuft, tress, ringlet, plait.

lodge 1. *v*. abide, live, stay, reside, dwell, inhabit 2. *v*. settle, fix, place 3. *n*. cottage, cabin, chalet.

lofty *adj*. 1. haughty, exalted, proud 2. tall, elevated, high **lowly**, **low**.

log *n*. 1. register, diary, record 2. timber, stump, branch, chunk, pole.

logical *adj*. sensible, rational, reasonable, sound **illogical**, **irrational**.

loiter *v*. saunter, dawdle, tarry, linger.

loll *v*. recline, lean, droop, sprawl, lounge **toil**.

lone *adj*. lonely, isolated, single, solitary LOAN.

lonely *adj*. solitary, secluded, apart, dreary, friendless, desolate.

long 1. *v*. crave, desire, covet 2. *adj*. extensive, lengthy, protracted, extended **short**.

look 1. *n*. glance, appearance, gaze 2. *v*. appear, seem 3. *v*. behold, see, observe, watch, regard, gaze.

loom *v*. threaten, menace, appear, emerge **recede**.

loop *n*. circle, ring, noose, coil.

loose *adj.* 1. vague, indefinite
2. slack, relaxed 3. free,
unattached, untied, unfastened
fastened*, *tied*, *secure*, *firm*, *fast.

loosen *v.* relax, release, free,
slacken, untie ***tighten*, *bind*, *tie***.

loot 1. *n.* plunder, spoils, booty 2. *v.*
rifle, rob, ransack, steal, plunder
LUTE.

A looted lute

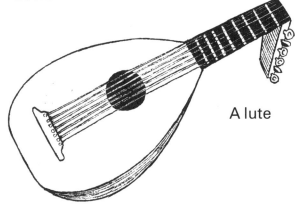

A lute

lop *v.* dock, sever, detach, cut, chop.

lord *n.* peer, nobleman, prince,
governor, master, ruler ***servant***.

lose *v.* mislay, fail, forfeit, misplace,
miss ***win*, *find*, *succeed*, *profit*,
gain, *triumph***.

loss *n.* 1. want, waste, deprivation
2. damage, detriment, destruction,
defeat ***gain*, *profit***.

lost *adj.* missing, wasted, mislaid,
forfeited ***found***.

lot *n.* 1. quantity, plenty, abundance
few 2. parcel, portion, division
3. doom, chance, hazard, destiny.

lotion *n.* cream, ointment, balm,
salve, liniment.

loud *adj.* 1. showy, vulgar, flashy,
gaudy 2. boisterous, blaring, noisy,
deafening ***soft*, *quiet***.

lounge 1. *n.* waiting room, lobby,
vestibule 2. *v.* loll, recline, idle,
laze, relax.

lout *n.* ruffian, hooligan, hoodlum,
boor, yokel, bumpkin.

lovable *adj.* dear, adorable, likable,
attractive, charming ***hateful***.

love 1. *n.* affection, adoration,
warmth, friendliness, tenderness
enmity*, *hate*, *lust*, *malice 2. *v.*
esteem, adore, cherish, worship,
delight ***loathe*, *hate*, *detest***.

lovely *adj.* beautiful, enchanting,
attractive, charming, sweet,
delightful, pleasing, adorable
ugly*, *hideous.

low *adj.* 1. humble, poor, meek
2. base, degraded, vulgar, ignoble
3. shallow, deep, sunken, subsided
tall*, *high 4. cheap, inexpensive,
moderate.

lower *v.* 1. reduce, diminish, lessen
increase 2. drop, sink, let down
raise*, *elevate*, *lift*, *hoist 3.
disgrace, reduce, degrade *She will
lower her opinion of you if you fail
her.*

lowly *adj.* poor, humble, plain,
commonplace ***lofty*, *majestic*,
*sublime***.

loyal *adj.* true, devoted, constant,
faithful, trustworthy ***disloyal*,
treacherous, *untrue***.

loyalty *n.* faithfulness, allegiance, patriotism, fidelity **treachery**, **treason**, **disloyalty**.

lucid *adj.* 1. clear, rational, distinct, intelligible **obscure** 2. light, clear, transparent.

luck *n.* chance, hazard, fate, lot, fortune **misfortune**.

lucky *adj.* happy, favored, successful, fortunate **unlucky**, **unfortunate**, **hapless**.

ludicrous *adj.* absurd, farcical, droll, ridiculous, laughable **serious**.

lug *v.* heave, tug, haul, pull.

luggage *n.* bags, baggage, tackle, gear.

lull 1. *n.* quiet, cessation, stillness, calmness 2. *v.* still, quiet, calm, hush, tranquilize.

lumber *n.* timber, wood.

luminous *adj.* lucid, fluorescent, radiant, shining.

lump *n.* piece, chunk, bump, swelling.

lunatic *n.* maniac, madman, crackpot, loony.

lunge *v.* thrust, attack, push, pass.

lurch *v.* roll, list, sway, topple, tumble, reel, stagger.

lure *v.* allure, attract, decoy, tempt, seduce, entice **repel**.

lurid *adj.* startling, glaring, terrible, shocking, sensational.

lurk *v.* prowl, snoop, creep, skulk, slink, sneak.

luscious *adj.* delightful, delicious, palatable, juicy **unpalatable**, **nauseous**, **sour**.

lust 1. *v.* desire, long for, crave, covet 2. *n.* passion, craving, longing.

luster *n.* brilliance, radiance, brightness, sheen, gloss, gleam.

lusty *adj.* sturdy, strong, robust, vigorous **weak**.

luxurious *adj.* lavish, splendid, opulent, rich, extravagant, self-indulgent **plain**, **self-denying**.

macabre *adj.* gruesome, grim, ghastly, horrible.

mace *n.* club, staff, cudgel, truncheon, bludgeon.

machine *n.* engine, contrivance, motor, device, mechanism, contraption, tool.

mad *adj.* 1. angry, furious, wrathful 2. crazy, deranged, idiotic, insane **sane**, **rational**, **lucid**.

madden *v.* enrage, infuriate, irritate, provoke **soothe**, **calm**, **pacify**.

magazine *n.* 1. publication, periodical, journal, review 2. arsenal, storehouse, warehouse, depository.

magic *n.* wizardry, sorcery, witchcraft.

magician *n.* conjuror, juggler, wizard, sorcerer.

magistrate *n.* judge, justice, syndic, mayor, governor.

magnate *n.* tycoon, financier, industrialist, bigwig, personage MAGNET.

magnetic *adj.* attractive, alluring, drawing, gripping, holding.

magnificent *adj.* superb, majestic, imposing, grand, gorgeous, impressive, splendid, luxurious **simple**, **plain**, **mean**.

magnify *v.* 1. amplify, enlarge, exaggerate, increase **diminish**, **reduce**, **decrease** 2. glorify, praise.

magnitude *n.* extent, mass, size, bulk, dimension, volume, importance **smallness**.

maid *n.* maidservant, housemaid, servant MADE.

mail *n.* 1. letters, correspondence, communication, post 2. armor, harness MALE.

maim *v.* disable, injure, cripple, mutilate, wound.

main *adj.* principal, important, foremost, chief, leading **minor**, **secondary** MANE.

maintain *v.* 1. assert, declare, allege, testify 2. support, uphold, sustain, keep, preserve **discontinue**, **relinquish**, **withdraw**.

maintenance *n.* preservation, upkeep, support, continuity.

majestic *adj.* stately, dignified, imposing, magnificent, royal, regal, splendid **lowly**, **base**, **squalid**.

major *adj.* chief, larger, greater, important, principal **minor**, **slight**, **small**.

majority *n.* most, mass, preponderance, bulk **minority**.

make 1. *v.* perform, execute, practice, do *Next week, we shall make the first attempt to cross the river* 2. *v.* form, fashion, produce, mold, shape **destroy** 3. *v.* get, earn, gain, secure 4. *v.* force, compel, require 5. *v.* select, appoint *The school will make Sally the new sports captain* 6. *n.* add up to 7. *n.* type, brand, kind, mark.

malady *n.* sickness, disease, infirmity, disorder, ailment, illness.

male *adj.* manly, masculine **female**, **feminine**.

malice *n.* rancor, resentment, hate, ill will, spite, enmity **love**, **kindness**.

malign *v.* defame, disparage, abuse, slander **praise**.

A main mane

mammoth 1. *n.* extinct elephant 2. *adj.* huge, enormous, colossal, gigantic **tiny**, **small**.

man *n.* 1. male, adult male, husband **woman** 2. attendant, servant, workman 3. humanity, mankind, homo sapiens.

manage

manage *v.* 1. maneuver, arrange, succeed 2. administer, guide, handle, supervise, superintend *bungle*, *mismanage*.

manager *n.* director, supervisor, overseer, boss, chief, skipper.

mandate *n.* order, commission, requirement, command.

maneuver 1. *v.* manage, intrigue, contrive 2. *n.* scheme, plot, tactics.

mangle *v.* destroy, lacerate, maim, mutilate.

mania *n.* insanity, craze, obsession, madness.

manifest 1. *adj.* apparent, obvious, plain, evident, open *hidden*, *obscure* 2. *v.* reveal, display, show, declare.

manipulate *v.* handle, conduct, work, operate.

manly *adj.* courageous, bold, brave, firm, dignified *weak*.

manner *n.* 1. aspect, behavior, appearance 2. mode, fashion, method, style, way MANOR.

manor *n.* mansion, hall, estate MANNER.

mansion *n.* manor house, residence, dwelling, seat.

mantle *n.* robe, wrap, cloak, cover, covering MANTEL.

manual 1. *n.* handbook, guide, vade mecum 2. *adj.* physical, by hand *automatic*.

manufacture 1. *n.* construction, production, fabrication 2. *v.* fabricate, make, assemble.

manuscript *n.* document, writing, copy.

many *adj.* various, abundant, divers, numerous, frequent, several *few*.

map *n.* chart, plan, diagram, outline.

mar *v.* ruin, harm, spoil, impair *adorn*.

march 1. *n.* procession, walk, parade 2. *v.* proceed, parade, walk.

margin *n.* edge, rim, limit, border.

mariner *n.* sailor, seaman, tar, salt, navigator, seafarer.

mark 1. *v.* note, observe, heed 2. *v.* imprint, indicate, distinguish, stamp 3. *n.* token, symbol, imprint, trace, sign, emblem.

market 1. *n.* store, mart, shop, exchange, forum 2. *v.* sell, vend, retail, dispose of, offer.

marriage *n.* wedding, matrimony, wedlock, nuptials, union *divorce*, *separation*.

marry *v.* join, unite, wed, betroth, espouse *divorce*.

marsh *n.* swamp, morass, quagmire, fen, bog.

marshal 1. *v.* arrange, array, draw up, organize, range 2. *n.* (military) general MARTIAL.

mart *n.* market, store, emporium, trading center.

martial *adj.* military, militant, warlike, belligerent *peaceful* MARSHAL.

martyr *n.* victim, sufferer, scapegoat.

marvel 1. *v.* admire, wonder, gape 2. *n.* wonder, phenomenon, miracle.

marvelous *adj.* amazing, stupendous, astonishing, miraculous, wonderful, incredible *commonplace*, *ordinary*.

masculine *adj.* male, manly, virile, robust *feminine*.

mask 1. *v.* conceal, hide, veil, disguise 2. *n.* cloak, screen, disguise, domino.

mass 1. *n.* bulk, size, pile, lump 2. *n.* eucharist 3. *v.* collect, assemble, gather.

massacre 1. *v.* kill, slay, butcher, murder, slaughter 2. *n.* slaughter, carnage, extermination, butchery.

massage *v.* knead, stimulate, rub, stroke.

massive *adj.* 1. bulky, weighty, heavy *light* 2. immense, gigantic, huge *small*, *little*, *tiny*.

mast *n.* pylon, spar, yard, boom, pole.

master 1. *v.* acquire, learn, grasp, vanquish, conquer 2. *n.* commander, governor, ruler, teacher, expert, boss, chief, head *servant*.

masterly *adj.* clever, adroit, skillful, expert *clumsy*, *awkward*.

mat *n.* carpet, rug, cover, pad.

match 1. *v.* harmonize, resemble, equal 2. *n.* game, contest, trial, competition.

mate 1. *v.* match, marry, pair, couple, breed 2. *n.* companion, fellow, pal, associate.

material 1. *adj.* tangible, physical, real *intangible*, *spiritual* 2. *n.* substance, matter, fabric, textile.

maternal *adj.* motherly, affectionate, matronly *paternal*.

mathematical *adj.* accurate, precise, rigid, strict.

matrimony *n.* union, wedlock, marriage, nuptials.

matron *n.* nurse, wife, dame, woman, warden, principal.

matter 1. *n.* topic, affair, subject 2. *n.* difficulty, trouble 3. *n.* body, material, substance 4. *v.* mean, signify, import.

mature 1. *v.* age, mellow, ripen 2. *adj.* adult, grown-up *young*, *naïve*, *innocent* 3. *adj.* complete, full, mellow, ripe *immature*.

maul *v.* bruise, wound, injure, beat, batter, disfigure.

maxim *n.* saying, saw, axiom, rule, adage, proverb.

maximum *adj.* largest, highest, most, greatest *minimum*.

maybe *adv.* possibly, probably, perhaps.

maze *n.* network, warren, labyrinth, intricacy MAIZE.

meager *adj.* 1. hungry, lank, lean, gaunt *plump* 2. poor, frugal, scanty *plentiful*, *profuse*, *excess*.

meal *n.* 1. grain, flour, cereal, groats 2. repast, banquet, collation, spread, snack.

mean 1. *v.* signify, indicate, denote, intend 2. *adj.* shabby, beggarly, servile, poor *stately* 3. *adj.* unkind, cruel *kind* 4. *adj.* selfish, miserly, mercenary, stingy *generous* 5. *adj.* middle, medium, average *The mean temperature over the city was 20 degrees* MIEN.

meaning *n.* 1. sense, explanation, significance 2. design, aim, intention, object.

means *n.* 1. method, mode, way, expedient *We shall have to find some means of reaching the island* 2. income, resources, wealth, revenue.

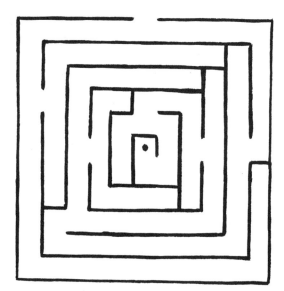

A maze

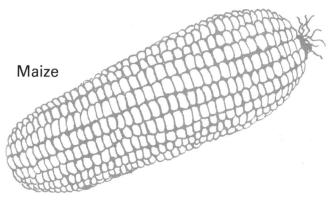

Maize

measure

measure 1. *v.* rule, gauge, appraise, estimate 2. *n.* rule, extent, gauge, size, dimension.

meat *n.* viands, victuals, fare, food, flesh MEET, METE.

mechanic *n.* craftsman, operative, artisan, technician, smith.

medal *n.* trophy, reward, medallion, award MEDDLE.

meddle *v.* intrude, pry, interfere, intercede MEDAL.

medicine *n.* physic, medicament, remedy, drug, potion, cure.

mediocre *adj.* inferior, average, commonplace, medium, so-so **superior**, **grand**.

meditate *v.* reflect, ponder, ruminate, contemplate.

medium 1. *adj.* average, mean, moderate, normal 2. *n.* means, agency, factor, method, instrument *Gold has been a medium of exchange for thousands of years.*

medley *n.* jumble, variety, hotchpotch, mixture, collection.

meek *adj.* mild, lowly, submissive, humble, docile, modest, gentle **undaunted**.

meet 1. *n.* meeting, contest, match 2. *adj.* proper, suitable, fit 3. *v.* comply, fulfill, discharge 4. *v.* assemble, collect, converge, encounter **miss**, **diverge**, **avoid**, **evade** MEAT, METE.

meeting *n.* gathering, congregation, assembly **parting**.

melancholy 1. *adj.* depressed, sad, sorrowful, dejected, unhappy, glum, gloomy **joyful**, **jubilant**, **happy** 2. *n.* dejection, depression, sadness, gloom **happiness**, **glee**.

mellow *adj.* 1. smooth, melodious, soft, silver-toned, sweet 2. mature, ripe **immature**, **unripened**.

melodious *adj.* musical, dulcet, harmonious, tuneful **discordant**, **unmelodious**, **harsh**, **hoarse**.

melody *n.* air, theme, tune, song, music.

melt *v.* dissolve, thaw, soften, liquefy **harden**, **freeze**, **solidify**.

A merry snowman melting

member *n.* 1. leg, arm, limb, component 2. associate, partner, fellow.

memento *n.* souvenir, remembrance, memorial, relic.

memoir *n.* diary, biography, narrative, record.

memorable *adj.* unforgettable, historic, remarkable, famous *passing*.

memorize *v.* learn, remember, retain.

memory *n.* remembrance, recall, recollection *forgetfulness*.

menace 1. *v.* alarm, frighten, intimidate, threaten *encourage* 2. *n.* threat, danger, peril, hazard.

mend *v.* repair, remedy, fix, refit, restore, improve, recover, heal *ruin*, *destroy*, *spoil*, *worsen*, *break*.

menial 1. *n.* domestic, servant, attendant 2. *adj.* low, servile.

mental *adj.* reasoning, rational, thinking, intellectual *physical*.

mention 1. *n.* reference, remark, allusion 2. *v.* declare, state, tell, refer to, speak of.

mercenary *adj.* 1. hired, paid 2. miserly, avaricious, covetous.

merchandise 1. *n.* stocks, goods, wares, produce 2. *v.* market, promote, sell.

merchant *n.* dealer, trader, tradesman, exporter, importer, retailer.

merciful *adj.* compassionate, lenient, kind, humane, forgiving, gracious *unjust*, *mean*, *harsh*, *merciless*, *ruthless*.

merciless *adj.* unfeeling, relentless, severe, ruthless, pitiless *merciful*, *benevolent*.

mercy *n.* 1. discretion, consideration *He threw himself on the mercy of the court* 2. compassion, pardon, grace, forgiveness, pity, clemency, sympathy *cruelty*, *ruthlessness*.

mere *adj.* sheer, simple, bare.

merely *adv.* purely, barely, hardly, simply, only, solely.

merge *v.* unite, join, mingle, submerge, combine.

merit 1. *v.* earn, deserve, have a right to 2. *n.* credit, worth, value, excellence, quality *fault*.

merry *adj.* cheerful, jovial, blithe, happy, jolly, lively *sad*, *doleful*, *gloomy*.

mesh *n.* net, web, screen, network.

mess *n.* 1. predicament, plight, difficulty 2. confusion, jumble, disorder, untidiness, muddle *order*.

message *n.* letter, missive, note, communication, dispatch, information.

messenger *n.* carrier, courier, bearer, envoy.

meter *n.* 1. gauge, record, measure 2. rhythm, measure, verse.

method *n.* manner, course, means, system, way, mode, process.

middle 1. *n.* midst, central, center *edge*, *beginning*, *end* 2. *adj.* center, halfway, mean, intermediate.

might 1. *v.* allow, permit, be possible 2. *n.* power, force, potency, strength MITE.

The might of a mite

mighty

A miner

A minor miner

mighty *adj.* powerful, strong, robust, potent, enormous **weak**, **frail**.

mild *adj.* gentle, bland, placid, tender, meek, kind, soft **turbulent**, **violent**, **stormy**, **incisive**, **severe**, **poignant**.

militant *adj.* belligerent, fighting, aggressive, contending **peaceful**.

military *adj.* soldierly, martial, warlike **civil**.

mimic 1. *n.* impressionist, impersonator 2. *v.* imitate, mime, ape, impersonate.

mince *v.* chop, grind, pulverize, cut up, crush, MINTS.

mind 1. *v.* attend, watch, observe 2. *v.* obey, pay attention to 3. mark, care, regard 4. *n.* spirit, intellect, brain, soul, intelligence, reason MINED.

mine 1. *v.* dig, excavate, quarry 2. *n.* pit, quarry, colliery, shaft, excavation.

mingle *v.* combine, blend, mix, join, merge **separate**, **sort**.

miniature 1. *n.* portrait 2. *adj.* small, diminutive, wee, tiny, little **large**, **giant**, **huge**.

minimum *adj.* lowest, smallest, least, limit, margin **maximum**.

minister *n.* 1. ambassador, administrator, official 2. parson, pastor, vicar, cleric, clergyman, priest.

minor 1. *n.* child, youth **major**, **adult** 2. *adj.* lesser, inferior, smaller, small, unimportant **chief**, **great**, **main**, **senior** MINER.

minority *n.* group, faction, contingent, few **majority**.

minstrel *n.* musician, bard, singer, troubadour.

mint 1. *v.* coin, stamp, forge, fashion, make, punch, strike 2. *adj.* fresh, untouched, new.

minute 1. *adj.* little, small, wee, microscopic, tiny **large**, **huge**, **immense** 2. *n.* jiffy, instant.

miracle *n.* wonder, prodigy, marvel, spectacle.

miraculous *adj.* wonderful, incredible, supernatural, extraordinary **ordinary**, **commonplace**, **everyday**.

mire *n.* ooze, mud, slime, slush.

mirror 1. *n.* reflector, looking glass 2. *v.* reflect, copy.

mirth *n.* laughter, joy, merriment, fun, jollity *gloom*, *sadness*, *seriousness*.

misbehavior *n.* naughtiness, rudeness, misconduct.

miscellaneous *adj.* various, mixed, diversified, mingled, diverse.

mischief *n.* 1. devilment, naughtiness, roguery, prankishness 2. harm, evil, injury, damage *good*.

mischievous *adj.* playful, naughty, troublesome *good*, *well-behaved*.

miscreant *n.* scoundrel, knave, rascal, rogue, villain.

miser *n.* niggard, tightwad, skinflint, hoarder *benefactor*, *spendthrift*.

miserable *adj.* 1. distressed, forlorn, unhappy, poor, wretched *joyful*, *content*, *happy* 2. mean, low, despicable 3. valueless, worthless.

misery *n.* woe, unhappiness, suffering, sorrow, grief, distress *delight*, *joy*, *bliss*, *ecstasy*, *rapture* 2. killjoy, drip, bore, moper.

misfortune *n.* calamity, mishap, disaster, blow, adversity *fortune*, *felicity*, *luck*, *welfare*.

misgiving *n.* mistrust, suspicion, hesitation, doubt *trust*.

mishap *n.* mischance, disaster, accident, calamity.

misjudge *v.* mistake, err, misunderstand, miscalculate.

mislay *v.* miss, misplace, lose *find*, *discover*.

mislead *v.* misguide, delude, deceive, misdirect, trick *guide*.

misplace *v.* miss, lose.

miss 1. *n.* damsel, girl, maid, maiden 2. *n.* failure, fault, slip, blunder *hit* 3. *v.* lose, forfeit, fail, mistake *succeed*, *catch* 4. *v.* yearn, want, need, wish.

missile *n.* weapon, rocket, projectile.

mission *n.* 1. legation, ministry, embassy 2. trust, business, errand, job, duty, assignment.

missionary *n.* evangelist, apostle, pioneer, preacher, minister.

mist *n.* haze, cloud, steam, vapor, fog, blur MISSED.

mistake 1. *v.* misjudge, confound, misunderstand 2. *n.* blunder, fault, error, oversight *accuracy*, *correctness*.

mistaken *adj.* erroneous, incorrect, wrong *correct*, *accurate*, *right*.

mistress *n.* paramour, courtesan, landlady, dame.

mistrust *v.* doubt, suspect, distrust, question *trust*, *confide*.

misunderstand *v.* misinterpret, misconceive, mistake *comprehend*, *understand*, *perceive*, *realize*.

misuse 1. *v.* maltreat, waste, squander, abuse 2. *n.* ill-treatment, abuse *use*.

mite *n.* atom, particle, scrap, molecule MIGHT.

mitigate *v.* 1. abate, lessen, relieve, moderate 2. soothe, mollify, allay, appease *aggravate*.

mix *v.* blend, mingle, compound, combine *separate*, *divide*.

mixture *n.* variety, miscellany, blend, hotchpotch, medley.

moan *v.* mourn, lament, wail, cry, grieve, complain, groan *rejoice* MOWN.

moat *n.* ditch, gully, fosse MOTE.

mob *n.* crowd, riffraff, throng, rabble, swarm, horde.

mobile *adj.* changeable, portable, movable, *immobile*, *fixed*, *stationary*, *still*.

mock 1. *adj.* counterfeit, imitation, sham, false *real*, *genuine*, *authentic* 2. *v.* ape, imitate, mimic 3. *v.* jeer, taunt, deride, gibe, ridicule, laugh at.

mockery

mockery *n.* 1. derision, scorn, ridicule *praise*, *admiration* 2. sham, pretense, counterfeit, show.

mode *n.* method, manner, way, style, fashion MOWED.

model 1. *n.* copy, imitation, replica, representation 2. *n.* version, type 3. *n.* prototype, original, pattern 4. *n.* mannequin 5. *v.* form, shape, plan, mold.

moderate 1. *v.* control, govern, judge 2. *v.* allay, quiet, lessen, soothe, appease *intensify* 3. *adj.* reasonable, fair, mild, temperate *extreme*, *excessive*, *immoderate*, *drastic*, *extreme*.

modern *adj.* late, novel, new, fresh, recent, present *antique*, *ancient*, *old-fashioned*, *obsolete*.

modest *adj.* 1. pure, chaste, virtuous *shameful*, *wanton*, *immodest* 2. moderate, reasonable 3. unassuming, humble, meek *proud*, *arrogant*, *showy*, *gaudy*.

modesty *n.* humility, simplicity, meekness, shyness, timidity *vanity*, *conceit*, *pride*.

modify *v.* alter, change, vary, shape, adjust.

moist *adj.* humid, dank, wet, damp, muggy *dry*, *arid*, *parched*.

moisture *n.* humidity, dampness, dankness, wetness *dryness*, *aridity*.

mold *n.* 1. mustiness, mildew, decay, blight 2. loam, earth 3. form, cast, shape, model.

molest *v.* pester, harass, disturb, assault, assail, harry, badger.

mollify *v.* relax, soften, tame, pacify, calm, tranquilize *tease*.

moment *n.* 1. significance, import, consequence, weight *insignificance* 2. second, jiffy, instant, twinkling.

momentous *adj.* serious, weighty, grave, important *trivial*, *trifling*, *unimportant*.

monarch *n.* king, queen, sovereign.

money *n.* coin, riches, wealth, currency, funds, cash.

mongrel *n. & adj.* hybrid, crossbred, half-bred.

monitor *n.* adviser, warner, supervisor, overseer.

monopolize *v.* hog, absorb, corner, control, dominate.

monotonous *adj.* tedious, boring, uniform, repetitious, humdrum, unvaried *fascinating*, *interesting*.

monster *n.* fiend, villain, demon, brute.

A monster

monstrous *adj.* 1. shocking, horrible, frightful, outrageous *agreeable* 2. vast, huge, enormous, colossal *tiny*.

monument *n.* cenotaph, memorial, tomb, pillar, statue.

monumental *adj.* stupendous, weighty, huge, important, exceptional, notable, remarkable *tiny*, *insignificant*, *trivial*.

mood *n.* humor, disposition, temper, vein.

moody *adj.* sullen, sulky, glum, pettish, morose, temperamental, ill-tempered *cheerful*, *good-natured*, *happy*.

moor 1. *v.* secure, fix, fasten 2. *n.* common, heath, bog.

mop *v.* swab, wipe, wash, clean.

mope *v.* be gloomy, grieve, sulk, despair, be sad *cheer up*.

moral *adj.* just, good, honest, virtuous, upright, ethical, law-abiding *immoral*, *dishonest*, *sinful*, *corrupt*, *infamous*, *unscrupulous*.

morale *n.* enthusiasm, confidence, spirit.

morass *n.* swamp, fen, bog, marsh, mire.

morbid *adj.* 1. depressed, pessimistic, gloomy *cheerful* 2. diseased, sick, unhealthy, unsound *healthy*.

more *adj.* greater, extra, further, in addition *fewer*, *less*.

moreover *conj. & adv.* further, also, likewise, besides, too.

morning *n.* sunrise, daybreak, dawn, forenoon *evening*.

morose *adj.* sour, churlish, moody, sullen, gloomy, depressed *cheerful*, *glad*, *sunny*.

morsel *n.* mouthful, fragment, bite, tidbit, piece, scrap.

mortal *adj.* 1. human, person, individual *immortal* 2. deadly, lethal, destructive, fatal.

mortify *v.* 1. corrupt, putrefy, fester *heal* 2. annoy, depress, vex, displease, upset *gratify*.

most 1. *adj.* extreme, greatest, maximum 2. *n.* greatest part *least*.

mostly *adv.* mainly, generally, principally, chiefly *seldom*.

mother 1. *v.* look after, nurse, care for 2. *n.* mama, mom.

motion *n.* 1. proposal, impulse, suggestion, gesture 2. passage, change, action, movement *stillness*, *immobility*.

motive *n.* incentive, reason, purpose, cause, spur, stimulus.

motley *adj.* mottled, mixed, speckled, dappled, mingled, assorted.

motor *n.* machine, car, engine, dynamo.

motto *n.* saying, maxim, adage.

mound *n.* hillock, hill, pile, knoll, heap.

mount 1. *n.* hill, mountain 2. *n.* steed, horse 3. *v.* scale, climb, go up 4. *v.* ascend, increase, rise *descend*.

A mount

103

mountain

Mounting the mountain

mountain *n.* mount, peak, height.

mourn *v.* deplore, bewail, bemoan, sorrow, grieve, lament **rejoice**, **celebrate**.

mournful *adj.* distressed, melancholy, sad, unhappy **cheerful**, **joyful**, **happy**, **festive**.

mouth *n.* 1. jaws, grimace, face 2. opening, entrance, inlet, aperture.

move 1. *n.* movement, motion, proceeding 2. *v.* push, propel, drive, stir **stop** 3. *v.* proceed, walk, go, advance, march **stay** 4. *v.* excite, rouse, affect, touch.

movement *n.* 1. party, faction, group 2. change, move, action, motion 3. melody, passage in music.

much 1. *adv.* long, frequently, often, nearly, almost 2. *adj.* plenteous, abundant **little**.

muck *n.* filth, dirt, refuse, mire, slime.

mud *n.* marsh, swamp, mire, dirt.

muddle 1. *v.* spoil, mix up, jumble, confuse 2. *n.* disorder, mess, plight, confusion, chaos.

muff *v.* spoil, muddle, bungle, miss.

muffle *v.* 1. dull, soften, deaden, mute, silence **amplify** 2. shroud, envelop, wrap, cover.

muggy *adj.* damp, stuffy, close, wet, dank, moist, humid.

multiply *v.* 1. procreate, reproduce 2. advance, gain, grow, increase **decrease**, **lessen**.

multitude *n.* legion, throng, assembly, crowd, swarm, host.

mum *adj.* mute, speechless, dumb, silent.

mumble *v.* murmur, mutter, babble, jabber.

munch *v.* nibble, crunch, eat, chew, bite.

murder 1. *v.* assassinate, kill, slay, slaughter, massacre 2. *n.* killing, death, homicide.

murky *adj.* dark, obscure, dim, gloomy, cloudy.

murmur 1. *n.* whisper, whimper, hum, grumble 2. *v.* whisper, whimper, mumble, mutter.

muscular *adj.* sinewy, strong, stalwart, brawny, powerful **weak**, **flabby**.

music *n.* harmony, symphony, tune, melody.

musical *adj.* harmonious, tuneful, melodious, dulcet.

must *v.* should, ought to, be obliged to, have to.

muster *v.* collect, gather, assemble, congregate.

musty *adj.* sour, stale, moldy, fusty.

mute *adj.* silent, speechless, dumb, voiceless.

mutilate *v.* cripple, injure, disfigure, maim, mangle, wound.

mutiny 1. *n.* rebellion, uprising, riot, revolt 2. *v.* revolt, rebel, rise up.

mutual *adj.* joint, reciprocal, common, alternate.

mysterious *adj.* hidden, secret, puzzling, unknown, obscure **open**, **direct**, **obvious**.

mystery *n.* enigma, riddle, puzzle, secret.

mystify *v.* puzzle, confuse, bewilder, perplex, baffle.

myth *n.* legend, fable, tradition, tale, fiction, fantasy.

mythical *adj.* fanciful, fictitious, fabulous, legendary **actual**, **historical**.

nab *v.* catch, grab, snatch, clutch, seize, arrest, grasp.

nag 1. *v.* pester, annoy, worry, bother, hector, vex **soothe**, **appease** 2. *n.* pony, horse.

nail *n.* claw, talon, spike, brad, pin, skewer, peg.

naïve *adj.* innocent, ingenuous, unsophisticated, artless, simple, unaffected **sophisticated**, **experienced**, **astute**, **cunning**.

naked *adj.* 1. unclothed, bare, nude, undressed 2. evident, open, manifest, unconcealed, simple.

name 1. *n.* reputation, character, repute 2. *n.* title, designation, appellation 3. *v.* call, entitle, term, christen, baptize.

nap *n.* sleep, slumber, doze, snooze, siesta.

narrate *v.* recite, recount, tell, describe, relate, detail.

narrative *n.* story, tale, account, history, description.

narrow *adj.* 1. thin, slender, close, confined, tight **wide**, **broad**, **spacious**, **extensive** 2. mean, avaricious, ungenerous.

nasty *adj.* 1. disagreeable, troublesome, annoying, unpalatable **sweet**, **palatable** 2. unclean, impure, filthy, foul, dirty **pleasant**, **nice**.

nation *n.* people, state, country, realm, population, society, land, community.

native 1. *n.* resident, citizen, aborigine **stranger**, **foreigner**, **outsider** 2. *adj.* aboriginal, local, indigenous, original, genuine, natural **foreign**, **alien**, **outlandish**.

natural *adj.* 1. native, inborn, natal, hereditary **alien** 2. ordinary, legitimate, normal, regular **unnatural**, **contrary**.

naturally *adv.* 1. simply, normally, freely 2. necessarily, usually, consequently, customarily, because of.

nature *n.* 1. disposition, temper, humor 2. species, type, character, sort 3. the universe, the earth, creation, the world.

naught *adv.* nothing.

naughty *adj.* bad, unruly, disobedient, mischievous, perverse, sinful, worthless **good**, **obedient**.

nausea

nausea *n.* sickness, queasiness, disgust, squeamishness.

nautical *adj.* naval, marine, maritime.

navigate *v.* direct, sail, steer, pilot, cruise.

navy *n.* fleet, shipping, vessels, ships.

near *adj.* close, nearby, adjacent, adjoining, nigh, neighboring **distant**, **remote**, **far**.

nearly *adv.* approximately, closely, almost.

neat *adj.* 1. clean, orderly, spruce, trim, tidy **untidy**, **sloppy**, **messy**, **unkempt** 2. handy, expert, clever 3. straight, pure, unadulterated, unmixed **diluted**.

A gnu

A new gnu

necessary *adj.* essential, indispensable, needed, obligatory, unavoidable **unnecessary**, **needless**, **optional**.

necessity *n.* requisite, essential, requirement, urgency **choice**.

need 1. *n.* poverty, distress, want, penury 2. *n.* urgency, lack, necessity, want **plenty** 3. *v.* require, lack, miss, want **have** KNEAD.

needless *adj.* superfluous, unnecessary, useless **necessary**.

needy *adj.* penniless, poor, destitute, poverty-striken **wealthy**, **affluent**, **rich**.

negative *adj.* canceling, denying, contradicting, opposed, conflicting, opposite, other, complaining **positive**.

neglect 1. *n.* default, disregard, failure, omission, negligence **care**, **attention**, **concern**, **regard** 2. *v.* leave out, disregard, ignore, omit **attend**, **care**, **concern**, **pamper**.

negligent *adj.* heedless, neglectful, careless, thoughtless, forgetful, indifferent **careful**, **vigilant**.

negotiate *v.* bargain, arrange, treat, discuss, settle, arbitrate, talk over.

neighbor *n.* countryman, nearby dweller, compatriot, acquaintance.

neighborhood *n.* locality, vicinity, nearness, district, community.

neighborly *adj.* friendly, kind.

nerve *n.* 1. impertinence, effrontery, cheek, sauciness **politeness** 2. power, force, vigor, courage, strength, pluck, bravery **cowardice**, **weakness**.

nervous *adj.* fearful, timid, weak, agitated, apprehensive, edgy **courageous**, **bold**, **confident**.

nestle *v.* huddle, snuggle, cuddle.

net *v.* 1. earn, obtain, clear, gain 2. *n.* trap, mesh, snare, web.

neutral *adj.* 1. dull, mediocre, drab 2. uninvolved, neuter, impartial **partial**, **partisan**.

never *adj.* not ever, at no time, not at all **always**, **ever**.

new *adj.* 1. modern, novel, fresh, latest, unused, original **old**, **ancient** GNU, KNEW.

newcomer *n.* entrant, beginner, novice, visitor, caller *veteran*.

news *n.* tidings, information, report, data, intelligence, word.

next *adj.* 1. following, after, subsequent *preceding*, *previous* 2. adjacent, closest, nearest, beside *distant*.

nibble *v.* bite, chew, nip, gnaw.

nice *adj.* 1. delightful, good, pleasant, agreeable, delicious *nasty*, *unpleasant*, *disagreeable* 2. accurate, precise, exact *careless*, *inexact*.

niche *n.* cranny, recess, corner.

nick *v. & n.* cut, score, notch, dent.

niggardly *adj.* mean, close, stingy, mercenary, miserly *generous*, *hospitable*.

nigh *adj.* adjacent, adjoining, near, close *distant*.

night *n.* dusk, evening, darkness, obscurity *day*, *light* KNIGHT.

nimble *adj.* brisk, active, spry, agile, light *awkward*, *clumsy*.

nip 1. *n.* pinch, bite 2. *n.* sip, drink, dram 3. *v.* bite, pinch, squeeze, clip, chill.

no 1. *adj.* none, not any, not one 2. *adv.* not at all, in no way, nay *yes* KNOW.

noble *adj.* 1. grand, lordly, stately, aristocratic *common*, *lowborn* 2. generous, superior, great, upright, magnanimous *ignoble*, *base*, *dishonest*.

nod *v.* 1. assent, agree, bow 2. sleep, nap.

noise *n.* clamor, uproar, din, racket, tumult, clatter, commotion, hubbub *silence*, *quiet*, *peace*.

nominate *v.* designate, choose, appoint, name, propose.

nonchalant *adj.* careless, indifferent, unconcerned, cool *excitable*.

nondescript *adj.* indescribable, abnormal, odd.

none *pron.* not any, not one, not a part NUN.

None

Nun

nonentity *n.* nobody, no one, nothing *celebrity*.

nonsense *n.* trash, absurdity, balderdash, moonshine, twaddle, folly, stupidity *sense*.

nook *n.* niche, corner, recess.

noose *n.* loop, rope, hitch, lasso.

normal *adj.* usual, natural, typical, customary, regular *abnormal*, *odd*, *irregular*, *peculiar*, *eccentric*.

nostalgia

nostalgia *n.* memories, memorabilia, homesickness, recollections.

notable *adj.* memorable, extraordinary, unusual, remarkable, noted, famous, distinguished ***ordinary***, ***commonplace***, ***usual***.

notch *v. & n.* cut, dent, nick, gash.

note 1. *n.* banknote, bill 2. *n.* fame, importance, repute, renown 3. *n.* notice, memo, report, comment 4. *v.* remark, record, notice, heed ***overlook***.

noted *adj.* famous, eminent, notable, celebrated ***unknown***.

nothing *n.* 1. naught, cipher, zero, 2. no thing, no part, nonexistence 3. small matter, trifle.

notice 1. *n.* advertisement, sign, poster 2. *n.* warning, intelligence, intimation 3. *n.* observation, heed, note 4. *v.* see, regard, observe, perceive ***ignore***.

notify *v.* announce, advise, inform, declare, acquaint.

notion *n.* fancy, impression, idea, belief, view, opinion, conception.

notorious *adj.* 1. famous, well-known, famed, celebrated 2. ill-famed, disreputable, infamous, nefarious ***creditable***.

nourish *v.* feed, support, nurture, nurse, cherish.

nourishment *n.* nutriment, food, sustenance, diet.

novel 1. *n.* tale, story, narrative, book, romance 2. *adj.* strange, unusual, new, modern, recent.

novice *n.* learner, tyro, beginner ***expert***, ***veteran***.

now *adv.* at present, at this time, right away, at once ***then***.

noxious *adj.* harmful, pernicious, injurious, toxic, malign ***fragant***.

nude *adj.* naked, bare, unclothed ***clothed***.

nuisance *n.* bother, trouble, bore, annoyance, irritation ***delight***, ***pleasure***.

null *adj.* invalid, useless, void.

nullify *v.* annul, cancel, repeal, abolish, invalidate ***establish***.

numb *adj.* insensible, dull, paralyzed, dead, unfeeling.

number 1. *n.* digit, figure 2. *n.* collection, horde, multitude, quantity 3. *v.* reckon, compute, count, total.

numeral *n.* figure, digit, number.

numerous *adj.* numberless, abundant, many ***few***, ***scanty***.

nurse 1. *n.* sister, matron, hospital worker 2. *v.* nourish, nurture, feed, suckle, mind, care for.

nurture *v.* nourish, support, train, educate, feed.

nutritious *adj.* strengthening, wholesome, nourishing, ***unwholesome***.

nymph *n.* girl, maid, maiden, damsel, lass.

oaf *n.* simpleton, blockhead, ruffian, lummox.

oath *n.* 1. curse, profanity, blasphemy 2. promise, vow, pledge.

obedient *adj.* dutiful, yielding, subservient, respectful ***rebellious***, ***disobedient***, ***perverse***, ***wayward***.

obey *v.* comply, follow, yield, submit, keep *disobey*, *resist*, *infringe*, *rebel*, *transgress*.

object 1. *n.* article, fact, thing, 2. *n.* goal, aim, target, end, objective 3. *v.* protest, oppose, refuse *agree*, *assent*, *approve*.

objection *n.* protest, opposition, disapproval, doubt, scruple *agreement*, *assent*, *concurrence*.

obligation *n.* agreement, contract, stipulation, bond 2. requirement, duty, responsibility.

oblige *v.* 1. force, coerce, compel, require *coax* 2. serve, gratify, please, favor *annoy*.

obliging *adj.* accommodating, kind, polite, friendly *discourteous*.

oblique *adj.* 1. indirect, devious 2. slanting, inclined, sloping.

obliterate *v.* cancel, delete, destroy, rub out, erase *create*.

oblivious *adj.* mindless, heedless, careless, forgetful, neglectful *heedful*.

obnoxious *adj.* odious, unpleasant, blameworthy, disagreeable, despicable, contemptible, loathsome, hateful *pleasant*.

obscene *adj.* impure, gross, indecent, smutty, filthy, foul, coarse, dirty, offensive *decent*.

obscure 1. *adj.* vague, incomprehensible, doubtful *lucid*, *clear*, *obvious* 2. *adj.* unknown, undistinguished *famous*, *distinguished* 3. *adj.* gloomy, dusky, dark, shadowy, indistinct *clear*, *legible* 4. *v.* hide, disguise, conceal darken *uncover*.

observant *adj.* watchful, alert, vigilant, attentive *inattentive*, *careless*.

observation *n.* 1. attention, observance, study, notice *neglect*, *inattention* 2. comment, note, remark.

observe *v.* 1. remark, note, see, behold, notice, detect *overlook*, *disregard* 2. celebrate, honor, keep up 3. express, mention, utter, say 4. obey, comply with, fulfill, keep, heed *infringe*.

obsolete *adj.* unfashionable, neglected, disused, antiquated, outmoded, old-fashioned *new*, *modern*, *current*, *fashionable*.

obstacle *n.* obstruction, check, barrier, hindrance, impediment, difficulty *aid*.

obstinate *adj.* dogged, perverse, pig-headed, stubborn, headstrong, unyielding *yielding*, *pliable*, *pliant*, *docile*.

obstruct *v.* oppose, stop, hinder, bar, delay, prevent, impede, block *help*, *further*, *aid*.

obstruction *n.* obstacle, impediment, hindrance, barrier.

obtain *v.* get, acquire, gain, achieve, procure *lose*.

obtuse *adj.* stupid, doltish, blunt, dull, slow-witted *sharp*, *quick*, *acute*, *keen*.

obvious *adj.* plain, clear, visible, evident, open, exposed, manifest, unmistakable *subtle*, *hidden*, *unobtrusive*, *obscure*, *inexplicable*.

occasion *n.* 1. opportunity, juncture, suitable time 2. event, incident, happening, occurrence.

occasional *adj.* irregular, casual, infrequent, rare *frequent*.

occult *adj.* mystical, supernatural, magical, hidden, secret *natural*.

occupant *n.* occupier, holder, resident, tenant.

occupation *n.* 1. calling, vocation, trade, craft, profession, employment 2. ownership, possession 3. handiwork, pastime.

occupy *v.* 1. inhabit, own 2. invade, seize, capture *evacuate* 3. possess, employ, use.

occur

occur *v.* happen, befall, come about, appear, arise.

occurrence *n.* happening, affair, incident, event.

ocean *n.* main, deep, sea.

odd *adj.* 1. singular, extraordinary, strange, unusual ***ordinary***, ***regular*** 2. uneven ***regular*** 3. single, unmatched.

odious *adj.* detestable, invidious, hateful, disagreeable.

odor *n.* aroma, scent, perfume, smell, bouquet.

offend *v.* 1. err, sin, transgress 2. annoy, vex, displease, mortify, irritate ***please***, ***flatter***.

offense *n.* 1. anger, displeasure, indignation ***delight***, ***pleasure*** 2. attack, assault, aggression 3. crime, sin, misdeed, wrong, fault.

offensive 1. *adj.* disagreeable, disgusting, revolting, ***pleasant*** 2. *adj.* aggressive, attacking, ***defensive*** 3. *adj.* rude, impertinent, insolent, unpleasant ***pleasant*** 4. *n.* attack ***inoffensive***.

offer 1. *n.* proposition, suggestion, proposal ***refusal***, ***denial*** 2. *v.* present, proffer, tender, submit ***refuse***, ***deny***, ***receive***.

office *n.* 1. post, situation, position, duty, job 2. bureau, room, place, studio, workplace, district.

official 1. *adj.* authorized, formal, authoritative ***informal*** 2. *n.* officer, bureaucrat, governor.

offshoot *n.* accessory, addition, by-product, branch.

offspring *n.* child, children, young, descendant.

often *adv.* frequently, many times, regularly, repeatedly rarely, ***seldom***, ***hardly***, ***sometimes***.

ogre *n.* fiend, giant, monster, goblin.

oil *n.* grease, lubricant, fat, petroleum.

old *adj.* 1. ancient, antique, old-fashioned ***fresh***, ***new*** 2. elderly, aged, mature ***young***, ***youthful*** 3. worn-out, decaying.

omen *n.* portent, augury, indication, sign, warning.

ominous *adj.* threatening, sinister, foreboding, unfavorable ***auspicious***.

omit *v.* ignore, exclude, leave out, miss, disregard ***include***.

onerous *adj.* weighty, difficult, burdensome, heavy ***light***.

only 1. *adv.* barely, simply, solely, merely 2. *adj.* sole, solitary, single, alone.

onset *n.* 1. beginning, outset, opening, start ***end*** 2. attack, charge, assault ***retreat***.

onslaught *n.* assault, attack, storm, charge, drive, push.

onward *adv.* in advance, ahead, forward ***backward***.

ooze *v.* percolate, drain, filter, leak, seep, drip, flow.

opaque *adj.* obscure, clouded, untransparent, filmy, murky ***transparent.***

Odd

open 1. *adj.* frank, fair, sincere, candid, honest ***secret, stealthy*** 2. *adj.* not closed, uncovered 3. *adj.* unobstructed, clear ***closed*** 4. *v.* unseal, uncover, unlock ***close*** 5. *v.* commence, begin, ***finish.***

opening *n.* 1. gap, hole, aperture 2. opportunity, vacancy, chance 3. commencement, beginning ***closure.***

openly *adv.* frankly, candidly, sincerely, plainly ***secretly.***

operate *v.* manage, run, perform, work, function, use, act.

operation *n.* function, working, performance, process.

opinion *n.* idea, viewpoint, belief, impression, estimation.

opponent *n.* adversary, enemy, foe, rival, competitor, antagonist ***ally, colleague, accomplice, friend.***

opportunity *n.* convenience, occasion, chance, time.

oppose *v.* confront, withstand, combat, thwart, contradict, resist ***support, cooperate, endorse.***

opposite *adj.* 1. facing, fronting 2. adverse, opposed, hostile, contrary, diverse, unlike ***same, like, similar.***

opposition *n.* antagonism, difference, defiance, obstruction, hostility, resistance ***cooperation, agreement, help, support.***

oppress *v.* crush, overwhelm, burden, torment, maltreat, persecute ***relieve.***

oppressive *adj.* 1. stifling, muggy, close, sultry 2. overwhelming, overpowering, hard ***light.***

optimistic *adj.* confident, cheerful, hopeful ***pessimistic.***

optional *adj.* voluntary, elective, discretional ***compulsory, obligatory, necessary.***

opulent *adj.* affluent, flush, rich, well-off, wealthy ***poor.***

oral *adj.* verbal, uttered, said, spoken, vocal ***written, printed.***

oration *n.* address, speech, lecture, discourse.

orb *n.* sphere, ball, globe.

orbit *n.* track, circuit, course, path, revolution.

ordain *v.* 1. prescribe, order, decree, enact 2. call, elect, consecrate, appoint.

Opposite

111

ordeal *n*. experience, proof, tribulation, test, trial, suffering, hardship.

order 1. *n*. shipment, requirement, consignment 2. *n*. rule, law, regulation 3. *n*. mandate, direction, instruction, command 4. *n*. method, plan, arrangement *disorder*, *chaos* 5. *v*. classify, arrange 6. *v*. direct, instruct, decree.

orderly 1. *adj*. well-behaved, peacable, quiet *unruly* 2. *adj*. neat, methodical *disorderly* 3. *n*. attendant, servant.

ordinary *adj*. 1. commonplace, mediocre, average, common *uncommon*, *superior*, *unusual*, *special*, *unique* 2. established, normal, customary, standard *extraordinary*, *fabulous*.

organization *n*. institute, association, management, establishment, group.

organize *v*. order, construct, arrange, establish, form *ruin*, *disorganize*.

orifice *n*. aperture, mouth, hole.

origin *n*. spring, fountain, foundation, source, root, derivation, birth *end*.

original *adj*. 1. novel, fresh, new, creative *hackneyed*, *trite*, *old* 2. aboriginal, primary, first, primitive *secondary*.

originate *v*. 1. discover, produce, invent, create 2. begin, start, arise *end*.

ornament 1. *v*. adorn, embellish, decorate, beautify 2. *n*. adornment, decoration.

ornate *adj*. embellished, decorated, adorned, ornamented *unadorned*, *plain*, *simple*.

orthodox *adj*. correct, normal, conventional, sound, true, accepted, traditional *unconventional*, *unorthodox*.

ostentatious *adj*. vain, pompous, pretentious, boastful, showy *modest*.

ought *adv*. should, must, need to.

oust *v*. expel, dislodge, deprive, eject, evict *admit*.

outbreak *n*. 1. explosion, outburst, eruption 2. fray, revolt, riot, brawl, conflict.

outburst *n*. eruption, torrent, outbreak.

outcast *n*. vagabond, castaway, exile, wretch.

outcome *n*. result, consequence, issue, conclusion.

outcry *n*. scream, clamor, uproar, cry *peace*, *silence*.

outdo *v*. exceed, beat, excel, surpass.

outfit *n*. gear, kit, clothing, rig, equipment.

outing *n*. expedition, trip, excursion, holiday, jaunt.

outlandish *adj*. alien, strange, foreign, uncouth, barbarous *native*.

outlaw *n*. bandit, freebooter, fugitive, robber, brigand, highwayman, criminal.

outlay *n*. costs, expenses, expenditure *receipt*, *income*.

outlet *n*. way out, exit, egress, opening, vent, break *entrance*.

outline 1. *n*. shape, silhouette 2. *n*. sketch, plan, draft, drawing, contour 3. *v*. draw, draft, sketch.

outlook *n*. 1. scene, prospect, view 2. chance, prospect, future 3. attitude, viewpoint.

output *n*. production, proceeds, crop, yield.

outrage 1. *v*. offend, shock, insult, abuse 2. *n*. affront, offense, insult, indignity, abuse *compliment*.

outrageous *adj*. exorbitant, extravagant, villainous, atrocious, excessive, monstrous.

outright *adv*. entirely, altogether, wholly, completely *partly*.

outset *n.* opening, start, commencement, beginning *climax*, *end*.

outside 1. *n.* utmost, limit 2. *n.* surface, exterior 3. *adj.* external, outer, exterior *inside*.

outspoken *adj.* plain, blunt, candid, bold, frank *reserved*.

outstanding *adj.* 1. conspicuous, eminent, distinguished *inconspicuous* 2. owing, due, unsettled, unpaid *paid*.

outward *adj.* exterior, outside, external, outer *inward*.

outwit *v.* defraud, confuse, baffle, cheat, trick, deceive.

over *prep.* above, on top of, across, more than, during *below*, *under*.

overall *adj.* complete, sweeping, comprehensive.

overbearing *adj.* domineering, arrogant, oppressive, imperious, overpowering *humble*.

overcast *adj.* murky, obscure, cloudy, hazy *clear*, *sunny*.

overcome *v.* conquer, vanquish, overwhelm, subdue, crush, defeat *yield*, *submit*.

overflow *v.* flood, cascade, inundate, run over.

overhaul *v.* 1. check, examine, repair 2. pass, overtake, gain upon.

overhear *v.* listen, eavesdrop, learn.

overjoyed *adj.* ecstatic, jubilant, delighted, rapturous *depressed*.

overlook *v.* 1. rise above, look down upon 2. excuse, pardon, forgive *punish* 3. neglect, miss, disregard *include*.

overpower *v.* overcome, vanquish, subdue, conquer, overwhelm *surrender*.

overrule *v.* 1. cancel, revoke, rescind, annul, repeal 2. govern, control, direct *allow*.

overseer *n.* inspector, foreman, superintendent.

oversight *n.* 1. mistake, neglect, fault, error, blunder 2. direction, management, control.

overtake *v.* overhaul, pass, catch.

overthrow *v.* conquer, destroy, defeat, vanquish, beat *restore*.

overture *n.* 1. [music] prelude, opening, introduction 2. offer, proposal, invitation.

overwhelm *v.* 1. sink, flood, swallow up, submerge, drown 2. overpower, conquer, defeat.

own *v.* 1. confess, avow, allow, admit *deny* 2. hold, possess, have.

owner *n.* possessor, holder, landlord, proprietor.

Overlooking
the overseer

pace

P

pace 1. *n.* walk, stride, step, amble 2. *n.* speed, rate 3. *v.* stride, walk, move, go.

pacific *adj.* peaceful, calm, gentle, mild, unruffled, tranquil *excited*, *rough*, *turbulent*.

pacify *v.* tranquilize, calm, appease, lull *inflame*, *excite*, *disturb*, *upset*, *madden*.

pack 1. *n.* clan, crew, gang, band, herd, mob 2. *n.* parcel, package, bale, bundle, burden 3. *v.* stow, fill, store, compress, cram.

package *n.* pack, packet, box, bundle, parcel.

pact *n.* agreement, treaty, contract, alliance, bond, bargain PACKED.

pad 1. *n.* pillow, wadding, cushion, bolster 2. *n.* blotter, notebook, tablet 3. *v.* expand, fill out, protect, stuff.

paddle 1. *v.* bathe, dip, wade 2. *n.* oar, scull, sweep, lever.

page *n.* 1. leaf, sheet, paper, blade 2. attendant, servant boy.

pageant *n.* spectacle, parade, review, display, show.

pain 1. *n.* ache, pang, agony, discomfort, suffering, distress *comfort*, *ease* 2. *n.* sorrow, grief, misery, heartache *joy*, *delight*, *pleasure* 3. *v.* grieve, disquiet, trouble 4. *v.* torture, torment PANE.

painful *adj.* racking, sore, aching, agonizing, distressing *soothing*.

painstaking *adj.* hardworking, exacting, careful, assiduous, thorough *slipshod*, *careless*.

paint 1. *n.* color, pigment, dye, stain, lacquer 2. *v.* draw, sketch, portray, picture, cover.

painting *n.* portrait, picture, sketch, composition.

pair *n.* couple, brace, two, twain, twins PARE, PEAR.

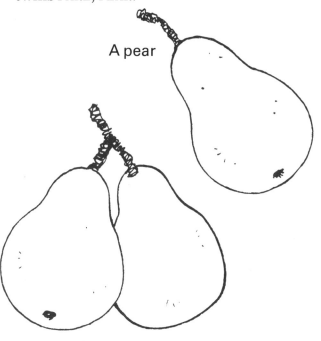

A pear

A pair of pears

pal *n.* fellow, friend, chum, companion, comrade *enemy*, *rival*.

palace *n.* mansion, stately home, castle *hovel*.

palatable *adj.* delicious, tasty, luscious, savory, enjoyable *nasty*.

pale 1. *n.* stake, fence, paling, picket 2. *adj.* obscure, faint, dim *bright* 3. *adj.* wan, ashen, pallid, white *ruddy*, *flushed* PAIL.

pall 1. *n.* cover, shroud, cloak 2. *v.* depress, discourage, dispirit.

palpitate *v.* flutter, tremble, quaver, throb, pulsate.

paltry *adj.* little, trifling, worthless, insignificant, petty, small *important*.

pamper *v.* favor, coddle, spoil, fondle *neglect*, *scourge*.

pamphlet *n.* leaflet, booklet, folder, brochure, handbill.

pan *n.* vessel, skillet, caldron, kettle, pot.

panel *n.* 1. group, committee, forum, team 2. partition, board, wall.

pang *n.* pain, twinge, hurt, gripe, throb, ache.

panic 1. *v.* terrify, stampede, frighten *soothe*, *tranquilize*, *calm* 2. *n.* terror, dread, fright, alarm.

pant *v.* blow, wheeze, puff, gasp.

paper *n.* 1. newspaper, journal 2. document, writing, record 3. essay, report, dissertation, article *At the society meeting, she read her paper on growing mushrooms* 4. notepaper, stationery.

par *n.* average, normal, equality.

parade 1. *v.* display, flaunt, strut, show off 2. *n.* ceremony, show, pageant, display.

paradise *n.* heaven, utopia, Eden, fairyland.

paradox *n.* reversal, ambivalence, enigma, mystery, absurdity, contradiction.

paragraph *n.* clause, section, sentence, passage, item.

parallel 1. *n.* counterpart, resemblance, equal 2. *adj.* similar, resembling, like *divergent* 3. *v.* match, equal, resemble.

paralyze *v.* transfix, deaden, unnerve, benumb, freeze, cripple, disable.

paramount *adj.* principal, supreme, eminent, chief, superior, foremost, leading *inferior*.

paraphernalia *n.* baggage, belongings, trappings, ornaments, equipment.

parasite *n.* flatterer, sycophant, hanger-on, toady.

parcel *n.* packet, collection, lot, bundle, package.

parch *v.* shrivel, scorch, brown, dry.

parched *adj.* arid, withered, dry, dehydrated, thirsty, scorched *wet*, *moist*.

pardon 1. *v.* absolve, excuse, discharge, clear, forgive, release *condemn*, *sentence*, *avenge*, *retaliate* 2. *n.* remission, absolution, grace, mercy, acquittal, forgiveness.

pare *v.* 1. shave, clip, skin, peel, cut 2. reduce, lessen, diminish PAIR, PEAR.

parentage *n.* birth, descent, lineage, pedigree, extraction, ancestry, forebears, family.

park 1. *v.* place, station, post, leave, put, settle 2. *n.* garden, enclosure, green, grassland, wood.

parley 1. *v.* talk, discourse, discuss, converse 2. *n.* talk, discussion.

parody 1. *v.* caricature, imitate 2. *n.* burlesque, imitation, satire.

parry *v.* prevent, avert, avoid, turn aside, ward off, side step.

parsimonious *adj.* close, mean, avaricious, miserly, closefisted, stingy *generous*.

parson *n.* minister, priest, clergyman, rector, pastor, vicar, presbyter.

part 1. *n.* character, role 2. *n.* share, lot, portion 3. *n.* portion, piece, fragment, section *whole*, *entirety* 4. *n.* division, component, element 5. *v.* divide, sever, break, split *unite*.

partial *adj.* 1. fond, favorably disposed 2. biased, unjust, prejudiced *impartial*, *just* 3. limited, imperfect, incomplete *whole*, *complete*.

participate *v.* share, take part in, partake, join in.

particle

particle *n.* scrape, speck, spot, grain, bit, piece.

particular *adj.* 1. distinctive, exceptional, unusual **general** 2. careful, precise, fastidious, fussy **careless** 3. special, specific.

parting 1. *adj.* declining, departing 2. *n.* separation, division, breaking 3. *n.* leave-taking, farewell **meeting**, **arriving**.

partisan *n.* supporter, disciple, follower **leader**.

partition 1. *n.* barrier, screen, wall 2. *n.* separation, division **unification**, **joining** 3. *v.* share, divide, apportion.

partner *n.* 1. spouse, companion, husband, wife, consort 2. collaborator, colleague, associate.

partnership *n.* association, alliance, company, connection, union.

party *n.* 1. gathering, social, get-together 2. group, company, assembly, crowd 3. circle, ring, league, set, alliance 4. individual, person *We were not alone together; Harry was the third party.*

pass *v.* 1. convey, deliver, send 2. occur, experience, suffer *We passed several months of very cold weather* 3. pass away, cease, elapse, lapse 4. move, proceed, go 5. enact, approve 6. ignore, disregard *He passed the question since he did not know the answer* **consider**, **notice**, **note** 7. excel, surpass, exceed 8. *n.* gorge, ravine 9. *n.* permit, license.

passage *n.* 1. gallery, corridor, lobby 2. trip, journey, voyage 3. transit, movement, passing 4. sentence, paragraph, clause.

passenger *n.* wayfarer, traveler, tourist.

passion *n.* 1. love, fondness, affection, attachment 2. fervor, zeal, rapture, excitement, rage **indifference**, **apathy**.

passionate *adj.* 1. excitable, angry, impatient **good-tempered** 2. enthusiastic, fervent, warm, ardent, zealous **apathetic**.

passive *adj.* unresisting, yielding, submissive, inactive, quiet **active**, **impassive**.

past 1. *n.* bygone time 2. *adj.* previous, former 3. *adj.* spent, ended, gone, over PASSED.

pastime *n.* entertainment, sport, relaxation, diversion, hobby, amusement **profession**.

pastry *n.* confection, sweet, cake, gateau, tart, pie.

pasture *n.* grass, meadowland, field, grassland, herbage.

pat *v.* & *n.* tap, hit, rap.

patch *v.* repair, restore, fix, mend.

patent 1. *adj.* apparent, clear, evident, obvious 2. *n.* invention, copyright, protection.

paternal *adj.* fatherly.

path *n* track, trail, way, route, passage, lane, road.

pathetic *adj.* touching, tender, pitiable, affecting **laughable**.

patience *n.* 1. composure, courage, calmness 2. perseverance, persistence, endurance **impatience** PATIENTS.

patient 1. *adj.* persistent, persevering 2. *adj.* calm, submissive, uncomplaining **impatient**, **excitable** 3. *n.* sufferer, invalid.

patriotic *adj.* nationalistic, chauvinistic, loyal.

patrol 1. *n.* watchman, guard, janitor, sentry 2. *v.* watch, protect, guard.

patronize *v.* 1. disdain, condescend, look down upon 2. support, assist, help, favor.

patter *n.* 1. tapping, rattle 2. jabber, prattle, chat, chatter.

pattern *n.* specimen, model, prototype, sample.

pause 1. *v.* cease, desist, wait, stop, delay *continue*, *perpetuate* 2. *n.* halt, rest, hesitation, break, stop *continuity*, *perpetuity* PAWS.

paw *n.* talon, claw, foot, pad, hoof.

pawn *v.* wager, stake, deposit, pledge.

pay *v.* 1. *n.* wages, salary, payment 2. *v.* settle, compensate, discharge, reward.

peace *n.* 1. concord, harmony *discord*, *war* 2. stillness, serenity, calm, quiet *tumult*, *outcry* PIECE.

peaceful *adj.* tranquil, serene, pacific, calm, friendly *disrupted*, *disturbed*, *martial*, *militant*, *restless*, *turbulent*.

peak *n.* summit, crest, crown, apex, pinnacle, top *base*, *bottom* PIQUE.

peal *v.* toll, sound, echo, boom, ring, chime PEEL.

peculiar *adj.* 1. particular, individual, special 2. uncommon, strange, unusual, exceptional, queer *ordinary*, *common*, *everyday*.

pedal *v.* push with foot, drive PEDDLE.

peddle *v.* vent, sell, hawk, retail PEDAL.

pedestrian 1. *adj.* slow, dull, stodgy, monotonous, prosaic, prosy 2. *n.* walker, hiker, tramper.

pedigree *n.* ancestry, breed, lineage, descent.

Peel

Peeling peel

peel *v.* skin, strip, pare PEAL.

peep *v. & n.* 1. cheep, chirp, cry 2. look, glimpse, peer, peek.

peer 1. *v.* examine, pry, peep, peek 2. *n.* nobleman, lord 3. *n.* companion, equal, equivalent PIER.

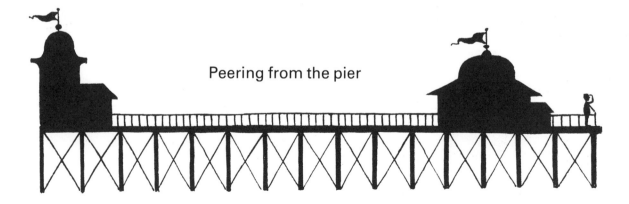

Peering from the pier

peevish

peevish *adj.* cross, testy, fretful, petulant, irritable *amiable*.

peg *n.* hanger, stopper, pin, fastening.

pelt 1. *n.* skin, coat, hide 2. *v.* dash, flash, streak, rush 3. *v.* beat, batter, throw, strike, assail 4. *v.* pour, rain, stream.

Pen

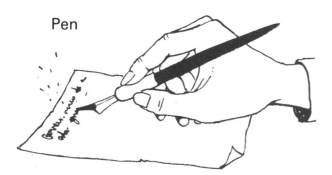

pen 1. *v.* compose, write, inscribe 2. *n.* sty, coop, enclosure, cage 3. *n.* quill, style, stylus, nib.

penalty *n.* fine, forfeit, punishment *reward*.

pencil 1. *v.* sketch, mark, depict, draw 2. *n.* brush, crayon, lead, pastel.

pendant *n.* pennant, hanging, earring, tassle.

pending 1. *prep.* during 2. *adj.* waiting, undecided, depending.

penetrate *v.* 1. perforate, bore, permeate, pierce, enter *extract* 2. understand, discern, comprehend, perceive.

penetrating *adj.* acute, keen, subtle, shrewd, sharp, discerning *blunt*, *stupid*.

penitence *n.* sorrow, contrition, regret, repentance, remorse.

pennant *n.* flag, banner, streamer, pendant.

penniless *adj.* needy, bankrupt, poverty-stricken, destitute, poor *rich*, *wealthy*.

pension *n.* 1. annuity, grant, allowance 2. guesthouse, hotel, hostel.

pensive *adj.* reflective, thoughtful.

people 1. *n.* folk, persons, human beings, population 2. *n.* race, family, tribe, nation 3. *v.* populate.

pep *n.* vim, punch, guts, vigor, power *apathy*, *listlessness*.

peppery *adj.* 1. irascible, testy, hasty, irritable, churlish 2. pungent, hot.

perceive *v.* 1. comprehend, grasp, understand *misunderstand* 2. notice, remark, discover, see, observe.

percentage *n.* proportion, ratio, part.

perch 1. *v.* settle, roost 2. *n.* pole, rod, staff.

percolate *v.* strain, drain, filter, ooze.

perfect 1. *adj.* total, entire 2. *adj.* excellent, complete, faultless, flawless, blameless *flawed*, *imcomplete*, *imperfect*, *defective* 3. *v.* finish, complete, accomplish.

perfidy *n.* treachery, faithlessness, disloyalty, treason, betrayal *fidelity*.

perforate *v.* drill, puncture, penetrate, pierce, bore.

perform *v.* 1. effect, achieve, do, execute, carry out *fail* 2. play, act, present.

performer *n.* player, actor, entertainer, musician *spectator*.

perfume *n.* smell, scent, fragrance, odor, aroma.

perhaps *adv.* maybe, conceivably, perchance, possibly *absolutely*, *definitely*.

peril *n.* hazard, risk, danger, jeopardy *safety*, *security*.

period *n.* 1. cycle, course 2. term, era, epoch, time, span, age, interval.

periodical *n.* 1. newspaper, magazine, journal, review, publication 2. *adj.* regular, recurrent, intermittent.

perish *v.* 1. decay, wither, waste, shrivel *endure* 2. expire, die, decease, pass away.

perky *adj.* jaunty, trim, pert, airy.

permanent *adj.* enduring, durable, stable, lasting, steadfast, constant, perpetual *passing*, *temporary*, *transient*, *fleeting*.

permeate *v.* spread through, pervade.

permission *n.* leave, license, liberty, consent, authorization.

permit 1. *n.* license, pass, permission, authority 2. *v.* let, allow, endure, tolerate *prohibit*, *disallow*, *forbid*.

pernicious *adj.* injurious, mischievous, fatal, hurtful, deadly, destructive *harmless*.

perpendicular *adj.* upright, vertical *horizontal*.

perpetrate *v.* perform, execute, commit, do, achieve.

perpetual *adj.* everlasting, ceaseless, permanent, endless, eternal, continual, unceasing *intermittent*, *inconstant*, *temporary*.

perplex *v.* mystify, confound, puzzle, confuse, bewilder *enlighten*.

persecute *v.* distress, torment, victimize, oppress, harass *befriend*.

persevere *v.* endure, continue, persist, keep on *lapse*, *desist*, *stop*, *discontinue*.

persist *v.* endure, continue, remain, last, persevere *stop*, *desist*, *refrain*.

persistent *adj.* enduring, determined, dogged, constant, stubborn *inconstant*.

personal *adj.* private, individual, particular, special *public*, *general*.

personality *n.* character, identity, individuality.

perspective *n.* view, aspect, prospect, vista, outlook.

persuade *v.* entice, coax, influence, urge, induce, convince *dissuade*, *discourage*.

persuasive *adj.* logical, compelling, convincing, enticing, inducing *unconvincing*, *dubious*.

pert *adj.* brisk, flippant, nimble, lively, dapper, smart, saucy, sprightly *polite*, *courteous*.

pertain *v.* belong, concern, appertain, befit, apply.

pertinent *adj.* suitable, appropriate, relevant, fit *inappropriate*.

perturb *v.* disturb, disquiet, confuse, trouble, agitate *compose*.

peruse *v.* observe, scrutinize, read, examine, study.

pervade *v.* spread, permeate, fill, penetrate.

perverse *adj.* willful, contrary, obstinate, dogged, stubborn *obedient*.

pervert *v.* entice, corrupt, distort, tempt, falsify.

pessimistic *adj.* gloomy, unhappy, doubtful, cheerless *optimistic*.

pest *n.* 1. insect, virus, vermin, germ 2. infection, nuisance, pestilence, plague, affliction.

pester *v.* plague, hector, bother, badger, annoy, harass, vex.

pestilence *n.* epidemic, plague, pest.

pet 1. *n.* darling, favorite 2. *v.* indulge, caress, fondle.

petition 1. *v.* solicit, beg, appeal, entreat, ask 2. *n.* appeal, application, request.

petrify *v.* 1. change to stone, ossify, fossilize, calcify 2. amaze, dumbfound, stun, astonish.

petty *adj.* 1. mean, miserly, stingy *generous* 2. trifling, insignificant, small, little, trivial, paltry, slight, unimportant *important*.

petulant

petulant *adj.* peevish, hasty, irritable, touchy.

phantom 1. *adj.* spectral, unreal, ghostly, imaginary **real** 2. *n.* vision, ghost, spook, specter, spirit, apparition.

phase *n.* aspect, state, condition, appearance, stage FAZE.

phenomenal *adj.* wondrous, marvelous, miraculous **commonplace**.

phenomenon *n.* marvel, wonder, occurrence, appearance, happening, manifestation.

philanthropic *adj.* gracious, charitable, benevolent, kind, generous, giving **selfish**.

philosophical *adj.* calm, tranquil, wise, unruffled **restless**.

phobia *n.* aversion, dread, fear, distaste, hatred, dislike.

phrase *n.* idiom, clause, sentence, expression FRAYS.

physical *adj.* 1. corporal, carnal, bodily 2. mortal, substantial, material, natural **spiritual**, **mental**.

physique *n.* build, shape, form.

pick 1. *n.* pike, pickax, mattock, adze, icepick, toothpick 2. *v.* gather, choose, pluck, select.

picket 1. *v.* stand watch, demonstrate, protest, boycott 2. *n.* guard, sentry, sentinel 3. *n.* pale, paling, fence, post.

pickle *n.* 1. plight, quandry, predicament, tough spot 2. sauce, chutney, relish.

picture 1. *v.* describe, draw, paint, imagine 2. *n.* drawing, painting, photograph, illustration, engraving.

piece *n.* part, bit, scrap, fragment, share, portion PEACE.

pierce *v.* 1. move, affect, thrill, excite 2. enter, perforate, stab, puncture.

pig *n.* hog, swine, sow, boar, porker.

pigment *n.* paint, dye, color, stain.

pike *n.* spear, point, spike, lance, harpoon, javelin.

pile 1. *v.* gather, heap up, collect 2. *n.* collection, heap, mass.

pilfer *v.* purloin, steal, thieve, rob.

pilgrim *n.* wayfarer, wanderer, crusader, traveler.

pilgrimage *n.* voyage, journey, trek, tour, trip, expedition.

pill *n.* tablet, capsule, lozenge, drug.

pillage *v.* despoil, rifle, plunder, rob, sack.

pillar *n.* prop, monument, column, post, pole, pylon.

pillow *n.* cushion, bolster, support, headrest.

pilot 1. *v.* direct, conduct, steer, guide 2. *n.* guide, steersman, helmsman, aviator, coxswain, navigator.

pimple *n.* spot, swelling, eruption, blotch, boil, pock.

pin 1. *v.* fix, transfix, fasten 2. *n.* bolt, clip, peg, fastener, brooch, clasp.

pinch 1. *n.* crisis, difficulty, emergency 2. *n.* pang, nip, squeeze 3. *v.* compress, tweak, nip, squeeze.

pinnacle *n.* top, summit, apex, turret, peak, zenith, minaret.

pious *adj.* devout, saintly, religious, godly, holy **impious**, **profane**.

pipe *n.* 1. tube, cylinder, hose, reed, straw 2. recorder, flute, fife, whistle 3. briar, corncob, meershaum, calumet.

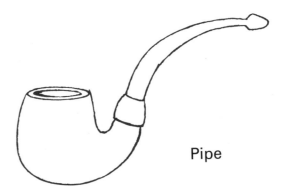

Pipe

pique 1. *n.* grudge, irritation, resentment 2. *v.* displease, vex, offend, affront PEAK.

pirate 1. *n.* privateer, sea rover, freebooter, buccaneer, corsair 2. *v.* copy, plagiarize, appropriate, annex, infringe, lift.

Pirate

pivot *n.* hinge, swivel, fulcrum, turn, spindle.

placard *n.* poster, advertisement, notice, bill, handbill.

placate *v.* appease, pacify, conciliate.

place 1. *n.* house, home, residence, dwelling 2. *n.* spot, district, site, area, position, situation, location 3. *n.* office, job, post, employment 4. *n.* town, city, village 5. *v.* set, locate, establish, put, deposit, lay, seat PLAICE.

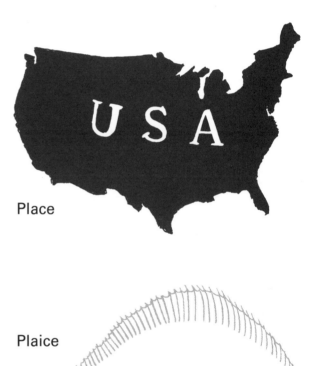

Place

pistol *n.* gun, revolver, firearm, repeater PISTIL.

pit *n.* hollow, hole, cavity, mine, well, crater.

pitch 1. *n.* slant, angle, slope 2. *v.* fall, plunge, collapse 3. *v.* cast, fling, toss, hurl 4. *v.* set up, erect, raise (a tent), encamp.

piteous *adj.* mournful, pitiable, sorrowful, miserable, woeful.

pitiless *adj.* ruthless, unfeeling, cruel, merciless ***kindly***, ***kind***, ***gentle***.

pity 1. *v.* sympathize, commiserate, condole, relent 2. *n.* mercy, sympathy, compassion, charity ***cruelty***.

Plaice

placid *adj.* calm, peaceful, quiet, composed, tranquil, serene ***temperamental***.

plague

plague 1. *n.* epidemic, disease, pestilence, contagion 2. *n.* trouble, annoyance, vexation ***boon*** 3. *v.* vex, trouble, annoy, molest *I've been plagued by mosquitoes all summer* ***please***.

plain 1. *adj. smooth, even, flat, level* ***uneven*** 2. *adj.* simple, ordinary, unadorned ***ornate***, ***fancy***, ***grand***, ***luxurious***, ***magnificent*** 3. *adj.* homely, unattractive, ugly ***beautiful***, ***pretty*** 4. *adj.* obvious, clear, certain, manifest, understandable 5. *adj.* frank, sincere, honest, straightforward 6. *n.* prairie, steppe, pampas, savanna, plateau PLANE.

plan 1. *v.* contrive, plot, devise, arrange, concoct 2. *n.* draft, chart, map, sketch, drawing, plot 3. *n.* system, design, scheme, proposal.

plane 1. *n.* airplane, aircraft 2. *adj.* flat, smooth, level, even PLAIN.

plant 1. *n.* herb, shrub, bush, flower, vegetable 2. *n.* workshop, shop, factory, equipment, works, mills 3. *v.* seed, sow, scatter.

Plant

plaster 1. *n.* cement, mortar, stucco, gypsum 2. *n.* bandage, lint, gauze, dressing 3. *v.* coat, cover, daub, smear.

plastic 1. *v.* soft, flexible, pliable, malleable 2. *n.* polythene, thermoplastic, polystyrene, latex, celluloid, Bakelite.

plate 1. *v.* coat, cover, laminate 2. *n.* silverware, dish, engraving, platter.

platform *n.* 1. program, plan, policy, principle *Senator Johnson's platform was based on free trade* 2. stage, podium, rostrum, pulpit.

plateau *n.* tableland.

platitude *n.* triteness, commonplace.

plausible *adj.* 1. likely, fair, reasonable, credible ***implausible*** 2. glib, deceptive, specious, superficial ***genuine***, ***real***.

play 1. *v.* frolic, skip, frisk, gambol, sport, caper 2. *v.* act, perform, represent, impersonate 3. *v.* trifle, dally, toy *Don't play with your fork; eat your food!* 4. *v.* operate, work *He played the violin superbly* 5. *v.* game, gamble, compete, contend 6. *n.* drama, comedy, tragedy, farce, melodrama, show 7. *n.* sport, game, recreation, amusement ***work***.

player *n.* contestant, competitor, sportsperson, actor.

playful *adj.* humorous, merry, lively, frisky, amusing ***serious***, ***ferocious***.

plea *n.* 1. excuse, cause, defense, apology 2. entreaty, request, appeal.

plead *v.* 1. beg, entreat, appeal, excuse 2. dispute, reason, defend, argue ***deny***, ***refuse***.

pleasant *adj.* delightful, charming, agreeable, amiable, pleasurable, gratifying ***unpleasant***, ***disagreeable***, ***obnoxious***, ***repulsive***, ***horrible***.

please *v.* 1. like, choose, wish, prefer 2. delight, content, gratify, satisfy *displease*, *annoy*, *vex*, *offend* PLEAS.

pleased *adj.* glad, content, satisfied, happy *irate*, *sorry*.

pleasing *adj.* welcome, pleasant, charming, agreeable *irritating*, *annoying*, *frightful*, *harsh*, *offensive*.

pleasure *n.* comfort, gladness, enjoyment, happiness, delight, joy *displeasure*, *pain*, *discomfort*, *anger*, *offense*.

pledge 1. *n.* vow, oath, promise, guarantee 2. *v.* deposit, plight, pawn 3. *n.* guarantee, promise, agree, warrant.

plentiful *adj.* ample, fruitful, enough, abundant, full *scarce*, *rare*, *scanty*, *meager*, *infrequent*.

plenty *n.* sufficiency, abundance, enough *need*, *want*, *scarcity*, *famine*.

pliable *adj.* pliant, adaptable, flexible, supple, lithe *inflexible*, *rigid*, *obstinate*.

plight *n.* state, dilemma, predicament, condition, scrape, situation.

plod *v.* labor, toil, trudge, tramp, lumber.

plot 1. *n.* story, outline, theme, fable 2. *n.* plan, intrigue, scheme, conspiracy 3. *v.* scheme, contrive, devise, plan, concoct.

plow *v.* cultivate, furrow, till, work.

pluck 1. *n.* courage, bravery, spirit, boldness, nerve *cowardice* 2. *v.* pick, snatch, gather, tug, pull, jerk *plant*.

plucky *adj.* courageous, valiant, brave, bold *cowardly*, *fearful*.

plug 1. *n.* cork, bung, stopper, peg, pin, spike 2. *v.* stuff, block, stop, obstruct 3. (colloq.) *v.* puff, advertise, hype, boost.

plump *adj.* fat, portly, round, stout, chubby, obese, stocky *slim*, *thin*, *skinny*, *lank*, *meager*.

plunder 1. *n.* booty, loot, robbery, spoils 2. *v.* rifle, rob, spoil, sack, ravage, loot, pillage.

plunge 1. *n.* dip, ducking, jump, dive 2. *v.* submerge, dive, immerse, dip.

ply 1. *v.* commute, oscillate, go, alternate, run 2. *v.* employ, practice, ask, use 3. *n.* laminate, layer, film, thickness, leaf.

poach *v.* steal, filch, purloin, fish or hunt illegally.

pocket 1. *n.* compartment, sack, pouch 2. *v.* take, steal.

poem *n.* lyric, sonnet, verse, ballad.

poignant *adj.* severe, distressing, sharp, pointed, piercing.

point *n.* 1. tip, end, prong, tine, spike, needle 2. headland, cape, bluff 3. moment, period, instant 4. speck, dot 5. end, aim, purpose, object 6. instant, period, moment 7. *v.* indicate, show 8. *v.* direct, guide, aim.

poise 1. *v.* hold in place, balance, hover, float 2. *n.* confidence, dignity, control, composure *awkwardness* 3. *n.* steadiness, balance *instability*.

poison 1. *v.* taint, corrupt, pollute, infect, contaminate 2. *n.* toxin, venom, taint, virus.

poisonous *adj.* noxious, deadly, toxic, lethal, baneful *harmless*, *beneficial*.

poke *v.* push, jab, jog, thrust, shove.

pole *n.* stick, post, staff, shaft, column, rod.

policy *n.* plan, system, stratagem, program, action, approach, tactics.

polish 1. *n.* sheen, luster, brightness, shine 2. *n.* refinement, elegance, grace 3. *v.* brighten, furbish, shine, burnish *dull*, *tarnish*.

polite

polite *adj.* affable, well-bred, courteous, respectful, gracious, civil **rude**, **impolite**, **impertinent**, **impudent**, **insolent**, **vulgar**.

poll 1. *v.* crop, lop, clip, shear, mow, shave 2. *n.* roster, enumeration, election, survey, questionnaire, canvass.

pollute *v.* defile, foul, contaminate, taint **clean**, **purify**, **purge**.

pomp *n.* splendor, show, pageantry, ceremony, display, magnificence, spectacle **simplicity**.

pompous *adj.* boastful, grandiose, bombastic, pretentious **unassuming**.

ponder *v.* study, examine, consider, meditate, contemplate.

pool 1. *n.* lake, pond, lagoon, puddle 2. *v.* combine, merge, contribute.

poor *adj.* 1. needy, destitute, penniless, impoverished, impecunious **wealthy**, **rich**, **opulent**, **prosperous** 2. unlucky, unfortunate, pitiable, faulty, unsatisfactory, unsound, inferior **good**, **excellent**, **satisfactory**.

pop *v.* 1. detonate, burst, bang, explode, report 2. insert, put into, slip in *While on Broadway, I popped in to see the new show.*

popular *adj.* 1. approved, accepted, favorite, famous **unpopular**, **disliked** 2. common, prevailing, current, general.

population *n.* inhabitants, people, residents, folk, populace.

port *n.* haven, harbor, anchorage, dock, wharf.

portable *adj.* light, convenient, movable, handy.

porter *n.* doorkeeper, doorman, caretaker, janitor, carrier, bellboy.

portion *n.* fragment, morsel, part, scrap, piece, bit **whole**, **all**.

portly *adj.* rotund, bulky, stout, plump **slim**, **thin**, **slender**.

Portrait

portrait *n.* painting, picture, likeness, image.

portray *v.* depict, sketch, paint, represent, draw, illustrate.

pose *v.* 1. affect, feign, pretend 2. model, sit 3. mystify, puzzle, embarrass *Her total silence posed a problem for everyone at the party* 4. *n.* position, posture, attitude.

Pose

poser *n.* enigma, mystery, puzzle, riddle.

position *n.* 1. situation, locality, station, place 2. posture, pose, attitude 3. condition, circumstances, state 4. job, situation, employment 5. *v.* situate, place, put.

positive *adj.* precise, clear, defined, definite, certain, sure 2. actual, substantial, real *negative*.

possess *v.* own, control, have, occupy, hold *want*.

possession *n.* ownership, control, property.

possible *adj.* feasible, practicable, likely, potential *impossible*, *impractical*.

post *n.* 1. mail, letters, correspondence 2. job, situation, employment 3. column, shaft, pole, pillar 4. seat, station, position 5. send, mail.

poster *n.* placard, bill, advertisement, sticker, sign.

postpone *v.* adjourn, put off, defer, delay, suspend, hold over, shelve *expedite*.

posture *n.* pose, deportment, position, attitude, carriage.

pot *n.* skillet, pan, caldron, jar, crock.

potent *adj.* mighty, strong, powerful *feeble*.

potential 1. *n.* capacity, ability, capability 2. *adj.* likely, latent, possible.

potion *n.* drink.

pottery *n.* ceramics, china, stoneware, earthenware.

pouch *n.* sack, bag, purse, pack, satchel.

pounce *v.* attack, swoop, seize, jump on, bound.

pound *v.* beat, bruise, pulverize, strike, crush.

pour *v.* stream, flow, discharge, spill, emit, issue PORE.

pout *v.* fret, sulk, scowl, frown, mope, glower.

poverty *n.* 1. necessity, penury, lack, want, beggary, need *wealth*, *comfort* 2. barrenness, sterility, scarcity *abundance*, *fruitfulness*.

powder *n.* dust, crumbs, grounds, ash, filings.

power *n.* 1. energy, strength, force 2. capacity, ability, potentiality *inability* 3. control, command, authority, rule.

powerful *adj.* strong, robust, mighty, commanding, potent *weak*, *ineffective*, *feeble*.

practical *adj.* efficient, qualified, attainable, sound, useful *impractical*, *unskilled*.

practice *n.* 1. drill, exercise 2. custom, usage, habit, tradition, use 3. performance, operation, application.

praise 1. *n.* approval, glorification, commendation, compliment *criticism*, *disapproval*, *scandal*, *ridicule* 2. *v.* approve, admire, commend, applaud *denounce*, *malign*, *rebuke*, *reprimand* PRAYS, PREYS.

prank *n.* joke, caper, trick, antic.

prattle *v. & n.* gabble, chatter, prate.

pray *v.* 1. adore, worship, supplicate 2. entreat, beseech, ask, request PREY.

prayer *n.* request, worship, entreaty, invocation, petition.

preach *v.* proclaim, urge, teach, lecture, discourse.

precarious *adj.* perilous, unreliable, hazardous, uncertain, doubtful *safe*, *secure*.

precaution *n.* prudence, wariness, forethought, care, providence, safeguard *carelessness*.

precede *v.* introduce, herald, go before, usher, head, lead, introduce, forerun *succeed*, *ensue*.

precedence *n.* lead, preference, priority, supremacy **inferiority**.

preceding *adj.* previous, preliminary, foregoing, prior **posterior**, **subsequent**.

precinct *n.* district, limit, boundary, ward, constituency.

precious *adj.* 1. dear, darling, beloved, prized, cherished **hated** 2. priceless, valuable, costly **cheap**.

precipice *n.* bluff, crag, cliff, steep.

precipitate 1. *adj.* hasty, rash, indiscreet, hurried, reckless 2. *v.* speed, expedite, hurry, hasten 3. *v.* hurl, throw.

precise *adj.* 1. strict, formal, scrupulous, rigid, careful **informal** 2. definite, explicit, exact, correct **incorrect**, **approximate**.

precision *n.* accuracy, exactness, correctness **inaccuracy**.

preclude *v.* hinder, stop, prevent, obviate, debar, shut out.

precocious *adj.* advanced, premature, forward.

predecessor *n.* forefather, forerunner, ancestor.

predicament *n.* condition, dilemma, situation, plight, state.

predict *v.* foretell, forecast, foresee, prophesy.

predominant *adj.* prevalent, supreme, dominant, prevailing **secondary**, **accessory**.

preface *n.* preamble, prologue, foreword, introduction.

prefer *v.* select, fancy, single out, favor, choose **reject**.

preference *n.* selection, priority, choice.

pregnant *adj.* 1. with child, gestant, gravid, gestational 2. meaningful, significant 3. fruitful, fertile.

prejudice 1. *v.* warp, influence, bias, sway 2. *n.* unfairness, partiality, bias.

preliminary *adj.* preparatory, introductory, opening.

premature *adj.* early, untimely, unexpected, unseasonable **prompt**, **considered**, **mature**.

premeditated *adj.* planned, deliberate, intended, prearranged **spontaneous**, **accidental**.

premium *n.* 1. enhancement, appreciation 2. recompense, prize, reward, bounty, bonus.

prepare *v.* procure, order, provide, arrange, get ready.

preposterous *adj.* unreasonable, ridiculous, absurd, extravagant.

prescribe *v.* order, decree, direct, ordain, recommend.

presence *n.* 1. appearance, bearing, air, demeanor 2. vicinity, attendance, neighborhood, nearness **absence** PRESENTS.

present 1. *v.* bestow, donate, give, proffer 2. *v.* display, introduce, exhibit, show 3. *n.* donation gratuity, gift, offering 4. *n.* now, this time, right now **past** 5. *adj.* instant, current, existing.

presently *adv.* 1. forthwith, immediately, directly 2. shortly, soon.

preserve 1. *n.* jelly, jam, conserve 2. *v.* keep, shield, guard, secure, save **squander**, **waste**, **use**.

press *v.* 1. smooth, iron 2. squeeze, compress 3. hasten, hurry 4. force, compel 5. push 6. hug, clasp, embrace.

pressing *adj.* urgent, compelling.

pressure *n.* force, power, urgency, influence, hurry.

prestige *n.* distinction, influence, credit, reputation, importance.

presume *v.* surmise, assume, suppose, believe, think.

presumption *n.* supposition, guess, belief, conjecture 2. boldness, arrogance, effrontery, audacity **humility**, **modesty**, **shyness**.

Presenting

A present

presumptuous *adj.* bold, impudent, arrogant, insolent forward.

pretend *v.* affect, sham, feign, deceive, simulate 2. claim, aspire, strive for 3. act, make believe.

pretentious *adj.* ostentatious, assuming, affected *simple*, *humble*.

pretext *n.* guise, semblance, appearance, cloak.

pretty *adj.* attractive, fair, beautiful, lovely, bonny, comely, cute *plain*, *ugly*.

prevalent *adj.* predominant, extensive, prevailing, customary, common, widespread *uncommon*, *rare*, *infrequent*.

prevent *v.* hinder, interrupt, obstruct, impede, slow, thwart *help*, *allow*, *enable*.

previous *adj.* former, preceding, earlier, prior *later*, *following*, *subsequent*.

price 1. *n.* value, expense, cost, charge 2. *v.* charge, mark up, value.

priceless *adj.* inestimable, precious, invaluable *cheap*.

prick 1. *v.* sting, wound 2. *v.* perforate, pierce, puncture 3. *n.* puncture, perforation.

pride *n.* 1. dignity, self-respect *shame* 2. conceit, haughtiness, self-esteem, vanity, egotism *humility*, *humbleness*, *modesty* PRIED.

priest *n.* pastor, minister, clergyman, parson.

priggish *adj.* prim, conceited.

prim *adj.* precise, proper, formal, straitlaced, stiff, prudish, stuffy *hearty*, *informal*.

primary *adj.* 1. principal, main, chief *secondary* 2. original, earliest, primitive, first.

prime *adj.* 1. first-rate, best, excellent *inferior* 2. original, primary, first.

primitive

primitive *adj.* 1. primeval, simple, aboriginal, ancient 2. uncivilized, rough, barbarous, archaic *sophisticated*, *cultivated*, *cultured*.

principal 1. *n.* head, leader, chief 2. *adj.* first, main, essential, leading, foremost *secondary*, *accessory*.

The principal

principle *n.* 1. rule, standard, doctrine, law, tenet 2. rectitude, honor, integrity, virtue *dishonesty*.

print 1. *n.* stamp, mark 2. *n.* lithograph, etching, engraving, picture 3. *v.* engrave, impress, imprint.

prior *adj.* preceding, former, previous, earlier *subsequent*, *later*.

prison *n.* jail, lockup, penitentiary, dungeon.

private *adj.* 1. personal, individual, special *public* 2. solitary, quiet, secluded 3. secret, confidential, concealed.

prize 1. *n.* premium, award, reward, bounty 2. *v.* value, appraise, esteem 3. *v.* lever up, lift, raise PRIES.

probable *adj.* credible, feasible, likely, reasonable *improbable*, *unlikely*, *impossible*.

probe *v.* scrutinize, explore, investigate, search, examine.

problem *n.* 1. dispute, difficulty, dilemma, doubt 2. riddle, puzzle, question *solution*.

procedure *n.* practice, operation, conduct, system, course.

proceed *v.* 1. originate, result, spring, follow 2. advance, move ahead, progress, continue *withdraw*, *retreat*, *hesitate*.

proceeds *n.* income, returns, product, yield, income.

process 1. *v.* treat, develop, convert 2. *n.* procedure, course, method.

procession *n.* parade, cavalcade, march.

proclaim *v.* declare, publish, announce, advertise.

procure *v.* acquire, cause, get, contrive, obtain, gain.

prod *v.* jab, poke, push, goad.

prodigal *adj.* lavish, profuse, wasteful, extravagant *thrifty*.

produce 1. *v.* bring forth, generate, bear 2. originate, cause, create, make 3. show, bring out, exhibit *The conjuror produced a rabbit out of the hat* 4. *n.* production, product.

product *n.* yield, goods, produce, harvest, result.

productive *adj.* fruitful, creative, fertile, efficient *wasteful*, *useless*.

profane *adj.* 1. blasphemous, impious, irreligious, wicked *religious*, *holy*, *pious* 2. secular, worldly *sacred*.

profess v. acknowledge, state, avow, own, affirm, confess.

profession n. 1. employment, calling, occupation *hobby*, *pastime* 2. avowal, declaration.

professional adj. competent, proficient, expert, businesslike *amateur*.

proficient adj. expert, capable, skilled, practiced, qualified *unskilled*, *inexperienced*.

profit 1. n. benefit, advantage 2. n. return, gain *loss* 3. v. gain, benefit, improve, exploit *lose* PROPHET.

profound adj. penetrating, intellectual, deep, skilled, thorough, wise, complete *shallow*, *superficial*.

profuse adj. lavish, bountiful, abundant, exuberant, liberal *meager*, *scanty*.

program n. record, agenda, schedule, calendar, plan, list.

prominent adj. 1. obvious, noticeable, conspicuous 2. distinguished, eminent, famous, celebrated *insignificant*, *unimportant*.

promise 1. v. assure, swear, agree, pledge 2. n. word, vow, pledge, assurance.

promote v. 1. raise, advance, elevate, exalt *demote*, *retard* 2. stir up, support, aid *hinder*.

prompt 1. v. suggest, hint 2 v. impel, incite, stimulate, urge 3. adj. quick, timely, ready, active, alert *late*, *slow*.

prone adj. 1. recumbent, flat, prostrate, face down 2. inclined, disposed, tending.

pronounce v. speak, declare, utter, affirm, articulate, enunciate.

pronounced adj. marked, obvious, distinct, clear, definite, evident *indistinguishable*, *vague*.

A progressing procession

progress 1. n. progression, advancement, furtherance, development *regression* 2. v. proceed, improve, advance, enhance, perfect.

prohibit v. prevent, disallow, hinder, forbid *allow*, *permit*, *help*, *encourage*.

project 1. v. bulge, jut, protrude 2. v. shoot, cast, throw 3. n. scheme, design, plan, proposal.

prolific adj. fertile, productive, fruitful, teeming *barren*.

prolong v. extend, lengthen, protract *shorten*.

proof n. 1. testimony, confirmation, evidence 2. essay, trial, test.

prop n. strut, brace, support, stay, pin.

propagate v. increase, diffuse, multiply, spread, continue, reproduce, breed, procreate, generate.

propel v. push, urge, impel, drive, move, shove, motivate, stimulate *draw*.

proper adj. 1. decent, polite, respectable *improper*, *rude* 2. suitable, just, fit, fitting, appropriate *unsuitable*.

properly

properly *adv.* strictly, accurately, suitably, correctly **wrongly**, **improperly**.

property *n.* 1. belongings, chattels, assets 2 feature, characteristic, quality 3. real estate, land, grounds.

prophecy *n.* foretelling, forecast, prediction, divination.

prophesy *v.* foretell, forecast, predict, divine.

proportion *n.* adjustment, portion, distribution, part, share, lot.

proposal *n.* scheme, offer, intent, suggestion, project.

propose *v.* suggest, mean, recommend, offer, intend, woo, court.

proprietor *n.* possessor, landowner, landlord.

prosecute *v.* 1. charge, summon, sue, bring suit 2. continue, pursue, finish, consummate.

prospect 1. *n.* expectation, hope, anticipation 2. *n.* survey, landscape, view, vision, scene 3. *v.* seek, dig, search, explore, scrutinize.

prosper *v.* thrive, succeed, flourish, make good, do well **sink**, **fail**, **decline**.

prosperity *n.* riches, wealth, fortune, opulence, affluence **hardship**.

prosperous *adj.* flourishing, fortunate, successful, rich **unfortunate**, **failing**, **poor**.

prostrate *adj.* flat, stretched out, prone, fallen, helpless **upright**.

protect *v.* guard, preserve, defend, screen, shelter **attack**, **endanger**.

protest 1. *n.* objection, complaint **approval** 2. *v.* dispute, challenge, demur, object **approve**.

prototype *n.* model, original, archetype.

protract *v.* lengthen, delay, prolong, continue **shorten**.

Protruding

protrude *v.* jut, project, extend, bulge, stick out **recede**.

proud *adj.* 1. noble, dignified, grand, lofty, stately 2. arrogant, boastful, haughty, supercilious **humble**, **modest**.

prove *v.* establish, verify, show, ascertain, justify **disprove**.

proverb *n.* maxim, saying, adage, aphorism.

provide *v.* produce, get, procure, furnish **deprive**.

provided *conj.* granted, supposing, on condition, if.

province *n.* 1. region, district, territory, area, tract 2. department, division.

provoke *v.* arouse, enrage, excite, kindle, cause, incite **appease**.

prowess *n.* courage, skill, bravery, daring, valor **cowardice**.

prowl *v.* roam, creep, rove, sneak, slink, lurk.

prudent *adj.* 1. frugal, saving, thrifty **extravagant** 2. cautious, wary, discreet, wise, careful **rash**, **reckless**, **foolish**, **impetuous**.

prudish *adj.* narrow-minded, coy, demure, overmodest, squeamish *tolerant*.

prune *v.* clip, cut back, trim, dock.

pry *v.* peep, peer, meddle, interfere.

public 1. *adj.* municipal, general, common *private*, *personal* 2. *adj.* unenclosed, unbounded, unrestricted *secluded* 3. *n.* society, people, persons.

publish *v.* announce, declare, proclaim, reveal, circulate, make known.

pucker *v.* crease, furrow, wrinkle, crinkle.

puff *v.* inflate, pant, blow, swell.

pull *v. & n.* haul, pluck, draw, tug, drag *push*.

punch *v.* 1. hit, push, strike 2. bore, puncture, perforate, pierce.

punctual *adj.* timely, punctilious, prompt, exact.

puncture *n.* wound, prick, sting, hole, perforate, bore.

pungent *adj.* biting, caustic, sharp, acid, piquant, piercing, penetrating *bland*, *mild*.

punish *v.* chasten, penalize, chastise, reprove, scold, discipline *praise*, *condone*, *reward*.

puny *adj.* feeble, small, weak, little, inferior *athletic*.

pupil *n.* scholar, beginner, student, learner.

puppet *n.* doll, marionette, dummy.

purchase 1. *n.* acquisition, bargain 2. *v.* bargain, obtain, get, buy.

pure *adj.* 1. clear, unpolluted, clean, unsullied *adulterated*, *foul* 2. real, simple, genuine 3. guiltless, innocent, virtuous *immoral*, *immodest*.

purely *adv.* entirely, merely, absolutely, completely.

purge *v.* 1. clear, purify, cleanse *pollute* 2. eliminate, remove, eradicate.

purloin *v.* rob, filch, steal, thieve, pilfer.

purpose *n.* 1. object, aim, intent, end 2. usage, application.

pursue *v.* 1. chase, track, follow, hunt 2. conduct, persist, continue *abandon*.

pursuit *n.* 1. activity, venture, undertaking 2. hunt, chase, search, race.

push *v.* impel, drive, thrust, force *pull*, *haul*, *draw*.

put *v.* 1. set, purpose, place, offer, lay, express 2. compel, oblige, urge *I was put to school at the age of four*.

putrid *adj.* corrupt, rotten, stinking, decayed.

puzzle 1. *n.* enigma, poser, problem, riddle 2. *v.* embarrass, mystify, perplex, bewilder.

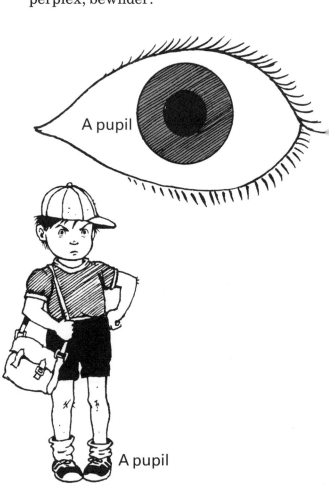

A pupil

A pupil

quack

quack *n.* impostor, pretender, faker, humbug, charlatan, phony.

quail *v.* flinch, tremble, cower, shrink, quake.

quaint *adj.* unusual, uncommon, strange, odd, curious.

quake *v.* tremble, quiver, shake, shiver, shudder.

qualification *n.* capability, fitness, accomplishment, suitability, ability.

qualify *v.* 1. modify, restrict, limit 2. suit, fit, entitle.

quality *n.* 1. soundness, condition, worth, excellence, goodness 2. nature, trait, characteristic.

qualm *n.* doubt, pang, twinge, uneasiness, throe.

quandary *n.* dilemma, difficulty, predicament.

quantity *n.* number, extend, amount, bulk, portion.

quarrel 1. *v.* squabble, argue, wrangle, bicker 2. *n.* disagreement, dispute, tiff, difference, brawl, argument, *accord*.

quarrelsome *adj.* dissident, hostile, acrimonious, churlish *agreeable*.

quarry *n.* 1. victim, prey, game 2. pit, mine, excavation.

quaver *v.* shake, vibrate, quiver, tremble, oscillate.

quay *n.* jetty, wharf, landing, pier KEY.

queasy *adj.* nauseous, sick, ill, sick to one's stomach.

queer *adj.* strange, uncommon, odd, peculiar, unusual, quaint *usual*, *ordinary*, *conventional*.

quell *v.* suppress, restrain, subdue, quiet, overcome, crush.

quench *v.* 1. slake, cool, allay 2. put out, extinguish.

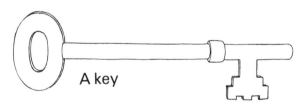

A key

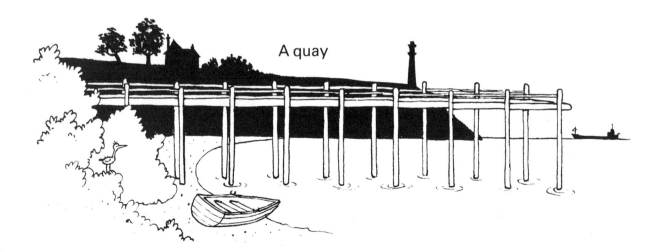

A quay

query 1. *v.* question, ask, inquire, doubt 2. *n.* inquiry, question, demand.

quest *v. & n.* hunt, search, desire.

question *n.* 1. dispute, doubt, controversy 2. inquiry, query, debate ***answer***, ***reply***, ***retort***.

questionable *adj.* uncertain, dubious, doubtful, debatable ***certain***.

queue 1. v. file, line up, wait 2. *n.* file, line, procession CUE.

quibble *v.* cavil, prevaricate, argue, bicker.

quick *adj.* 1. nimble, sprightly, active, agile ***sluggish*** 2. swift, fleet, rapid, speedy, fast ***tardy***, ***slow*** 3. expert, skillful ***obtuse*** 4. touchy, impatient, hasty.

quicken *v.* accelerate, hurry, hasten ***delay***.

quiet 1. *adj.* still, silent, calm, tranquil ***loud***, ***turbulent*** 2. *v.* pacify, lull, soothe 3. *n.* repose, ease, calm, rest ***noise***, ***clamor***, ***din***, ***hubbub***.

quip *n.* joke, jibe, jest, witticism, wisecrack.

quirk *n.* caprice, foible, whim, peculiarity, fancy, whimsy, notion.

quit *v.* 1. abandon, stop, discontinue, cease 2. renounce, leave, resign, relinquish.

quite *adv.* 1. considerably, rather, very 2. entirely, completely, totally, wholly.

quiver *v.* shiver, quake, tremble, shake.

quixotic *adj.* bizarre, fantastic, imaginative, freakish, visionary.

quiz 1. *v.* interrogate, examine, question, test 2. *n.* riddle, puzzle, test, questionnaire.

quota *n.* proportion, portion, share.

quotation *n.* extract, passage, citation, selection, saying.

quote *v.* recite, mention, cite, echo, repeat.

race 1. *n.* contest, chase, match, pursuit 2. *n.* clan, tribe, breed, stock, people, nation 3. *v.* hurry, speed, run, hasten ***dawdle***, ***linger***.

rack 1. *v.* torment, pain, torture, distress 2. *n.* holder, stand, frame, bracket WRACK.

racket *n.* 1. noise, din, uproar, fuss, hubbub ***silence*** 2. swindle.

racy *adj.* lively, sharp, spirited, strong, vigorous.

radiant *adj.* beaming, luminous, shining, sparkling, brilliant, glowing ***dim***, ***dark***.

radiate *v.* gleam, emit, shine, beam.

radical *adj.* basic, fundamental, essential.

rag 1. *n.* fragment, bit, tatter, cloth, shred 2. *v.* needle, lark, bully, jest.

rage 1. *v.* storm, ravage, rave, fume 2. *n.* wrath, anger, fury, frenzy 3. *n.* vogue, mode, craze, fashion, fad.

ragged *adj.* torn, jagged, rough, tattered, rent.

raid 1. *v.* invade, attack, assault, pillage, loot 2. *n.* attack, foray, invasion RAYED.

rail 1. *v.* censure, abuse, upbraid, scoff ***praise*** 2. *n.* bar, fence, line, railing.

rain *v. & n.* shower, storm, drizzle, sprinkle REIGN, REIN.

raise *v.* 1. heave, lift, hoist, advance, elevate, lift up ***lower*** 2. rouse, stir up, excite, 3. cultivate, rear, bring up RAZE.

rake

rake *v.* collect, scrape, gather, scour, ransack.

rally 1. *v.* assemble, gather, meet *disperse* 2. *v.* revive, improve, recover, get better 3. *n.* gathering, meeting.

ransom *n.* 1. redemption, deliverance, release, liberation 2. payoff, price, payment.

rap *v.* & *n.* thump, whack, knock, bang WRAP.

Ram

ram *v.* 1. strike, push, thrust, drive, 2. stuff, force, cram.

ramble 1. *n.* trip, tour, excursion, stroll, amble 2. *v.* rove, range, roam, stroll, amble, wander.

ramp *n.* slope, gradient, rising plane, grade.

rancid *adj.* sour, moldy, rank, musty, tainted.

rancor *n.* spite, venom, malice, malevolence, animosity, bitterness *benevolence* RANKER.

random *adj.* casual, fortuitous, chance, haphazard *specific*, *definite*.

range 1. *v.* arrange, order, class 2. *v.* wander, pass over, rove 3. *n.* row, class, extent, rank, scope, sort.

rank 1. *adj.* wild, dense, luxuriant, excessive 2. *adj.* foul, putrid, rotten coarse 3. *v.* arrange, class, group, order 4. *n.* grade, level, class, dignity, position.

rankle *v.* inflame, fester, rile, gall, irritate, exasperate.

ransack *v.* ravage, sack, plunder, rummage, search, rifle, pillage.

Ram

rape *v.* ravish, violate, assault, outrage.

rapid *adj.* fast, quick, hasty, speedy, swift, *slow*, *sluggish*, *tardy*.

rapt *adj.* charmed, fascinated, enraptured, delighted RAPPED, WRAPPED.

rapture *n.* joy, exaltation, ecstasy, delight, bliss *misery*.

rare *adj.* 1. fine, excellent, choice, exquisite 2. scarce, infrequent, uncommon, extraordinary *common*, *ordinary*, *usual* 3. nearly raw, undercooked.

rarely *adv.* seldom, hardly, scarcely, infrequently **always**, **often**.

rascal *n.* villain, scoundrel, rogue, scamp, knave.

rash 1. *adj.* hasty, impetuous, reckless, headstrong, foolhardy **prudent**, **thoughtful**, **careful**, **cautious**, **discreet** 2. *n.* eruption, infection, inflammation.

rate 1. *n.* speed, ration, proportion 2. *n.* cost, price, measure, duty, tax, standard 3. *v.* estimate, assess, price.

rather *adv.* more, especially, preferable, sooner, somewhat, moderately.

ratify *v.* sanction, approve, authorize, endorse, support, uphold **revoke**.

ration 1. *v.* distribute, share, apportion, divide 2. *n.* allowance, portion, allotment, amount.

rational *adj.* right, moderate, fair, reasonable, just, sane **irrational**, **crazy**, **insane**, **mad**.

rattle 1. *v.* upset, unsettle, disturb 2. *v.* oscillate, vibrate, shake 3. *n.* patter, clatter, clangor, din.

raucous *adj.* husky, harsh, hoarse, gruff, rough **melodious**.

ravage *v.* ransack, devastate, pillage, despoil, sack, wreck, ruin **restore**.

rave *v.* babble, wander, ramble, rage, rant.

ravenous *adj.* famished, insatiable, hungry, rapacious, greedy, starved **satisfied**.

ravine *n.* defile, gully, gorge.

ravishing *adj.* delightful, alluring, enchanting, charming, captivating **repulsive**.

raw *adj.* 1. fresh, uncooked **cooked**, **processed** 2. green, unripe, crude, unfinished 3. unskilled, immature, inexperienced, callow **experienced** 4. cold, damp, chilly, freezing.

ray *n.* light, beam, gleam, shaft, flash.

raze *v.* destroy, obliterate, level, overthrow, demolish, ruin **restore**, **rebulid** RAISE.

reach 1. *v.* get to, attain, achieve, arrive at 2. *v.* stretch, extend, outstretch 3. *n.* extent, compass, range.

read *v.* study, peruse, decipher, interpret, pore over, scrutinize REED.

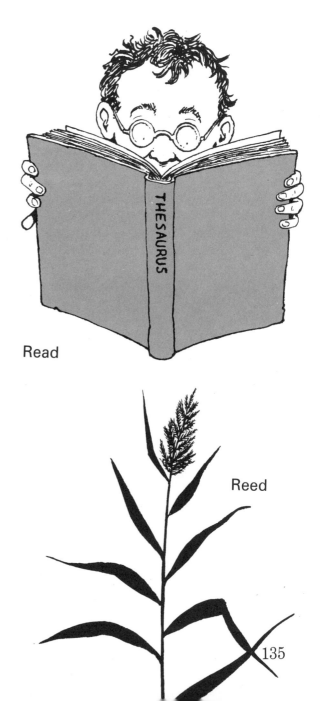

Read

Reed

readable

readable *adj.* 1. interesting, enjoyable, spellbinding, entertaining 2. clear, legible, distinct *illegible*.

readily *adv.* easily, quickly, willingly, promptly, eagerly *unwillingly*.

ready *adj.* 1. expert, apt, prompt, quick 2. arranged, prepared, fitted *unprepared*, *unwilling*, *reluctant*.

real *adj.* certain, authentic, actual, genuine, absolute *false*, *counterfeit*, *sham*, *bogus*, *artificial*, *spurious*, *imaginary* REEL.

reality *n.* existence, actuality, fact, truth *imagination*, *dream*, *hallucination*, *illusion*.

realize *v.* 1. effect, complete, accomplish, earn, gain 2. grasp, comprehend, appreciate, conceive *misunderstand*.

really *adv.* absolutely, actually, certainly, truly.

realm *n.* region, kingdom, domain, province.

reap *v.* 1. gather, harvest, garner *sow* 2. obtain, receive, gather, gain.

rear 1. *adj.* hind, posterior, back, after *front*, *fore* 2. *n.* end, tail, back, behind 3. *v.* nurse, foster, bring up, breed, educate, 4. *v.* lift, rise, elevate, hoist *If anyone attempted to ride it, the horse reared up.*

reason 1. *n.* principle, cause, motive, aim 2. *n.* judgment, mind, sense, intellect *instinct* 3. *v.* dispute, argue, think, debate.

reasonable *adj.* 1. suitable, fair, right, just, sensible, logical *irrational* 2. moderate, tolerable *immoderate*.

reassure *v.* cheer, comfort, console, hearten, encourage *discourage*, *intimidate*, *frighten*.

rebel 1. *v.* defy, disobey, revolt, rise up *conform*, *obey* 2. *n.* mutineer, malcontent, revolutionary, traitor *loyalist*.

rebellious *adj.* mutinous, subversive, rebel *obedient*.

rebuff 1. *v.* reject, repel, snub, resist *encourage* 2. *n.* defeat, repulse, resistance, snub *approval*.

rebuke 1. *v.* blame, chide, reprove, scold 2. *n.* reproof, reprimand, censure *praise*.

recall *v.* 1. cancel, summon, withdraw, call back, annul *reaffirm* 2. remember, recollect *forget*.

recede *v.* return, desist, ebb, go back, withdraw, retire, retreat *advance*, *protrude*.

receipt *n.* voucher, acceptance, acknowledgment, admission RESEAT.

receive *v.* 1. obtain, get, take, accept, acquire *give*, *offer*, *send* 2. greet, entertain, welcome.

recent *adj.* late, new, modern, novel, fresh *old*, *dated*.

reception *n.* 1. entertainment, party 2. admission, admittance.

recess *n.* 1. niche, retreat, nook, cavity, corner 2. respite, break, vacation, intermission.

recipe *n.* directions, receipt, formula, prescription.

recite *v.* describe, report, repeat, relate, rehearse.

reckless *adj.* rash, foolhardy, careless, negligent, heedless *careful*, *heedful*, *conservative*, *prudent*.

reckon *v.* 1. estimate, number, guess, count, compute *miscalculate* 2. infer, consider, regard, esteem, suppose.

reclaim *v.* rescue, improve, recover, restore.

recline *v.* rest, lounge, lie down, repose.

recognize *v.* identify, remember, know, recollect *ignore* 2. confess, admit, acknowledge *repudiate*.

recoil *v.* shrink, rebound, flinch, react, spring back *advance*.

recollect *v.* recall, remember, bring back, *forget*.

recommend *v.* 1. approve, commend, praise *disparage* 2. counsel, advise.

recompense *v.* repay, reward.

reconcile *v.* 1. appease, reunite, harmonize, pacify *devastate*, *wreck* 2. adjust, settle, make up.

record 1. *n.* account, memo, register, note, document 2. *n.* disk, recording 3. *n.* championship, leadership, supremacy 4. *v.* chronicle, note, register, enter.

recount *v.* 1. narrate, describe, report, tell 2. tally, check, number.

recover *v.* 1. cure, get better, heal, revive *worsen* 2. retrieve, get back, regain, reclaim.

recreation *n.* relaxation, amusement, diversion *work*.

recruit *1. n.* beginner, learner, trainee, helper, novice *veteran* 2. *v.* sign up, draft, enlist.

rectify *v.* improve, straighten, set right, correct, amend *falsify*, *err*.

recur *v.* return, reappear, persist, re-occur, be repeated.

redeem *v.* 1. deliver, free, liberate, release 2. recompense, make good, compensate, recover.

redress 1. *v.* set right, repair, remedy, amend 2. *n.* reparation, compensation.

reduce *v.* 1. lessen, shorten, contract, decrease *increase*, *augment*, *enlarge*, *magnify* 2. ruin, impoverish.

redundant *adj.* excessive, superfluous, surplus, unnecessary.

reel *v.* waver, totter, stagger REAL.

refer *v.* 1. allude, relate, indicate, denote 2. commit, consign, direct.

referee *n.* judge, arbitrator, umpire.

refine *v.* 1. polish, improve, cultivate 2. purify, cleanse.

refined *adj.* 1. polished, genteel, cultivated, elegant *rude*, *coarse*, *uncivilized*, *vulgar*, *tawdry* 2. clarified, purified *raw*.

reflect *v.* 1. meditate, consider, think, deliberate, muse 2. send back, mirror.

reform 1. *v.* correct, amend, improve, better *worsen* 2. *n.* correction, change, amendment.

refrain 1. *v.* abstain, desist, restrain, forbear, withhold *persist* 2. *n.* tune, melody, chorus, song.

refresh *v.* enliven, invigorate, revive *tire*, *exhaust*.

refrigerate *v.* chill, cool, keep in freezer.

refuge *n.* asylum, protection, shelter, safety, sanctuary.

refugee *n.* fugitive, exile, emigré, deportee.

refund 1. *v.* return, repay, restore, reimburse 2. *n.* reimbursement, repayment.

refusal *n.* denial, disapproval, negation, repudiation *offer*.

refuse 1. *n.* trash, waste, rubbish, dregs, garbage 2. *v.* reject, repel, deny, exclude, decline *accept*,

Refuse

refute

refute *v.* rebut, contradict, disprove, deny, invalidate **agree**.

regal *adj.* splendid, kingly, magnificent, royal, majestic, stately.

regard 1. *n.* concern, care 2. *n.* reference, relation *With regard to your recent letter, we have dispatched the goods direct* 3. *n.* gaze, view, look 4. *v.* behold, estimate, observe, notice, consider 5. value, respect, esteem.

regardless *prep.* despite, besides, notwithstanding.

region *n.* area, district, country, territory, province.

register *n.* roll, record, catalog, list, chronicle.

Reigning in the rain

regret 1. *n.* concern, grief, remorse, sorrow 2. *v.* bewail, be sorry for, repent, lament **rejoice**.

regular *adj.* 1. steady, uniform, constant **irregular, intermittent** 2. usual, normal, customary, formal **unusual, odd**.

regulate *v.* 1. correct, adjust, set 2. order, govern, direct, manage.

regulation *n.* law, rule, statute, order, precept.

rehearse *v.* narrate, practice, recite, prepare, repeat.

reign 1. *n.* power, sovereignty, sway, rule 2. *v.* govern, rule, prevail RAIN, REIN.

rein *v.* control, bridle, check, hold, restrain RAIN, REIGN.

reinforce *v.* augment, assist, strengthen, support, fortify.

reject *v.* refuse, repel, exclude, decline, discard **accept, acclaim, admit, adopt**.

rejoice *v.* delight, please, cheer, celebrate, gladden **grieve, lament, mourn, regret, rue**.

relapse *v.* regress, reverse, revert, fall back **improve, advance**.

relate *v.* 1. narrate, describe, tell, report, recite 2. concern, compare, connect.

relation *n.* 1. kinship. relative, kindred 2. bearing, connection, relationship.

relative 1. *adj.* respecting, corresponding, referring, pertain to 2. *n.* kin, relation.

relax *v.* 1. repose, recline, ease, rest 2. weaken, loosen, slacken **tighten, strain**.

relaxed *adj.* 1. loose, loosened, slack, flabby 2. serene, tranquil placid, cool **tense**.

release 1. *n.* discharge, liberation, freedom **imprisonment** 2. *v.* let go, quit 3. *v.* free, extricate, liberate, relinquish, loose **fasten, confine, imprison, arrest**.

relent *v.* relax, give in, yield, submit.

relentless *adj.* persistent, steadfast, remorseless, hard, merciless, cruel, heartless, strict.

relevant *adj.* fit, appropriate, pertinent, applicable, suitable *irrelevant*.

reliable *adj.* dependable, true, trustworthy, honest *erratic*, *unreliable*, *unsound*.

relic *n.* souvenir, remains, memento, vestige, token, keepsake.

relief *n.* 1. aid, help, support, assistance 2. ease, comfort, *distress*.

relieve *v.* 1. comfort, ease, cure, soothe 2. replace, substitute, change.

religion *n.* faith, creed, virtue, piety.

religious *adj.* faithful, holy, devout, reverent, conscientious, pious *impious*, *lax*.

relinquish *v.* renounce, abandon, surrender, yield, quit, give up, waive, forego *maintain*.

relish 1. *n.* liking, partiality, zest, gusto *disgust*, *distaste*, *dislike* 2. *n.* flavor, taste, savor 3. *n.* sauce, appetizer, pickle 4. *v.* appreciate, like, enjoy.

reluctance *n.* aversion, distaste, dislike, hesitancy, unwillingness *inclination*.

reluctant *adj.* averse, unwilling, disinclined, loath *eager*, *ready*, *willing*.

rely *v.* depend, lean, count, swear by, trust in *distrust*.

remain *v.* abide, tarry, stay, linger, continue, last *depart*, *leave*, *go*, *forsake*.

remainder *n.* rest, remains, remnant, surplus.

remark 1. *v.* observe, say, utter, express 2. *v.* observe, note, heed, notice, regard *ignore*, *disregard* 3. *n.* utterance, comment, observation, statement.

remarkable *adj.* unusual, strange, extraordinary, special, uncommon *ordinary*, *commonplace*, *average*.

remedy 1. *n.* solution, answer 2. *n.* antidote, medicine, cure 3. *v.* relieve, cure, heal, restore.

remember *v.* memorize, recall, retain, recollect *forget*.

remind *v.* prompt, cue, jog the memory, bring back.

remiss *adj.* slack, careless.

remit *v.* 1. forward, pay, transmit, send 2. excuse, overlook, forgive, pardon.

remnant *n.* remains, scrap, fragment, residue, remainder, rest.

remorse *n.* sorrow, regret, penitence, contrition.

remote *adj.* 1. slight, inconsiderable 2. distant, far, removed, isolated, secluded *near*, *close*, *imminent*.

remove *v.* transport, extract, displace, transfer, withdraw *retain*.

render *v.* 1. contribute, submit, furnish 2. make, effect, create.

renegade *n.* rebel, vagabond, traitor, deserter *loyalist*.

renew *v.* rebuild, refresh, restore, renovate, revive.

renounce *v.* 1. disclaim, disown, repudiate 2. abdicate, relinquish, give up, abandon, quit *accept*.

renown *n.* honor, glory, repute, fame, reputation *obscurity*.

rent *v. & n.* 1. hire, lease, let 2. tear, hole, gap, break.

repair 1. *v.* restore, mend, make good, patch *shatter*, *smash*, *break* 2. *n.* patch, restoration, renovation.

repeal *v.* abolish, set aside, revoke, reverse, cancel *confirm*.

repeat *v.* 1. reproduce, do again, duplicate *discontinue* 2. reiterate, recite, say again.

repel *v.* 1. offend, nauseate, disgust 2. refuse, reject, decline 3. rebuff, drive off, repulse *attract*, *charm*, *entice*, *tempt*, *lure*.

repellent *adj.* offensive, revolting, disgusting, abominable *attractive*, *charming*, *inviting*.

repent *v.* regret, atone, rue, lament, deprecate, deplore *rejoice*.

replace *v.* 1. substitute, supplant, succeed 2. return, put back, restore, reinstate *remove*.

replenish *v.* stock, supply, fill, reload, recharge *empty*, *exhaust*.

reply 1. *n.* answer, rejoinder, response 2. *v.* respond, answer *ask*, *question*.

report 1. *n.* explosion, noise, sound 2. *n.* declaration, statement, account, description 3. *v.* declare, tell, announce, relate, mention.

repose 1. *n.* respite, quiet, relaxation, sleep, ease 2. *v.* sleep, lie, recline, rest, lounge.

represent *v.* 1. personate, stand for, deputize, simulate 2. depict, describe, portray, reproduce.

repress *v.* crush, restrain, suppress, curb, subdue *encourage*, *support*, *revive*.

reprimand *v.* reproach, reprove, chide, rebuke *praise*.

reproach *v.* rebuke, reprimand, blame, reprove, denounce, condemn *approve*.

reproduce *v.* imitate, copy, simulate, duplicate.

reprove *v.* chide, condemn, rebuke, blame, reprimand *approve*.

repudiate *v.* deny, renounce, disclaim, disown, reject *avow*, *recognize*, *adopt*.

repugnant *adj.* distasteful, repellent, offensive, noisome, revolting *agreeable*.

repulsive *adj.* loathsome, repellent, disgusting, forbidding *agreeable*, *pleasant*, *ravishing*.

reputation *n.* character, distinction, repute, name, fame, renown.

request 1. *n.* demand, appeal, entreaty, petition 2. *v.* demand, ask, desire, solicit, beg *deny*.

require *v.* 1. request, demand, ask, direct *refuse* 2. want, need.

rescue 1. *n.* release, salvation, liberation 2. *v.* free, save, liberate, release, deliver *imperil*.

research 1. *v.* study, examine, look into, explore, investigate 2. *n.* study, investigation, scrutiny.

resemblance *n.* likeness, similarity.

resentful *adj.* revengeful, exasperated, irritable, angry *kind*.

reserve 1. *n.* shyness, coldness, coyness 2. *v.* retain, save, keep, hold.

reserved *adj.* 1. modest, shy, timid, secretive *outspoken* 2. engaged, booked, saved.

reside *v.* abide, dwell, inhabit, remain, live.

residence *n.* abode, home, house, dwelling, habitation, apartment RESIDENTS.

resign *v.* forsake, relinquish, quit, leave, give up, renounce.

resist *v.* withstand, hinder, oppose, check, thwart, confront, curb, *yield*, *submit*, *surrender*, *obey*, *give up*.

resolute *adj.* firm, unwavering, determined, decided, steady *weak*, *wavering*, *irresolute*, *undecided*.

resolve 1. *v.* determine, settle, decide 2. *v.* unravel, solve, interpret, decipher 3. *n.* resolution, determination, intention *hesitation*.

resort 1. *n.* refuge, haunt, spa, holiday place, retreat, sanctuary 2. *n.* relief, recourse, reserve 3. *v.* retreat, go, repair to, turn to.

resourceful *adj.* ready, flexible, adaptable, skillful, ingenious.

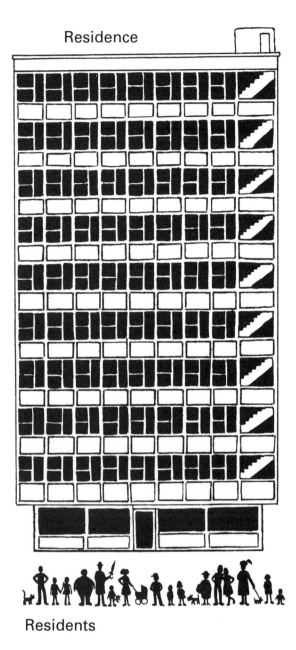

Residence

Residents

respect 1. *n*. admiration, esteem, honor, regard **contempt** 2. *n*. point, matter, particular, feature *She was polite in every respect* 3. *v*. honor, esteem, venerate **abuse, insult, ridicule, taunt**.

respectable *adj*. honest, estimable, reputable, worthy, deserving **unworthy, disreputable**.

respectful *adj*. polite, deferential, formal, courteous **impolite, impertinent, impudent**.

respite *n*. rest, delay, interval, pause, lull, break.

respond *v*. retort, reply, rejoin, answer, accord **question**.

responsible *adj*. 1. able, trustworthy, reliable, capable 2. liable, answerable, accountable, **irresponsible**.

rest 1. *n*. sleep, repose, relaxation, quiet 2. *n*. remainder, remnant, residue 3. *n*. stay, pause, cessation, stop 4. *v*. relax, repose **labor, work** WREST.

restaurant *n*. bistro, café, dining room, buffet, diner, delicatessen.

restful *adj*. relaxing, tranquil, reposeful, peaceful **restless, disturbed**.

restive *adj*. restless, nervous, uneasy, impatient **relaxed**.

restless *adj*. restive, nervous, uneasy, sleepless, disturbed **peaceful, tranquil, calm, restful**.

restore *v*. 1. mend, renew, renovate, recover 2. reinstate, replace, return **raze, spoil, erase, erode**.

restrain *v*. suppress, prevent, check, repress, curb, hold back **free, impel**.

restrict *v*. confine, limit, bound **free, liberate**.

result 1. *v*. follow, arise, happen, ensue 2. *n*. outcome, effect, end, consequence, upshot, product, conclusion **cause**.

resume *v*. restart, recommence, continue, pick up, begin again **stop, interrupt**.

retain *v*. 1. reserve, keep, withhold, hold **abandon, scrap, abolish, eject, lose** 2. hire, employ, engage **dismiss**.

retaliate *v*. avenge, retort, take revenge, repay **pardon, ignore**.

retard *v*. hinder, check, defer, obstruct, delay **advance**.

retire

retire *v.* 1. quit, relinquish, resign, abdicate 2. retreat, leave, withdraw, remove, depart *advance*.

retiring *adj.* timid, modest, bashful, diffident, shy, *bold*, *impudent*.

retort 1. *v.* answer, reply, respond *question* 2. *n.* reply, answer, repartee, response.

retract *v.* rescind, recant, take back, revoke, repeal *affirm*.

retreat 1. *n.* withdrawal, departure, retirement 2. *n.* shelter, asylum, refuge 3. *v.* fall back, withdraw, retire, give way, leave *advance*, *attack*, *charge*, *proceed*.

retrieve *v.* restore, bring back, regain, recover *lose*.

return 1. *v.* restore, repay, give back 2. *v.* revisit, go back, come back 3. *n.* list, form, account, summary *The survey of population returns are filed at city hall.*

reveal *v.* divulge, make known, disclose, tell, discover *conceal*, *hide*.

revel 1. *n.* feast, spree, festivity, merrymaking, fling 2. *v.* celebrate, rejoice, carouse, make merry.

revenge 1. *v.* avenge, vindicate, retaliate *forgive* 2. *n.* vengeance, retaliation, reprisal *forgiveness*.

revenue *n.* profit, income, proceeds, receipts *expenditure*.

reverberate *v.* reflect, echo, resound.

revere *v.* honor, idolize, venerate, admire, adore *despise*.

reverent *adj.* deferential, respectful, humble *disrespectful*, *impious*, *irreverent*.

reverse 1. *n.* opposite, contrary *obverse* 2. *n.* hardship, setback, misfortune, mishap *success* 3. *adj.* contrary, opposite, converse 4. *v.* turn, go back, invert, transpose, overturn *advance*.

review 1. *v.* criticize, survey 2. *v.* reconsider, revise 3. *n.* criticism, examination 4. *n.* magazine, journal REVUE.

revise *v.* amend, rewrite, review, update, alter, correct, change.

revive *v.* renovate, cheer, restore, recover, refresh *depress*, *repress*.

revoke *v.* repeal, annul, recall, reverse, recant *ratify*.

revolt 1. *v.* shock, sicken, repel, nauseate *please* 2. *v.* rise, rebel, mutiny 3. *n.* revolution, rebellion, uprising, mutiny.

revolution *n.* 1. rebellion, insurrection, mutiny, revolt 2. turning, rotation, circuit, orbit, cycle.

revolve *v.* spin, rotate, twist, turn, gyrate, circle.

reward 1. *v.* compensate, recompense, pay *punish* 2. *n.* compensation, bounty, recompense, prize *penalty*.

rhyme *n.* verse, jingle RIME.

rhythm *n.* beat, harmony, rhyme, meter, timing.

ribald *adj.* coarse, gross, bawdy, smutty, base, blue, nasty *pure*.

Reverse

rich *adj*. 1. affluent, opulent, wealthy, well-off **poor** 2. abundant, plentiful, ample **scarce** 3. fruity, luscious, nutritious, full-flavored **tasteless**.

rid *v*. clear, destroy, eliminate, free, release, do away with.

riddle 1. *v*. perforate, pierce, honeycomb *His clothes were old and riddled with holes* 2. *n*. enigma, mystery, puzzle, problem.

ride 1. *n*. spin, jaunt, journey, voyage 2. *v*. guide, drive, perch, tour, travel.

ridicule 1. *n*. sarcasm, burlesque, derision, mockery **respect**, **praise** 2. *v*. satirize, jeer, deride, taunt, mock.

ridiculous *adj*. laughable, preposterous, absurd, ludicrous **sensible**, **sound**.

rife *adj*. common, prevailing, prevalent, abundant **uncommon**.

rifle 1. *n*. gun, shotgun, musket 2. *v*. rob, fleece, seize, plunder, snatch, loot, pillage.

rift *n*. 1. cleavage, falling-out, disagreement, divergence 2. crack, breach, cleft, rent, fissure.

rig *v*. outfit, furnish, dress, put on, clothe, equip.

right 1. *adj*. just, good, upright, fair erect, lawful **wrong**, **evil**, **bad**, **dishonest** 2. *adj*. accurate, correct, proper, true, exact **mistaken**, **untrue**, **erroneous** 3. *adv*. directly, straight 4. *adv*. suitably, properly, fairly 5. *n*. title, claim, privilege, ownership 6. *n*. goodness, uprightness, fairness, justice RITE, WRIGHT, WRITE.

righteous *adj*. pious, virtuous, honest, religious, moral, good, saintly, holy **dishonest**, **immoral**.

rigid *adj*. 1. strict, sharp, severe, stern **lax**, **slack**, **soft** 2. inflexible, stiff, unbending **pliable**, **pliant**, **elastic**.

Ride

rigorous *adj*. stern, rigid, severe, precise, harsh, austere, exact **lenient**.

rim *n*. edge, lip, border, margin, brim.

rind *n*. hull, crust, skin, peel, bark, shell.

ring 1. *v*. jingle, peal, sound, tingle 2. *v*. surround, encircle 3. *n*. hoop, circle, band, loop 4. *n*. group, set, clique, crew 5. *n*. circus, stadium, arena WRING.

riot 1. *n*. affray, disturbance, brawl, tumult, disorder **peace**, **quiet** 2. *v*. revolt, brawl, rebel, rise up.

rip *v*. & *n*. slash, break, tear, slit, rent.

ripe *adj*. mellow, aged, ready, mature, finished, prepared **immature**, **unripe**.

ripple 1. *n*. undulation, wave 2. *v*. undulate, wave, swell.

rise 1. *v*. ascend, levitate, arise, go up **descend**, **fall**, **sink**, **subside** 2. *v*. awake, get up 3. *v*. progress, improve, be advanced, be promoted 4. *n*. rising, elevation, ascent **descent** 5. *v*. increase, addition, advance **decrease**, **downfall**.

risk

risk 1. *n.* hazard, peril, danger, chance *safety* 2. *v.* hazard, imperil, endanger, gamble.

risky *adj.* dangerous, perilous, chancy, daring *risky*.

ritual *n.* ceremony, formality, custom, liturgy.

rival 1. *n.* opponent, antagonist, competitor *partner* 2. *v.* compete, oppose, contest 3. *adj.* opposing, competing.

river *n.* brook, stream, torrent, watercourse, bourn.

road *n.* street, way, path, route, lane RODE, ROWED.

On the road

Rowed away

roam *v.* wander, range, ramble, stroll, meander.

roar *v. & n.* yell, cry, bellow, boom, shout, bawl, howl *whisper*.

rob *v.* plunder, pilfer, steal, fleece, loot, sack, strip, thieve.

robber *n.* thief, bandit, plunderer, brigand, pirate, burglar.

robe *n.* gown, vestment, dress.

robust *adj.* stout, sturdy, strong, muscular, brawny, hale *feeble*, *weak*, *wan*.

rock 1. *v.* swing, reel, sway, totter 2. *n.* boulder, pebble, stone.

rod *n.* wand, scepter, staff, pole, cane, perch.

rogue *n.* rascal, scoundrel, knave, villain, scamp *gentleman*.

role *n.* 1. task, function, duty, position 2. character, part ROLL.

roll 1. *v.* rotate, whirl, turn, spin, revolve 2. *v.* press, flatten, level 3. *v.* wrap, bind, swathe 4. *n.* bun, biscuit, scone 5. *n.* document, register, scroll, list ROLE.

romance *n.* 1. tale, fable, novel, story 2. betrothal, love affair, idyll, engagement.

romantic *adj.* 1. fictional, fanciful, idyllic, imaginative *practical*, *realistic* 2. lovelorn, sentimental.

roof *n.* canopy, shelter, cover, ceiling, shade.

room *n.* 1. compartment, apartment, chamber, accommodation 2. expense, space, extent RHEUM.

root *n.* origin, stem, bottom, radical, base, cause ROUTE.

rosy *adj.* 1. blooming, healthy 2. promising, optimistic.

rot 1. *n.* putrefaction, decay 2. *v.* decompose, putrefy, spoil, decay, crumble, go bad.

rotate *v.* turn, spin, revolve, turn around, whirl.

rotten *adj.* moldy, foul, putrid, decaying, corrupt *pure*, *sweet*.

rough *adj.* 1. coarse, shaggy, bristly, hairy *sleek* 2. rugged, unfinished, uneven, craggy *smooth* 3. impolite, rude, churlish, uncivil *suave*, *sophisticated* 4. crude, austere, harsh 5. stormy, tempestuous *calm*, *pacific* RUFF.

round 1. *adj.* spherical, circular, globular, curved 2. *n.* circuit, tour, compass, cycle.

rouse *v.* 1. wake, awaken 2. stir, excite, animate, stimulate ROWS.

rout 1. *n.* flight, defeat, overthrow 2. *v.* ruin, conquer, defeat.

route *n.* path, course, way, road ROOT.

routine *n.* custom, order, practice, system, habit.

rove *v.* roam, stroll, wander, stray, ramble, drift.

row (rhymes with toe) *n.* line, rank, file ROE.

row (rhymes with how) *n.* brawl, squabble, quarrel, noise, affray.

rowdy *adj.* boisterious, rough, noisy, disorderly.

royal *adj.* regal, majestic, imperial, kingly, noble.

rub *v.* scour, polish, scrape, wipe, smooth, chafe, massage.

rubbish *n.* 1. trash, garbage, refuse, debris, litter 2. balderdash, nonsense, drivel.

ruddy *adj.* rosy, reddish, glowing, florid *pale*.

rude *adj.* 1. crude, raw, unpolished 2. brusque, vulgar, impolite, coarse, impudent *polite*, *courteous*, *gracious*, *refined* ROOD, RUED.

rudimentary *adj.* primary, fundamental, elementary, basic *advanced*.

rue *v.* regret, deplore, grieve, lament *rejoice*.

ruffian *n.* rascal, wretch, villain, scoundrel *gentleman*.

ruffle *v.* 1. cockle, pucker, wrinkle 2. disturb, torment, vex, trouble.

rug *n.* mat, carpet, covering.

rugged *adj.* 1. sturdy, robust, stalwart, hardy, stout *weak*, *feeble* 2. jagged, rough, craggy, uneven *smooth*.

ruin 1. *v.* pauperize, bankrupt, impoverish 2. *v.* demolish, destroy, overthrow 3. *n.* remains, destruction.

rule 1. *v.* command, manage, govern, control 2. *v.* establish, settle 3. *n.* domination, command, government, control 4. *n.* order, law, precept, regulation.

ruler *n.* governor, monarch, leader, king, sovereign.

Rulers

rumble

rumble *v.* roll, drone, roar, thunder, boom.

rumor *n.* gossip, tidings, report, scandal, hearsay *fact*.

run 1. *v.* hasten, hurry, race, scamper, speed 2. *v.* pass, go, operate, proceed, work 3. *v.* glide, stream, flow 4. *v.* lie, extend, stretch 5. *n.* sprint, race, dash 6. *n.* excursion, trip.

rupture *n.* break, breach, fracture, hernia, burst.

rural *adj.* pastoral, rustic, countrified, provincial *urban*.

ruse *n.* maneuver, dodge, trick, artifice, deception.

rush 1. *n.* haste, hurry, dash, drive 2. *v.* dash, scurry, run, hasten, speed *linger*, *tarry*.

rustic *adj.* countrified, simple, rural, plain.

rusty *adj.* 1. corroded, worn, fusty, musty 2. unprepared, unpracticed.

rut *n.* 1. furrow, track, groove, hollow 2. routine, habit.

ruthless *adj.* cruel, pitiless, relentless, merciless, hard-hearted *humane*, *merciful*.

sack 1. *v.* despoil, pillage, ravage, plunder 2. *n.* pouch, bag, pack SAC.

sacred *adj.* consecrated, divine, hallowed, holy *profane*.

sacrifice 1. *n.* offering, oblation, gift, atonement 2. *v.* give up, surrender, yield, relinquish, forgo, cede *accept*, *gain*, *receive*.

sad *adj.* dejected, tragic, sorrowful, melancholy, dismal, depressed, downcast, gloomy, mournful *joyous*, *cheerful*, *happy*, *merry*, *glad*, *droll*.

saddle 1. *n.* seat, pillion, perch, pad 2. *v.* burden, encumber, load.

sadness *n.* depression, gloom, melancholy, misery *happiness*, *joy*, *mirth*.

safe 1. *n.* chest, vault, strongbox, coffer 2. *adj.* reliable, sure, trustworthy 3. *adj.* guarded, protected, secure *unsafe*, *dangerous*, *insecure*, *precarious*.

safeguard *n.* protection, shield, defense, security.

safety *n.* preservation, security, protection *danger*, *peril*, *risk*.

sag *v.* hang, dangle, droop, slump.

sage 1. *n.* philosopher, savant, wise person, pundit, scholar *fool*, *idiot* 2. *adj.* acute, wise, prudent, shrewd, sensible *stupid*.

sail 1. *n.* canvas, sailcoth, sheet 2. *n.* trip, journey, cruise, voyage 3. *v.* skim, cruise, voyage, navigate, float SALE.

sailor *n.* mariner, seafarer, tar, seaman, salt SAILER.

sake *n.* 1. regard, cause, account, respect 2. purpose, reason, end.

salary *n.* stipend, compensation, wages, allowance, pay.

sale *n.* 1. auction, clearance, sellout 2. vending, disposal, selling, marketing SAIL.

sally 1. *n.* raid, sortie, attack 2. *n.* frolic, trip, escapade, run 3. *n.* joke, quip, jest 4. *v.* issue, go forth, rush out.

salute 1. *n.* address, kiss, greeting 2. *v.* address, greet, receive, hail, accost.

salve 1. *n.* remedy, antidote, ointment 2. *v.* raise, save, rescue.

same *adj.* like, equivalent, identical, corresponding, similar *different, opposite*.

sample 1. *v.* try, taste, test 2. *n.* example, model, specimen.

sanction 1. *n.* support, permission, confirmation, authority 2. *n.* punishment, embargo, penalty 3. *v.* legalize, allow, support, authorize.

sanctity *n.* godliness, piety, purity, grace, holiness *evil*.

sanctuary *n.* 1. altar, temple, church, shrine 2. refuge, shelter, asylum.

sane *adj.* lucid, normal, sound, rational, sober *insane, crazy, mad* SEINE.

sanguine *adj.* enthusiastic, cheerful, confident, hopeful *despondent*.

sanitary *adj.* clean, pure, hygienic, sterile *insanitary*.

sap *v.* weaken, exhaust, mine, drain, undermine, debilitate.

sarcastic *adj.* taunting, cynical, severe, sardonic, cutting, satirical.

sardonic *adj.* derisive, ironical, sarcastic.

sash *n.* belt, band, girdle, scarf.

satellite *n.* 1. moon, spacecraft, sputnik, skylab, space station 2. disciple, follower, subordinate, minion.

satiate *v.* sate, glut, satisfy, fill, gorge.

satire *n.* irony, ridicule, burlesque, sarcasm, lampoon.

satisfaction *n.* 1. discharge, amends, payment, atonement 2. contentment, enjoyment, comfort, gratification *disappointment, discontent*.

satisfactory *adj.* sufficient, adequate, pleasing.

satisfy *v.* 1. suffice, please, content, gratify *frustrate* 2. persuade, meet, convince, assure.

saturate *v.* soak, steep, drench, souse.

sauce *n.* dressing, relish, condiment, appetizer, seasoning.

saucy *adj.* cheeky, rude, cocky, impertinent, flippant, insolent.

saunter *v.* lounge, amble, loiter, stroll, linger *hurry*.

savage 1. *adj.* ferocious, inhuman, fierce, brutish 2. *adj.* crude, wild, rough, uncivilized 3. *n.* aborigine, barbarian, brute.

save *v.* 1. reserve, hold, store, keep, *spend, squander, waste* 2. redeem, liberate, preserve, rescue, deliver.

savor 1. *v.* partake, relish, taste, enjoy 2. *n.* odor, flavor, smell, taste, savory.

say *v.* tell, remark, speak, express, utter, declare, mention.

saying *n.* maxim, axiom, proverb, adage, saw.

scale 1. *v.* ascend, mount, climb *descend* 2. *n.* range, gradation, measure *The company's losses were on a huge scale* 3. *n.* layer, plate, flake, laminate.

scamp *n.* cheat, scoundrel, rascal, villain, knave, rogue *gentleman*.

scamper *v.* scuttle, scoot, run, hurry, rush, tear.

scan *v.* 1. browse through, dip into, glance at 2. inspect, sift, search, scrutinize, examine.

scandal *n.* shame, slander, disgrace, infamy, dishonor *praise*.

scanty *adj.* small, niggardly, meager, sparse, scant, small *abundant, ample, lavish, plentiful, profuse*.

scar *v. & n.* mark, wound, blemish, hurt.

scarce

scarce *adj.* rare, infrequent, scanty, deficient, wanting, uncommon ***abundant, plentiful***.

scarcely *adv.* barely, hardly.

scarcity *n.* want, need, dearth, deficiency, lack ***plenty***.

scare 1. *v.* terrify, startle, frighten, shock 2. *n.* panic, alarm, fright, terror, shock.

scatter *v.* disperse, strew, spread, sprinkle ***gather, huddle, flock***.

scene *n.* exhibition, sight, spectacle, show, view SEEN.

scent *n.* fragrance, aroma, odor, perfume, smell CENT, SENT.

Cent

Scent

scepter *n.* wand, baton, staff, rod, cane.

schedule 1. *v.* adjust, time, list, plan 2. *n.* list, table, inventory, record, program.

scheme 1. *v.* plot, frame, plan, conspire, contrive 2. *n.* theory, design, project, plan, system.

scholar *n.* 1. professor, academic, don, savant, highbrow, egghead, ignoramus 2. disciple, student, pupil, learner.

school *n.* institute, college, academy.

scintillate *v.* shine, flash, sparkle, gleam, twinkle.

scoff *v.* jeer, deride, sneer, ridicule, jibe, taunt ***praise***.

scold *v.* criticize, rebuke, reprimand, blame, reprove, chide, admonish, ***encourage***.

scoop *v.* hollow out, gouge, excavate, ladle.

scope *n.* space, amplitude, extend, room, range.

scorch *v.* blister, char, roast, singe, burn.

score 1. *n.* tally, total, record, sum 2. *v.* notch, furrow, mark, cut 3. *v.* earn, record, gain, tally.

scorn 1. *v.* disdain, despise, spurn 2. *n.* mockery, contempt, disdain, ***esteem***.

scoundrel *n.* villain, scamp, knave, rascal, rogue ***gentleman***.

scour *v.* cleanse, whiten, scrub, rub.

scourge 1. *n.* plague, curse, punishment, pest 2. *v.* punish, whip, chastise, lash, torment ***pamper***.

scowl *v. & n.* glower, frown, glare ***smile***.

scramble *v.* 1. blend, combine, mix 2. climb, clamber, struggle.

scrap 1. *n.* morsel, bite, bit, fragment, crumb 2. *v.* abandon, discard, demolish ***retain***.

scrape 1. *n.* fix, trouble, predicament *As a boy, I was always getting into some scrape or other* 2. *v.* grate, scour, scratch, rub, rasp.

scratch *v. & n.* scrape, scribble, mark, score.

scrawl *v.* scribble, doodle, scratch.

scream *v. & n.* yell, cry, shriek, shrill, bawl.

screech *v. & n.* yell, shriek, scream.

screen 1. *v.* shelter, protect, hide, conceal 2. *n.* shield, guard, protection.

screw *v.* force, turn, rotate, twist, fasten, tighten ***unscrew***.

scribble *v.* scratch, scrawl, doodle.

scribe *n.* writer, clerk, notary.

script *n.* alphabet, calligraphy, handwriting, writing, manuscript, text, typescript.

scroll *n.* schedule, list, parchment.

scrub *v.* clean, scour, rub, cleanse.

scrupulous *adj.* strict, meticulous, conscientious, careful, vigilant *careless*.

scrutinize *v.* probe, examine, study, inspect *glimpse*.

scuffle *v.* contend, struggle, tassle, squabble, fight.

sculpture 1. *v.* chisel, carve, sculpt 2. *n.* carving, statue, figure, marble, bronze, statuary.

scuttle *v.* run, dash, hurry, scamper, bustle.

sea *n.* ocean, high sea, the main, the deep, waters, billow, brine.

seal 1. *n.* sea mammal 2. *n.* mark, endorsement, stamp 3. *v.* fasten, secure, close.

seam *n.* 1. crevice, layer, fissure, stratum 2. stitching, hem, suture SEEM.

sear *v.* burn, scorch, singe.

search 1. *n.* exploration, scrutiny, examination, inspection 2. *v.* explore, investigate, examine, inspect.

season 1. *n.* period, time, 2. *v.* spice, flavor.

seat *n.* 1. chair, stool, bench, pew, hassock 2. site, place, situation.

secluded *adj.* isolated, private, remote *busy*, *public*.

secondary *adj.* minor, lower, subordinate, inferior *primary*, *superior*, *principal*, *main*, *original*.

secret 1. *n.* confidence, mystery 2. *adj.* concealed, private, hidden, mysterious, clandestine *open*, *apparent*, *public*.

secrete *v.* discharge, exude.

section *n.* portion, piece, part, division, segment, sector.

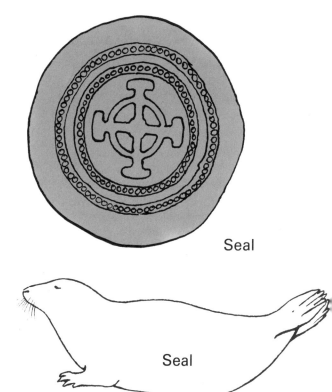

Seal

Seal

secure 1. *v.* fix, lock, fasten, shut 2. *v.* guard, defend, protect, *endanger* 3. *v.* acquire, gain, get, procure 4. *adj.* fast, firm, fixed, stable *precarious*, *loose*, *free* 5. *adj.* assured, confident, certain, sure *insecure*.

security *n.* 1. defense, safety, shelter, protection *peril* 2. deposit, pledge, pawn, bond.

sedate *adj.* calm, serene, collected, quiet, genteel, proper *hasty*.

seduce *v.* entice, tempt, decoy, allure, lead astray.

see *v.* 1. visit, call on 2. behold, observe, regard, perceive, discern, look at *disregard*, *ignore* 3. experience, suffer, feel *During the war, many people saw much suffering* 4. escort, wait upon, attend *Mary and I saw the children home* 5. understand, comprehend.

seed

seed *n.* kernel, grain, sperm, embryo.

seedy *adj.* shabby, needy, old, worn, miserable, faded **smart**, **thriving**.

seek *v.* solicit, attempt, search for, endeavor, strive, follow **shun**.

seem *v.* look, appear, exhibit, show, be obvious SEAM.

seemly *adj.* proper, decent, becoming, suitable **unbecoming**, **unseemly**.

seep *v.* leak, percolate, trickle, ooze, emit.

seethe *v.* simmer, boil, stew, steam, froth, bubble.

seize *v.* snatch, capture, grip, clutch, grasp, catch **release**, **loosen** SEAS, SEES.

seldom *adj.* scarcely, rarely, hardly, infrequently **often**, **frequently**, **mostly**.

select 1. *adj.* rare, choice, chosen, picked **cheap**, **inferior** 2. *v.* pick, choose, prefer.

selfish *adj.* narrow, miserly, mean, greedy, possessive, egotistical **generous**, **liberal**, **philanthropic**, **altruistic**.

sell *v.* exchange, trade, peddle, barter, vend **buy**, **purchase**.

send *v.* forward, post, dispatch, convey, transmit **receive**.

senior *adj.* elder, superior, higher, leading, eminent, main **junior**, **minor**.

sensation *n.* 1. excitement, thrill, surprise 2. impression, feeling, sense, perception.

sensational *adj.* thrilling, spectacular, exciting, startling **dull**, **humdrum**.

sense 1. *n.* mind, intellect, understanding 2. *n.* sensation, feeling, perception 3. *n.* judgment, conviction, discernment **folly** 4. *v.* appreciate, understand, perceive, feel CENTS, SCENTS.

sensible *adj.* rational, discreet, intelligent, wise **foolish**, **frivolous**, **fatuous**, **ridiculous**, **silly**, **inept**, **inane**, **idiotic**.

sentence *n.* 1. axiom, phrase, maxim 2. judgment, doom, condemnation **acquittal**, **pardon**.

sentiment *n.* emotion, feeling, sensibility, tenderness.

sentimental *adj.* emotional, affectionate, compassionate, melodramatic **cynical**, **unromantic**.

separate 1. *adj.* disconnected, apart, detached, alone **connected**, **joined**, **mingled** 2. *v.* sever, disconnect, divide, part, detach **unite**, **join**, **mingle**.

sequel *n.* consequence, result, continuation, outcome.

sequence *n.* series, succession, arrangement, order.

serene *adj.* tranquil, quiet, peaceful, calm, placid **disturbed**, **agitated**, **turbulent**, **temperamental**.

series *n.* sequence, course, succession, order.

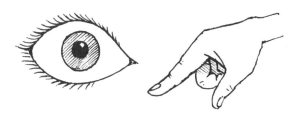

Senses

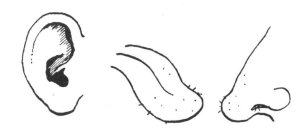

150

serious *adj.* earnest, grave, important, solemn **frivolous, trivial, jocular, flippant, funny, light, playful**.

sermon *n.* talk, discourse, address, homily, lecture.

servant *n.* employee, drudge, maid, attendant, domestic, slavery **master, lord**.

serve *v.* 1. help, aid, wait on, oblige, assist 2. content, satisfy.

service *n.* 1. aid, duty, employment, assistance 2. mass, rite, worship, ceremony.

servitude *n.* slavery, bondage, captivity, enslavement **freedom, liberty**.

set 1. *n.* collection, group 2. *n.* backcloth, setting, scene 3. *v.* fix, determine, establish, settle 4. *v.* place, locate, put 5. *v.* harden, solidify, congeal 6. *adj.* standard, firm, normal, unchanging.

setting *n.* background, scenery.

settle 1. *v.* abide, inhabit, dwell 2. *v.* establish, fix 3. *v.* discharge, square, pay, balance 4. *n.* stool, seat, settee, bench.

sever *v.* divide, cut, separate, part **join, connect, adhere, unite, link**.

several *adj.* different, many, numerous, various, some, diverse, distinct **few**.

severe *adj.* 1. strict, harsh, bitter, rigid, stern **lenient** 2. hard, intense, rigorous, violent **mild** 3. plain, simple, unadorned.

severity *n.* rigor, harshness, extremity, austerity, gravity **clemency**.

sew *v.* stitch, seam, baste, hem, make, mend SO, SOW.

shabby *adj.* 1. threadbare, ragged, worn, tattered **smart, gorgeous** 2. despicable, mean, low, base **praiseworthy**.

shack *n.* hut, cabin, shanty, shed.

shackle *v. & n.* manacle, handcuff, fetter, chain.

shade *n.* 1. hue, color, tint 2. shadow, gloom, dusk, darkness **light** 3. phantom, ghost, specter.

shadow *n.* darkness, gloom, shade **brightness**.

shaft *n.* 1. handle, rod, pole, staff 2. missile, arrow, barb.

shaggy *adj.* hairy, rough, rugged.

shake 1. *n.* jar, shock, tremor, convulsion, jolt 2. *v.* quiver, jolt, tremble, shudder, vibrate, agitate.

shallow *adj.* slight, superficial, foolish, silly **profound**.

sham *adj.* counterfeit, spurious, pretended, mock, false **real**.

shame 1. *v.* humiliate, discredit, abash, disgrace, mortify 2. *n.* dishonor, embarrassment, disgrace, ignomity **pride, honor**.

shameful *adj.* humiliating, mortifying, disgraceful, infamous **honorable**.

A sow sewing

151

shameless

shameless *adj.* brazen, insolent, impudent, unashamed, immodest *decent*, *modest*.

shanty *n.* cabin, hut, shack, shed.

shape 1. *v.* mold, fashion, create, design, make 2. *n.* figure, form, pattern, outline.

share 1. *v.* distribute, apportion, divide, allot, ration 2. *n.* dividend, part, interest, portion *whole*.

sharp *adj.* 1. quick, shrewd, witty, smart *obtuse*, *dull* 2. cutting, keen, fine, acute *blunt* 3. piercing, shrill *faint* 4. pungent, sour, biting, acrid.

shatter *v.* 1. despair, shock, upset 2. smash, break, destroy, burst, fragment *repair*.

shave *v.* smooth, graze, trim, smooth, clip.

shear *v.* strip, cut, fleece, clip SHEER.

shed 1. *v.* let fall, cast off, spill 2. *n.* cabin, shanty, hut, hovel, shack.

sheen *n.* luster, shine, polish, gloss.

sheer *adj.* 1. clear, pure, absolute, utter 2. transparent, thin, clear, diaphanous, fine 3. abrupt, perpendicular, steep SHEAR.

sheet *n.* 1. bed linen 2. leaf, page, foil, plate, wafer, layer.

shelf *n.* bracket, ledge, rack, mantel, projection.

shell *n.* framework, crust, case, husk, covering.

shelter 1. *n.* haven, asylum, retreat, refuge 2. *v.* protect, shield, screen, hide, guard, defend.

shield 1. *n.* guard, shelter, protection, defense 2. *v.* protect, defend, ward off *betray*.

shift 1. *n.* move, transfer, alteration 2. *n.* stretch, period, turn, bout, stint 3. *v.* alter, remove, change, move.

shifty *adj.* furtive, deceitful, crafty, evasive, foxy, sly *honest*.

shimmer *v.* sparkle, glimmer, glisten, gleam.

A bulb shining

shine 1. *n.* luster, sheen, gloss, glimmer *dullness* 2. *v.* glisten, glow, sparkle.

ship 1. *n.* vessel, liner, craft, boat, barque, launch, tug 2. *v.* send, dispatch, cart, haul.

A ship

shirk *v.* avoid, shun, evade, dodge, malinger.

shiver 1. *n.* shudder, shake, tremor 2. *v.* tremble, shake, shudder, quiver, quake.

shock 1. *v.* upset, outrage, offend, disgust 2. *v.* dismay, stun, horrify, frighten 3. *n.* clash, stroke, impact, collision, blow.

shoot 1. *n.* sprout, bud, twig 2. *v.* explode, dart, fire, emit, discharge CHUTE.

shop *n.* store, market, workshop, plant, factory.

shore *n.* strand, coast, seaside, beach.

short *adj.* 1. puny, slight, small, little *long*, *tall* 2. concise, pithy, brief, condensed *lengthy* 3. severe, terse, curt.

shorten *v.* lessen, reduce, diminish, abbreviate, abridge *lengthen*, *extend*, *elongate*, *prolong*, *protract*.

shortly *adv.* soon, briefly, tersely, quickly.

shout *v. & n.* yell, bellow, call, roar, cry, scream.

shove *v. & n.* thrust, push, prod, press, jostle.

show 1. *n.* exhibition, performance, spectacle, parade 2. *v.* point out, indicate 3. *v.* display, present, exhibit 4. *v.* guide, conduct, usher 5. *v.* reveal, teach, disclose *hide*.

shred 1. *v.* dice, mince, strip, tear, chop 2. *n.* bit, fragment, piece, scrap, particle.

shrewd *adj.* 1. quick, ingenious, clever, sharp, wise *stupid* 2. sly, wily, artful, astute, cunning.

shriek *v. & n.* yell, screech, scream.

shrill *adj.* piercing, acute, sharp, high-pitched, harsh *soft*.

shrink *v.* 1. flinch, recoil, draw back 2. dwindle, shrivel, wither, contract *swell*, *enlarge*, *grow*, *increase*, *lengthen*, *stretch*.

shrivel *v.* dry up, wrinkle, parch, wither.

shudder *v. & n.* shake, tremble, quiver, shiver.

shuffle *v.* 1. trudge, falter, struggle, crawl 2. mix, jumble.

shun *v.* elude, avoid, eschew, evade, escape *seek*, *face*.

shut *v.* bar, seal, close, fasten, lock *open*.

shy *adj.* bashful, timid, coy *bold*, *brazen*, *confident*, *smug*.

sick *adj.* weak, unhealthy, ill, unwell, ailing *healthy*, *well*.

sickness *n.* disease, malady, disorder, illness, affliction *remedy*.

side 1. *v.* support, join, take sides 2. *adj.* secondary, indirect, oblique 3. *n.* edge, border, verge, margin 4. *n.* sect, team, faction SIGHED.

sieve *n.* riddle, strainer, sifter.

sift *v.* 1. strain, sort, filter, 2. examine, investigate, scrutinize, probe.

sigh *v.* mourn, cry, grieve, lament, groan.

sight *n.* 1. look, spectacle, vision, scene, view 2. vision, seeing, eyesight *blindness* CITE, SITE.

sign 1. *v.* initial, subscribe, endorse 2. *n.* symbol, emblem, token, symptom, mark 3. *n.* hint, manifestation, indication.

A sign

Sign

153

signal

signal 1. *adj.* extraordinary, remarkable, conspicuous, famous 2. *n.* sign, indicator, beacon, mark.

significance *n.* weight, effect, impressiveness, meaning, force, importance.

significant *adj.* 1. meaningful, profound, suggestive, indicative 2. consequential, momentous, eventful, historic, vital *insignificant*, *slight*.

signify *v.* denote, imply, express, mean, indicate.

silence *n.* peace, quiet, stillness, calm, noiselessness *clamor*, *noise*, *outcry*, *racket*.

silent *adj.* quiet, still, hushed, tranquil, calm, soundless, noiseless *vociferous*.

silly *adj.* foolish, frivolous, senseless, weak, stupid, simple *sensible*.

similar *adj.* resembling, like, uniform *dissimilar*, *different*, *diverse*, *opposite*.

simmer *v.* seethe, stew, bubble, boil.

simple *adj.* 1. unmistakable, easy, clear, intelligible *difficult*, *puzzling*, *complex*, *intricate* 2. unaffected, natural, plain, unadorned, unaffected *ornate*, *elaborate*, *pretentious*, *fancy* 3. open, naïve, frank *sophisticated*, *subtle*.

simply *adv.* truly, barely, plainly, merely, sincerely.

sin 1. *v.* do wrong, err, trespass, offend, transgress 2. *n.* wrong, trespass, crime, depravity, wickedness *goodness*.

since 1. *prep.* after, from the time of 2. *adv.* before this, ago.

sincere *adj.* 1. open, direct, honest, candid, frank *insincere* 2. unfeigned, genuine, real, true *false*.

sinful *adj.* wrong, immoral, wicked, bad, unholy *good*, *upright*, *moral*, *holy*.

sing *v.* warble, croon, carol, chant, hum.

singe *v.* burn, sear, scorch.

single *adj.* 1. unwed, celibate, unmarried *married* 2. lone, sole, alone, solitary 3. individual, separate, particular *married*.

singular *adj.* rare, peculiar, unusual, strange, uncommon *commonplace*.

sinister *adj.* 1. wrong, evil, unlucky, unfortunate, bad *auspicious*, *good* 2. left, on the left.

sink *v.* 1. degrade, ruin, depress 2. immerse, submerge, submerse, lower *rise*, *float*.

A ship sinking

sip *v. & n.* taste, swallow, drink, sup, suck.

sit *v.* repose, remain, perch, settle, rest *stand*.

site *n.* position, place, station, location CITE, SIGHT.

situation *n.* 1. condition, predicament, plight, state 2. job, post, employment, office 3. position, locality, place.

size *n.* largeness, extent, bulk, volume SIGHS.

skeleton *n.* framework, outline, bones.

sketch 1. *v.* design, draw, rough, draft, trace 2. *n.* drawing, outline, picture, draft, plan, diagram.

skill *n.* ability, aptitude, facility, talent, dexterity **clumsiness**.

skillful *adj.* proficient, able, skilled, clever, competent, adept **clumsy**, **inept**, **awkward**.

skim *v.* 1. glide, coast, graze, sail, brush, touch 2. scan, browse *This morning, I just skimmed through my mail, as I had very little time.*

skin *n.* hull, rind, husk, peel, hide, pelt.

skinny *adj.* lank, gaunt, lean, poor, thin, scrawny, shrunk **chubby**, **portly**.

skip *v. & n.* spring, gambol, leap, hop, caper, jump, bound.

skirmish *n.* combat, encounter, conflict, collision, brush, contest.

skirt *n.* 1. border, rim, edge, fringe, margin, verge 2. dress, petticoat.

skulk *v.* sneak, prowl, hide, lurk, slink.

sky *n.* firmament, heavens, atmosphere, air.

slack *adj.* 1. tardy, sluggish, slow 2. inactive, lazy, idle **active**, **busy** 3. limp, loose, hanging, relaxed **taut**, **stiff**, **rigid**, **tight**.

slam *v.* shut, close, push, bang.

slander *v.* libel, discredit, defame, lie, malign, decry **praise**.

slang *n.* dialect, vulgarity, cant, jargon, argot.

slant *v. & n.* lean, incline, slope.

slap *v. & n.* pat, spank, blow, smack.

slash *v. & n.* gash, slit, cut.

slaughter 1. *v.* murder, slay, butcher, kill 2. *n.* carnage, butchery, massacre, bloodshed, murder.

slave 1. *v.* toil, drudge, work 2. *n.* captive, vassal, serf **freeman**.

slavery bondage, servitude.

slay *v.* murder, kill, massacre, slaughter **spare** SLEIGH.

sleek *adj.* glossy, silky, smooth **rough**.

sleep *v. & n.* repose, nap, slumber, drowse, rest, doze **wake**.

slender *adj.* thin, frail, slim, lean, slight, narrow **fat**, **heavy**, **portly**.

slice *v.* sever, cut, split, slit.

slide *v.* skim, glide, skid, slip.

slight 1. *v.* disregard, ignore, neglect, snub **flatter** 2. *adj.* trivial, petty, small, trifling **large**, **enormous**, **huge**, **major**, **significant**, **intense** SLEIGHT.

slim *adj.* 1. poor, weak, insignificant, slight 2. narrow, gaunt, slender, lank, thin **fat**, **corpulent**, **plump**, **portly**, **thick**.

slime *n.* mire, muck, mud, ooze.

sling 1. *n.* dressing, support, bandage 2. *v.* hurl, throw, fling, cast.

A sling

A sling

slink *v.* prowl, sneak, steal, skulk.

slip 1. *n.* blunder, mistake, oversight, error 2. *v.* err, blunder, mistake 3. *v.* slide, skid, glide.

slit *v. & n.* tear, cut, slash, gash.

slogan *n.* expression, catchword, phrase, motto, cry.

slope *v. & n.* tilt, incline, slant.

sloppy *adj.* 1. slovenly, careless, untidy, unkempt 2. wet, mushy, oozy, slimy.

sloth *n.* laziness, idleness, indolence, inertia, inactivity **haste**.

slovenly *adj.* lazy, untidy, slipshod, disorderly **neat, tidy**.

slow 1. *adj.* heavy, tedious, dull **lively** 2. *adj.* slack, tardy, sluggish, leisurely **fast, quick, fleet, rapid, swift** 3. *v.* retard, slacken, delay, detain SLOE.

sluggish *adj.* slothful, drowsy, idle, inactive, lazy, slow **quick, fast, active, rapid, swift, brisk**.

slumber *v. & n.* doze, repose, sleep, rest, nap.

slur 1. *v.* slander, defame, discredit 2. *v.* pass by, skim over, pass over 3. *n.* stigma, mark, disgrace, stain.

sly *adj.* crafty, subtle, cunning, artful, wily, shrewd.

smack *v. & n.* 1. smell, savor, taste, scent 2. whack, hit, slap, strike, wallop, belt.

small *adj.* 1. trivial, petty, unimportant, trifling **important, major** 2. puny, little, minute, tiny **large, big, great, huge, immense, massive, enormous**.

smart 1. *adj.* quick, clever, intelligent **stupid** 2. *adj.* trim, neat, spruce, stylish, fine **untidy, slovenly, dowdy** 3. *v.* ache, sting, pain, hurt.

smash 1. *n.* destruction, crash, ruin 2. *v.* shatter, break, crush, destroy **repair**.

smear *v.* stain, mark, daub, soil, spread, tarnish.

smell 1. *n.* odor, perfume, scent, aroma 2. *v.* scent, sniff.

smile *v. & n.* grin, laugh, beam, smirk **scowl, frown**.

smog *n.* fog, smoke, cloudiness.

smoke *n.* vapor, fume, fog, mist.

smooth 1. *v.* flatten, level, even 2. *adj.* level, sleek, flat, even **rough, uneven, rugged**.

smother *v.* suffocate, choke, stifle.

smug *adj.* complacent, self-satisfied, conceited **modest, shy**.

smut *n.* blight, dirt, smudge, blemish.

snack *n.* light meal, lunch, morsel, tidbit.

snag *n.* 1. problem, handicap, obstacle 2. projection, knob, snare, knot, jag.

snap *v.* 1. snarl, bite 2. crack, break, burst, split.

snare 1. *v.* trap, catch, capture **free** 2. *n.* net, trap, hook.

snatch *v.* grab, seize, grasp, grip, clutch.

sneak 1. *n.* spy, snoop, informer, grass, scoundrel 2. *v.* skulk, slink, lurk, prowl.

sneer *v. & n.* jeer, taunt, scoff, jibe.

sniff *v.* breathe, inhale, snuff, smell.

snip *v.* cut, nip, clip.

snivel *v.* blubber, whine, cry, weep, whimper.

snobbish *adj.* pretentious, vulgar, arrogant, haughty, ostentatious, assuming, supercilious, vain, stuck-up.

snub 1. *n.* slight, insult, humiliation 2. *v.* put down, slight, insult, humiliate **compliment**.

snug *adj.* cozy, comfortable, compact, intimate.

soak *v.* steep, wet, drench, saturate **dry**.

soar *v.* fly, hover, rise, glide, ascend **fall**.

sob *v.* sigh, lament, weep, cry.

sober *adj.* 1. temperate, abstemious, not drunk **tipsy, drunk, intoxicated, tight** 2. serious, grave, sedate, solemn **humorous** 3. steady, calm, collected, moderate **frivolous**.

sociable *adj*. affable, friendly, social, neighborly.

social *adj*. 1. communal, civic, tribal, civil, fraternal, public 2. sociable, convivial, gregarious, companionable.

society *n*. 1. humanity, the public, people 2. association, organization, group, club 3. company, association, fellowship, companionship.

soft *adj*. 1. plastic malleable, pliable, smooth, flexible ***solid***, ***hard***, ***rigid*** 2. silly, foolish, simple 3. quiet, subdued, mellow ***shrill***, ***loud***.

soil 1. *v*. stain, smudge, dirty, sully 2. *n*. loam, mold, dirt, ground, earth, land.

sojourn *v*. remain, reside, abide, dwell, stay, live.

solace *v*. & *n*. cheer, comfort, succor, aid, help.

sole *adj*. unique, single, exclusive, only, individual SOUL.

solemn *adj*. ceremonial, grave, formal, serious, ritual, sacred ***lighthearted***, ***frivolous***, ***jovial***.

solicit *v*. entreat, implore, request, beg, ask.

solid *adj*. 1. compact, hard, firm ***soft***, ***hollow***, ***liquid*** 2. reliable, sound, substantial ***unreliable***.

solitary *adj*. isolated, only, lone, remote, lonely.

solution *n*. 1. explanation, answer, result ***problem***, ***question*** 2. melting, liquefaction, emulsion.

solve *v*. answer, explain, make plain, interpret, decipher.

somber *adj*. 1. gloomy, dark, serious, dull 2. doleful, sad, dismal, mournful ***happy***, ***cheerful***, ***jolly***, ***humorous***, ***glad***.

sometimes *adv*. now and then, occasionally, at times, at intervals ***often***.

soon *adv*. presently, early, shortly, before long ***late***.

soothe *v*. pacify, calm, cajole, quiet, humor ***disquiet***, ***upset***, ***aggravate***, ***agitate***, ***alarm***, ***annoy***, ***arouse***, ***harass***, ***harrow***.

sophisticated *adj*. knowing, wordly-wise, civilized, experienced, urbane ***unsophisticated***, ***simple***, ***ingenuous***, ***innocent***, ***rough***, ***primitive***.

sorcery *n*. magic, witchcraft, divination, wizardry.

sordid *adj*. squalid, low, slovenly, vile.

sore 1. *adj*. tender, irritated, painful, aching 2. *adj*. annoyed, irritated, peeved, vexed 3. *n*. injury, ulcer, wound, cut.

sorrow *n*. misery, anguish, grief, trouble, sadness ***happiness***, ***glee***.

sorry *adj*. 1. regretful, remorseful, apologetic, repentant ***pleased***, ***glad*** 2. wretched, shabby, miserable, pitiful ***splendid***.

sort 1. *v*. arrange, classify, distribute, order ***mingle*** 2. *n*. variety, species, type, kind.

soul *n*. life, spirit, mind, essence SOLE.

sound 1. *adj*. entire, healthy, whole, unhurt ***unsound***, ***unhealthy*** 2. *adj*. true, rational, correct, sensible ***ridiculous***, ***foolish***, ***wrong*** 3. *n*. tone, noise, report, din, racket 4. *v*. utter, resound, pronounce.

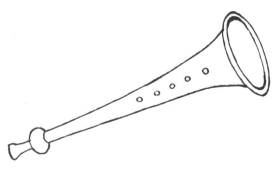

A musical instrument makes sound

sour *adj.* 1. surly, harsh, cross, morose *pleasant*, *benevolent* 2. tart, acid, sharp *sweet*, *luscious*.

source *n.* beginning, origin, cause, spring, derivation.

souvenir *n.* token, memento, relic, keepsake.

sovereign 1. *adj.* regal, supreme, chief, royal 2. *n.* ruler, monarch, king, queen.

sow (rhymes with cow) *n.* female pig, hog, swine.

sow (rhymes with dough) *v.* strew, propagate, scatter, plant *reap* SEW SO.

space *n.* 1. room, area, extent, capacity 2. universe firmament, cosmos.

spacious *adj.* vast, broad, wide, extensive, roomy *cramped*, *small*, *narrow*, *confined*.

span 1. *n.* distance, length, spread, extent 2 *v.* stretch, cross, reach.

spar 1. *v.* fight, wrangle, box 2. *n.* beam, pole.

spare 1. *adj.* superfluous, extra 2. *adj.* meager, skinny, lean 3. *v.* save, set aside, reserve *squander* 4. *v.* forgive, be merciful *slay*.

sparkle 1. *v.* glisten, scintillate, glitter, twinkle 2. *n.* luster, spark.

sparse *adj.* thin, meager, scattered, spread thin, scanty *dense*, *excess*.

spasm *n.* fit, convulsion, twitch, paroxysm.

speak *v.* discourse, utter, talk, express, say.

spear *n.* javelin, lance, pike, halberd, harpoon.

special *adj.* unusual, specific, exceptional, particular *ordinary*, *usual*, *standard*.

species *n.* collection, type, group, sort, class, kind.

specific *adj.* special, precise, peculiar, definite, particular *vague*, *general*, *random*.

specimen *n.* model, example, pattern, copy, sample.

speck *n.* particle, blemish, bit, spot, mite, atom.

spectacle *n.* sight, display, show, exhibition, scene.

spectator *n.* observer, looker-on, beholder, witness *performer*.

specter *n.* phantom, ghost, apparition, spirit.

speculate *v.* 1. hazard, gamble, venture, risk 2. muse, meditate, ponder, reflect.

speech *n.* 1. address, oration, lecture, discourse 2. dialect, language, tongue, talk, words.

speed *n.* swiftness, haste, velocity, hurry, dispatch *slowness*.

spell *n.* 1. term, time, season, period 2. magic power, incantation, charm.

spend *v.* 1. pay out, expend, disburse *save*, *hoard*, *earn* 2. use up, exhaust, consume *store*.

sphere *n.* 1. ball, globe, orb 2. department, field, capacity, area.

spice *n.* relish, seasoning, savor, flavor.

spill *v.* pour out, overflow, shed, drop.

spin *v.* 1. rotate, twirl, revolve, whirl 2. prolong, draw out, lengthen, twist.

spine *n.* 1. spike, thorn 2. ridge, backbone.

spirit *n.* 1. disposition, mood, temper, humor 2. fire, energy, courage, vitality 3. life, mind, soul 4. intent, meaning, significance *She loved her work, really entering into the spirit of the job* 5. ghost, specter, apparition, goblin.

spiritual *adj.* 1. sacred, religious, divine, holy 2. intellectual, mental, moral *material*, *worldy*, *physical*.

spite *n.* rancor, pique, malice, ill will, venom *goodwill*, *affection*.

spiteful *adj.* hateful, vindictive, malicious *benevolent*.

splash *v.* wet, sprinkle, splatter.

splendid *adj.* 1. sumptuous, magnificent, superb, gorgeous *dreadful*, *horrible*, *sorry* 2. brilliant, distinguished, remarkable *dull*, *ordinary*.

splinter *v.* chip, break, split, rend.

split 1. *n.* fissure, breach, break, crack 2. *v.* rend, divide, cleave, burst, splinter *join*, *connect*.

spoil *v.* 1. mar, ruin, injure, damage, harm *mend*, *restore* 2. corrupt, decay, go bad *enhance*.

sponsor *n.* supporter, patron, backer, promoter.

spontaneous *adj.* unbidden, instinctive, impulsive, natural *studied*, *cautious*, *planned*, *deliberate*, *premeditated*.

sport *n.* 1. game, recreation, play, amusement, fun, diversion 2. ridicule, mockery, derision *It is quite wrong to make sport of children's mistakes.*

spot 1. *v.* distinguish, identify, recognize 2. *n.* locality, place, site 3. *n.* stain, blemish, flaw, blot, speck.

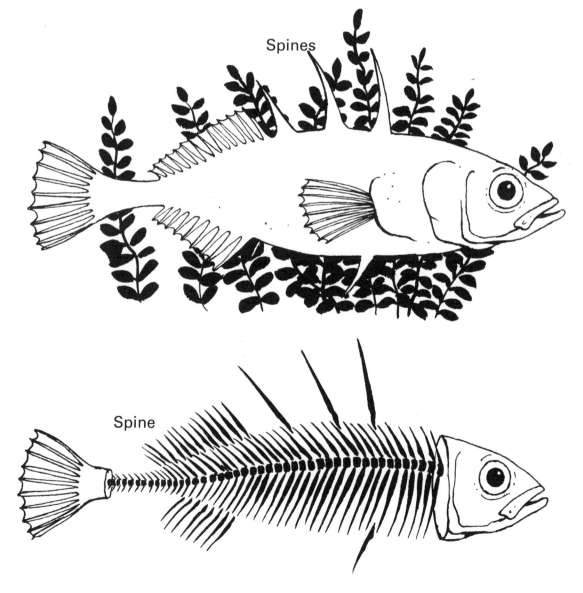

Spines

Spine

spotless

spotless *adj.* unstained, clean, immaculate *dirty*, *impure*.

spouse *n.* married person, mate, wife, husband.

spout 1. *v.* squirt, gush, spurt, pour 2. *v.* rant, utter, declaim 3. *n.* nozzle, tube, jet.

sprawl *v.* loll, relax, spread, lounge.

spray 1. *v. & n.* splash, sprinkle, shower 2. *n.* shoot, bunch, twig, nosegay, posy.

spread *v.* 1. unfold, disperse, extend, scatter, expand, stretch *contract* 2. divulge, circulate, publish, broadcast *conceal*.

spree *n.* celebration, revel, fling.

spring 1. *v. & n.* jump, hop, leap, vault, bound 2. *v.* originate, arise, emerge, issue 3. *n.* source, origin, fountain.

sprinkle *v.* strew, scatter, rain.

sprite *n.* spirit, ghost, specter, pixie, elf, fairy.

sprout *v.* germinate, shoot, flourish, grow.

spruce *adj.* jaunty, tidy, neat, natty, trim, smart *dowdy*.

spry *adj.* nimble, dapper, active, alert, brisk, lively *awkward*, *inactive*.

spur *v. & n.* urge, goad, boost.

spurious *adj.* false, fake, counterfeit, bogus, sham, feigned *real*, *genuine*.

spurn *v.* disdain, reject, scorn, disregard, despise *approve*.

spurt *v. & n.* stream, spout, gush, push, spring, spew.

spy 1. *v.* discern, scrutinize, see, discover, behold, detect 2. *n.* scout, informer, agent.

squabble *v.* dispute, brawl, quarrel, row, wrangle *agree*.

squad *n.* crew, company, gang, set, band, body.

squalid *adj.* filthy, unclean, dirty, nasty, foul *clean*, *gorgeous*, *majestic*, *stately*.

A spout spouting

squall *n.* 1. blast, gust, storm 2. yell, cry, bawl, scream.

squander *v.* dissipate, fritter, spend, lavish, expend, waste *save*, *conserve*, *hoard*, *preserve*, *spare*.

square 1. *v.* settle, balance 2. *adj.* just, honest, exact, true, right 3. *adj.* old-fashioned.

squash *v.* mash, squeeze, crush, press, pulp.

squat 1. *adj.* dumpy, thickset, crouching, stubby 2. *v.* cower, settle, crouch.

squeak *v.* yell, cry, squawk, creak, squeal.

squeal *v.* cry, yell, squeak.

squeeze *v.* squash, press, compress, pinch, nip.

squirm *v.* wriggle, twist, writhe.

squirt *v.* expel, splash, spout, emit, spurt, spray, gush.

stab *v.* spear, transfix, gore, pierce, wound.

stable 1. *adj.* solid, staunch, fixed, firm, steadfast **flimsy** 2. *n.* stall, mews, byre.

stack *v.* & *n.* heap, load, pile.

staff *n.* 1. pole, cane, rod, stick, club 2. employees, workforce, gang, personnel, crew.

stage 1. *n.* platform, theater, scaffold, playhouse, boards 2. *n.* degree, point, period, step 3. *v.* present, put on, arrange, direct, produce.

stagger *v.* 1. waver, reel, falter, totter 2. astound, surprise, shock, astonish 3. vary, alternate *Shopping times were staggered to help people who worked late.*

stagnant *adj.* still, sluggish, dormant, inactive.

staid *adj.* serious, sedate, sober, solemn, grave **giddy**, **flighty** STAYED.

stain 1. *v.* tarnish, blot, soil, blemish, sully 2. *v.* color, tinge, dye 3. *n.* spot, imperfection, blemish 4. *v.* & *n.* dishonor, disgrace, taint **honor**.

stair *n.* rung, step STARE.

stake *n.* 1. pole, peg, stick, post, rod 2. interest, share, 3. wager, hazard, bet, risk STEAK.

stale *adj.* 1. fusty, old, decayed, dry, musty 2. uninteresting, dull, trite, flat **fresh**, **new**.

stalk 1. *v.* pursue, track, follow, hunt, walk 2. *n.* stem, trunk, shaft, shank.

stall 1. *v.* delay, hesitate, stop, hinder, dawdle 2. *n.* recess, booth, cell, stable, stand, shop.

stalwart *adj.* 1. manly, brave, valiant, bold, daring 2. brawny, strong, muscular, robust **weak**.

stammer *v.* falter, pause, stutter, hesitate.

stamp 1. *v.* mark, imprint, print, impress 2. *v.* pound, tread, trample, crush, 3. *n.* seal, mark, block..

stand 1. *n.* booth, stall, kiosk 2. *n.* table, platform, rest 3. *v.* remain, stay, stop, rest 4. *v.* get up, arise, be erect **sit**, **lie** 5. *v.* sustain, endure, tolerate, bear **resist**.

standard 1. *adj.* normal, uniform, constant, consistent **unusual**, **special** 2. *n.* rule, scale, model, measure 3. *n.* banner, flag, ensign.

staple 1. *adj.* important, principal, chief, necessary 2. *n.* clasp, fastening, hasp.

stare *v.* gape, gaze, gawk, goggle, look intently STAIR.

stark *adj.* downright, entire, sheer, absolute, bare.

start 1. *v.* initiate, commence, begin, **cease**, **discontinue**, **halt**, **stop**, **terminate** 2. *v.* flinch, startle, shrink, jump 3. *n.* spasm, surprise, twitch 4. *n.* outset, beginning **end**, **finish**.

startle *v.* alarm, shock, frighten, dismay, disturb, perturb.

starve *v.* perish, die, be hungry, famish **feed**, **satiate**.

state 1. *n.* country, land, nation, commonwealth 2. *n.* condition, situation, plight 3. *v.* say, affirm, express, narrate, assert.

stately *adj.* magnificent, grand, majestic, dignified **squalid**, **mean**.

statement *n.* 1. report, declaration, announcement 2. record, account.

statesman *n.* politician, official, minister.

station 1. *n.* location, situation, place 2. *n.* stop, terminus, halt, depot 3. *v.* locate, fix, place, post.

stationary

Stationary stationery

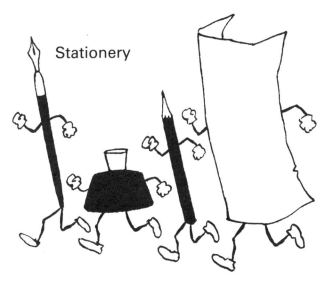

Stationery

stationary *adj.* still, at rest, fixed, motionless, stable **mobile** STATIONERY.

stationery *n.* paper, pens, ink, pencils STATIONARY.

statue *n.* figure, sculpture, monument, image.

status *n.* station, position, standing, condition, rank.

statute *n.* edict, regulation, law, rule, decree, ordinance, act.

staunch *adj.* firm, steadfast, constant, loyal, faithful **unfaithful**.

stay 1. *n.* rest, sojourn, repose, halt 2. *n.* stop, check, bar, restraint, halt 3. *n.* prop, brace, support, buttress 4. *v.* restrain, check, stop, hold 5. *v.* tarry, remain, dwell, lodge, abide **go, leave, depart, move, stray**.

steadfast *adj.* fixed, keen, direct, steady, reliable, devoted **fickle**.

steady *adj.* stable, constant, fixed, firm, regular **changeable, unsteady, erratic, inconstant, volatile, inconsistent**.

steal *v.* filch, rob, purloin, poach, pinch, pilfer.

stealthy *adj.* sneaking, sly, skulking, furtive, secret **open, direct, obvious**.

steam *n.* mist, fume, vapor.

steed *n.* mount, stallion, nag, horse, charger.

steep 1. *v.* drench, submerge, soak, immerse 2. *adj.* abrupt, sheer, precipitous.

steeple *n.* turret, tower, spire.

steer *n.* guide, govern, direct, conduct, pilot.

stem 1. *v.* check, stop, oppose 2. *v.* originate, arise, emanate 3. *n.* trunk, stalk, branch, shoot, stock.

step 1. *n.* degree, stage, grade 2. *n.* rung, tread, stair 3. *n.* walk, pace, stride, gait 4. *n.* measure, expedient, means 5. *v.* walk, move, go, proceed STEPPE.

sterilize *v.* decontaminate, cleanse, disinfect.

stern *adj.* forbidding, strict, austere, harsh, severe, hard, exacting **lenient, forgiving**.

stew 1. *n.* casserole, ragout, fricassee, hash 2. *v.* seethe, simmer, boil.

stick 1. *v.* attach, adhere, cement, glue 2. *v.* stab, pierce, spear, penetrate 3. *v.* abide, cleave, remain, cling 4. *n.* club, cane, staff, rod, switch, cudgel.

sticky *adj.* glutinous, gluey, adhesive, gummy, viscous.

stiff *adj.* 1. rigorous, austere, severe, strict *lax*, *lenient* 2. inflexible, solid, rigid, firm, unbending *limp*, *slack* 3. laborious, difficult, formidable *easy*, *simple*.

stifle *v.* 1. suffocate, choke, smother, 2. hush, repress, still, check, stop *encourage*.

stigma *n.* disgrace, mark, stain, blemish, blot.

still 1. *adj.* tranquil, serene, quiet, placid *noisy* 2. *adj.* inert, motionless, stationary *mobile* 3. *adv.* ever, always, continually 4. *v.* stifle, calm, silence, quiet, muffle 5. *adv.* yet, however, nevertheless, till now.

stimulate *v.* provoke, urge, incite, animate, encourage, excite *depress*, *frustrate*.

sting *v.* pain, wound, prick, afflict.

stingy *adj.* miserly, niggardly, tightfisted, close, mean *generous*, *lavish*, *liberal*.

stink *v. & n.* reek, smell, taint.

stint 1. *n.* job, chore, work, task 2. *v.* restrain, cease, limit, bound, stop.

stir *v.* 1. arouse, prompt, disturb, stimulate 2. shake, mix, churn, whisk, agitate, beat 3. budge, go, move.

stitch *v.* tailor, sew, needle.

stock *v. & n.* supply, reserve, store, hoard.

stocky *adj.* thickset, stubby, stout, solid, burly *lank*.

stolid *adj.* slow, stupid, dull, foolish *intelligent*.

stomach 1. *n.* abdomen, belly 2. *v.* bear, endure, put up with.

stone *n.* boulder, pebble, rock, jewel, gem.

stool *n.* chair, seat, hassock.

stoop 1. *v.* crouch, squat, bend, lean, bow 2. *n.* porch, veranda, portico, patio, terrace.

stop 1. *n.* halt, pause, rest 2. *v.* impede, obstruct, hinder, check, close 3. *v.* end, terminate, cease, halt, desist, finish *start*, *continue*, *commence*, *move*, *resume*.

store 1. *v.* reserve, stock, keep, provide *spend*, *disperse* 2. *n.* hoard, stock, provision, supply 3. *n.* depot, market, shop, warehouse.

storm 1. *n.* hurricane, gale, squall, tornado, tempest 2. *v.* fume, rant, rage *calm* 3. *v.* assault, attack *repel*.

story *n.* 1. tale, romance, yarn, narrative, legend 2. floor, tier, level, stage.

stout *adj.* 1. valiant, brave, intrepid, bold *cowardly*, *meek* 2. brawny, sturdy, robust, strong *fragile*, *frail* 3. chubby, portly, plump, fat *thin*.

stow *v.* store, pack, load, stuff.

straight *adj.* 1. fair, honorable, upright, honest *crooked* 2. direct, unswerving, undeviating *crooked*, *twisted* 3. right, faultless, perfect 4. *adv.* immediately, at once, directly STRAIT.

straighten *v.* adjust, rectify, unbend, disentangle *bend*, *contort*.

straightforward *adj.* steadfast, direct, downright, steady, unswerving *odd*, *wily*.

strain 1. *v.* injure, sprain, wrench 2. *v.* tighten, pull, stretch 3. *v.* purify, percolate, filter 4. *n.* music, tune, melody 5. *n.* exertion, effort *relaxation*.

strait *n.* 1. distress, hardship, difficulty *The charity was set up to help those in hard straits* 2. channel, passage, narrows STRAIGHT.

strand 1. *n.* string, thread, line 2. *n.* shore, coast, beach 3. *v.* cast away, abandon, wreck.

strange

strange *adj.* 1. outlandish, foreign, alien 2. singular, odd, peculiar, uncommon **familiar**, **ordinary**.

stranger *n.* foreigner, alien, outsider, visitor **friend**, **acquaintance**.

strangle *v.* choke, throttle, suffocate.

strap *n.* belt, strip, thong, band.

stray 1. *v.* roam, swerve, wander, straggle, rove 2. *adj.* lost, abandoned, vagrant.

stream 1. *v.* pour, spout, flow, rush, issue 2. *n.* rivulet, brook, current, river.

street *n.* highway, lane, road, avenue.

strength *n.* 1. spirit, fortitude, courage 2. force, vigor, power, might 3. soundness, solidity, sturdiness **weakness**, **frailty**.

strenuous *adj.* ardent, vigorous, determined, strong, energetic **ineffective**.

stress 1. *n.* strain, pressure, force 2. *n.* accent, weight, emphasis 3. *v.* underline, accentuate, emphasize.

stretch *v.* 1. lengthen, elongate, extend **contract**, **shrink** 2. exaggerate, amplify.

strict *adj.* 1. stern, austere, severe, rigorous **lenient** 2. precise, exact, accurate.

stride 1. *v.* walk, pace, march 2. *n.* pace, step, gait.

strife *n.* quarrel, animosity, conflict, discord, contest **accord**, **peace**, **tranquility**.

strike 1. *n.* walkout, revolt, boycott, lockout 2. *n.* assault, offensive, attack 3. *v.* beat, pound, smite, hit, knock.

striking *adj.* impressive, surprising, wonderful, admirable.

string *n.* twine, thread, cord, line.

stripe *n.* chevron, belt, stroke, streak, line.

strive *v.* aim, attempt, endeavor, struggle, toil.

stroke 1. *n.* effort, accomplishment, feat 2. *n.* knock, tap, rap, blow 3. *n.* seizure, attack, shock 4. *v.* smooth, massage, caress, rub.

stroll *v.* & *n.* saunter, walk, amble, ramble.

strong *adj.* 1. brawny, sinewy, hardy, robust, sturdy **frail**, **feeble**, **weak** 2. secure, solid, firm, compact **fragile**, **tenuous**, **flimsy** 3. sharp, pungent, spicy, piquant **bland**, **tasteless**.

structure *n.* 1. edifice, building, erection 2. form, construction, arrangement.

struggle 1. *n.* exertion, labor, effort 2. *n.* fight, conflict, contest 3. *v.* fight, contend, strive **yield**.

stubborn *adj.* headstrong, rigid, obstinate, perverse, willful **yielding**, **flexible**, **docile**, **pliable**, **tractable**.

student *n.* learner, pupil, scholar.

studious *adj.* zealous, scholarly, diligent, learned, eager **inattentive**.

study 1. *n.* sanctum, studio, den, office 2. *n.* inquiry, research, investigation 3. *v.* learn, consider, meditate, examine, muse.

stuff 1. *n.* textile, fabric, cloth 2. *n.* twaddle, balderdash, nonsense 3. *n.* matter, substance, material 4. *v.* fill, cram, stow, ram, pack.

stuffy *adj.* 1. prim, pompous, staid, prudish 2. close, musty, confined.

stumble *v.* fall, falter, trip, flounder.

stun *v.* 1. astonish, bewilder, amaze, stupefy, overcome 2. knock out, deaden, benumb, anesthetize.

stunt 1. *n.* feat, exploit, performance 2. *v.* dwarf, shorten, arrest, restrain.

stupefy *v.* deaden, dull, stun, benumb, drug, daze.

stupendous *adj.* amazing, wonderful, astonishing, surprising **ordinary**.

stupid *adj*. senseless, silly, foolish, dull, brutish ***intelligent***, ***smart***, ***bright***, ***clever***, ***keen***, ***alert***.

sturdy *adj*. stout, strong, firm, robust, stalwart, lusty ***frail***, ***flimsy***, ***fragile***.

stutter *v*. falter, stumble, hesitate, stammer.

style *n*. 1. elegance, fashion, chic 2. method, mode, manner, way 3. phraseology, diction 5. name, title, label STILE.

suave *adj*. polite, urbane, affable, sophisticated, agreeable ***boorish***, ***rough***, ***uncouth***.

subdue *v*. vanquish, soften, conquer, beat, overcome, quell ***yield***.

subject 1. *n*. point, topic, theme, matter 2. *n*. subordinate, dependent 3. *v*. control, subdue, expose 4. *adj*. obedient, subordinate ***superior***, ***independent***.

sublime *adj*. grand, magnificent, high, noble, exalted ***lowly***.

submerge *v*. sink, drown, immerse, submerse, plunge ***rise***, ***surface***.

submit *v*. 1. surrender, resign, yield ***resist***, ***fight***, ***overcome*** 2. offer, refer, tender.

subordinate *adj*. subservient, subject, inferior ***superior***.

subscribe *v*. 1. consent, approve, agree 2. support, donate to, contribute.

subsequent *adj*. succeeding, following, after ***previous***, ***preceding***, ***prior***.

subside *v*. descend, diminish, sink, lower ***rise***, ***increase***.

substance *n*. 1. material, stuff, matter, texture 2. gist, meaning, essence, import.

substantial *adj*. 1. solid, strong, firm, sound ***flimsy*** 2. actual, real 3. affluent, wealthy 4. considerable, important, major, grand ***unimportant***, ***trivial***.

Style

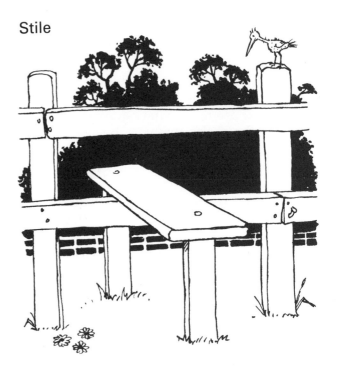

Stile

substitute

substitute 1. *v.* change, exchange, replace 2. *n.* replacement, proxy, makeshift.

subtle *adj.* 1. ingenious, deep, suggestive, delicate, fine **blunt**, **obvious** 2. crafty, tricky, artful, cunning **simple**.

subtract *v.* take, reduce, deduct, take away, withdraw **add**, **supplement**.

succeed *v.* 1. flourish, prosper, thrive **fail**, **lose**, **miss** 2. ensue, come after, follow **precede**.

success *n.* good fortune, prosperity, accomplishment, luck, **failure**.

successful *adj.* fortunate, lucky, prosperous, thriving **unsuccessful**, **vain**.

succession *n.* course, order, sequence, series.

suck *v.* absorb, engulf, imbibe, swallow up, draw in.

sudden *adj.* hasty, unusual, unexpected, abrupt, rapid **deliberate**, **foreseen**, **gradual**.

sue *v.* take action against, litigate, prosecute.

suffer *v.* 1. endure, bear, undergo, sustain, feel, tolerate **resist** 2. admit, let, permit, allow.

sufficient *adj.* enough, ample, adequate, satisfactory, plenty **insufficient**, **inadequate**, **scarce**.

suffocate *v.* smother, strangle, stifle, choke, asphyxiate.

suggest *v.* propose, advise, hint, intimate, advise **withdraw**.

suit 1. *n.* habit, dress, outfit, costume 2. *n.* case, action, trial 3. *v.* adapt, befit, adjust, become **differ**.

suitable *adj.* apt, applicable, fit, appropriate, proper **inappropriate**, **unsuitable**, **inept**, **unfit**, **unseemly**.

sulk *v.* scowl, glower, fret, mope.

sullen *adj.* sour, gloomy, morose, sulky, cross, somber, dismal **cheerful**.

sum *n.* total, whole, amount SOME.

summary *n.* abstract, outline, synopsis, digest.

summit *n.* peak, zenith, top, acme, apex, pinnacle **base**, **foot**.

summon *v.* send for, call, request, invite, cite **dismiss**.

sumptuous *adj.* splendid, rich, magnificent, gorgeous, costly, luxurious **austere**, **cheap**.

sundry *adj.* various, miscellaneous, several, divers, assorted.

sunny *adj.* shining, clear, bright, happy, cheerful, brilliant **dark**, **morose**, **overcast**.

sunrise *n.* daybreak, morning, dawn **sunset**, **evening**.

sunset *n.* nightfall, evening, dusk, sundown **sunrise**.

superb *adj.* exquisite, excellent, splendid, elegant, marvelous **inferior**.

supercilious *adj.* overbearing, disdainful, haughty, arrogant, proud **humble**.

A suitable suit

superficial *adj.* 1. slight, trivial, cursory, shallow 2. exterior, outer, external *deep*, *profound*.

superfluous *adj.* unnecessary, needless, excessive, redundant *deficient*, *essential*.

superintendent *n.* manager, warden, overseer, supervisor.

superior 1. *n.* boss, chief, principal 2. *adj.* higher, upper, better, greater *inferior*, *secondary*, *subject*, *subordinate*, *mediocre*.

supernatural *adj.* abnormal, mysterious, miraculous.

supersede *v.* succeed, displace, supplant.

superstition *n.* illusion, delusion, false belief, myth, fable, folklore.

supervise *v.* manage, command, direct, oversee, regulate.

supple *adj.* flexible, lithe, pliant, yielding *stiff*, *inflexible*.

supplement 1. *v.* extend, add, complement, supply *subtract* 2. *n.* extra, appendix, sequel.

supply 1. *n.* store, hoard, reserve, stock 2. *v.* stock, store, funish, provide *withhold*.

support 1. *v.* assist, help, patronize, aid *oppose* 2. *v.* uphold, bear, sustain 3. *v.* substantiate, confirm 4. *v.* cherish, provide for, maintain *oppress* 5. *n.* help, assistance, aid *hindrance*, *opposition* 6. *n.* supporter, prop, brace.

suppose *v.* 1. surmise, think, believe 2. imagine, presume, assume, conceive, deduce.

suppress *v.* subdue, crush, stifle, overpower *free*, *liberate*.

supreme *adj.* principal, best, highest, chief, greatest, foremost *least*, *lowest*.

sure *adj.* 1. positive, convinced, certain, confident *uncertain*, *doubtful* 2. stable, safe, firm, secure 3. infallible, indisputable, unfailing.

surface 1. *n.* face, covering, outside, exterior 2. *v.* rise, emerge *submerge*.

surge 1. *v.* flow, heave, swell, gush *ebb*, *wane*, *diminish* 2. *n.* breaker, billow, wave, roller SERGE.

surly *adj.* testy, touchy, morose, peevish, cross *genial*.

surmise 1. *n.* guess, supposition, conjecture 2. *v.* suppose, presume, suspect, guess.

surpass *v.* outdo, pass, excel, exceed *fail*.

surplus *n.* residue, remainder, excess *deficit*.

surprise 1. *n.* astonishment, amazement, wonder 2. *v.* startle, amaze, astound, astonish.

surrender *v.* relinquish, renounce, yield, give up *resist*, *conquer*, *defeat*, *overpower*.

surround *v.* enclose, circle, encircle, encompass.

survey 1. *n.* scrutiny, inspection, review 2. *v.* scan, inspect, view, observe, contemplate.

survive *v.* endure, persist, remain, outlive *fail*, *die*, *succumb*, *perish*.

susceptible *adj.* impressionable, responsive, sensitive *unimpressionable*, *impassive*.

suspect *v.* 1. doubt, distrust, mistrust 2. fancy, believe, surmise.

suspend *v.* 1. postpone, discontinue, break off, hold over *continue* 2. sling, dangle, hang.

suspense *n.* anxiety, concern, uncertainty, doubt, fear, apprehension *certainty*.

suspicion *n.* distrust, doubt, mistrust *trust*.

sustain *v.* 1. uphold, keep, bear, maintain, support *hinder*, *neglect* 2. endure, undergo *flinch*.

swagger *v.* bully, boast, bluster, parade, strut.

swallow

A swallow

A swallow swallowing

swallow 1. *n*. gulp, mouthful 2. *n*. bird 3. *v*. eat, gulp, engulf, devour 4. *v*. accept, believe, credit.

swamp 1. *v*. deluge, capsize, engulf, overwhelm 2. *n*. quagmire, bog, marsh, fen.

swarm 1. *v*. crowd, throng, collect 2. *n*. crowd, throng, flock, multitude ***disperse***.

swat *v*. hit, strike, clout.

sway *v*. 1. influence, direct, control 2. wave, turn, bend, move, swing.

swear *v*. 1. affirm, vow, assert, declare, promise, vouch 2. curse, blaspheme.

sweep *v*. clear, remove, brush, clean.

sweet *adj*. 1. pleasant, charming, agreeable ***nasty*** 2. fresh, clean, pure 3. honeyed, luscious, sugary ***sour***, ***bitter*** 4. harmonious, tuneful, soft, melodious ***discordant***, ***harsh*** SUITE.

swell *v*. distend, enlarge, dilate, increase, expand ***shrink***, ***diminish***, ***lessen***.

swerve *v*. swing, veer, deviate, diverge, dodge.

swift *adj*. rapid, quick, speedy, fast, fleet ***slow***, ***sluggish***.

swim *v*. glide, skim, bathe, paddle, float.

swindle 1. *n*. fraud, trickery, deception, cheat 2. *v*. deceive, cheat, defraud, trick.

swine *n*. pig, hog, sow.

swing *v*. dangle, sway, vibrate, wave.

swirl *v*. gyrate, reel, eddy, whirl, spin.

switch 1. *n*. push button, control 2. *v*. turn, replace, change, shift, substitute, swap.

swoon *v*. pass out, faint.

swoop *v*. seize, plummet, dive, pounce.

sword *n*. cutlass, blade, rapier, saber SOARED.

symbol *n*. device, figure, emblem, token, sign CYMBAL.

sympathetic *adj*. kind, considerate, compassionate, understanding, tender ***unsympathetic***, ***intolerant***, ***indifferent***.

sympathy *n*. 1. harmony, concord, agreement 2. compassion, understanding, tenderness, feeling.

symptom *n*. sign, indication, mark.

synthetic *adj*. artificial, manufactured, sham, mock.

system *n*. method, order, scheme, procedure, plan, arrangement.

T

A tank

table *n*. 1. index, statement, list, tabulation 2. tablet, board, slab, platform.

tablet *n*. 1. slab, table, stone 2. pill, lozenge, capsule.

taboo *v*. ban, forbid, prohibit.

tack *v*. 1. attach, pin, fasten, nail 2. zigzag, yaw, warp, stray.

tackle *v*. 1. attempt, try, undertake 2. grab, attack, seize.

tact *n*. judgment, diplomacy, discrimination, skill TACKED.

tactful *adj*. discreet, prudent, shrewd, adroit, skillful ***indiscreet***.

tactics *n*. method, strategy, plan, diplomacy.

tag *n*. ticket, label, sticker, card.

taint *v*. pollute, infect, contaminate, corrupt.

take *v*. 1. clasp, seize, grasp, grab ***give*** 2. choose, pick, select ***reject*** 3. accept, receive 4. interpret, understand *You may take it that our agreement is at an end* 5. catch, capture 6. demand, acquire *My journey takes a long time* 7. lead, conduct.

tale *n*. fable, account, story, legend TAIL.

talent *n*. ability, aptitude, skill, gift.

talk 1. *v*. confer, reason 2. *v*. converse, speak 3. *n*. discourse, lecture 4. *n*. parley, conversation.

tall *adj*. big, lofty, high, towering ***short***, ***low***, ***little***.

tally *v*. 1. count, calculate 2. conform, match, agree.

tame 1. *v*. domesticate, break, gentle 2. *adj*. domesticated, docile, mild ***wild***, ***savage***, ***fierce*** 3. *adj*. flat, dull, tedious.

tang *n*. taste, flavor, quality.

tangible *adj*. substantial, real, material, certain ***intangible***, ***vague***.

tangle *v*. & *n*. muddle, twist, knot ***unravel***.

tank *n*. 1. armored vehicle, combat car 2. reservoir, cistern, vat.

A tale

A tail

tantalize

tantalize *v.* irritate, frustrate, torment *appease*.

tantrum *n.* outburst, whim, temper, fit, scene, fury.

tap 1. *v. & n.* strike, knock, rap, hit 2. *n.* stopper, cock, faucet, valve, plug.

tape 1. *v.* tie, bind, wrap 2. *n.* ribbon, strip, strap.

taper *v.* lessen, narrow, contract, diminish.

tardy *adj.* slack, slow, late, leisurely *early*, *quick*, *rapid*.

target *n.* goal, object, end, aim.

tariff *n.* tax, levy, schedule, duty.

tarnish *v. & n.* spot, blemish, stain, soil *brighten*, *polish*.

tarry *v.* loiter, remain, wait, delay, stay, linger, dawdle *depart*, *hurry*.

tart 1. *n.* pie, pastry, puff 2. *adj.* sharp, sour, acid, bitter *sweet*, *sugary* 3. testy, peevish, waspish, surly *mild*.

task *n.* job, chore, work, labor, undertaking.

taste 1. *n.* savor, flavor, relish 2. *n.* judgment, discernment 3. *v.* sample, savor, try, experience.

tasteful *adj.* restrained, correct, proper, fitting *tasteless*.

tasteless *adj.* insipid, vapid, dull, tactless, gauche *strong*.

tattle *v.* chat, chatter, babble, prattle.

taunt *v. & n.* insult, ridicule, jeer, scoff *respect*.

taut *adj.* tight, stretched, strained, tense, rigid, stiff *loose*, *slack* TAUGHT.

tavern *n.* hostelry, bar, inn, saloon, pub.

tawdry *adj.* flashy, gaudy, showy *refined*.

tax 1. *v.* burden, assess, load 2. *n.* impost, duty, excise, levy TACKS.

teach *v.* inform, drill, instruct, show, educate, train *learn*.

teacher *n.* schoolmaster, lecturer, instructor, schoolmistress, tutor, trainer.

team *n.* company, party, crew, band, gang, group TEEM.

tear 1. *n.* rent, rip, fissure, split 2. *v.* rip, split, rend, pull, slash, cut TARE.

tearful sad, sobbing, lacrymose.

tease *v.* badger, provoke, vex, pester, tantalize *mollify*, *pacify* TEAS, TEES.

Teas tease

technique *n.* procedure, system, method.

tedious *adj.* irksome, wearisome, boring, tiresome, dreary, humdrum *exciting*, *interesting*, *impressive*.

teem *v.* swarm, abound, proliferate, increase TEAM.

tell *v.* 1. divulge, reveal 2. narrate, describe, relate 3. command, order, bid 4. discover, discern.

temper 1. *v.* moderate, soften 2. *v.* harden, anneal 3. *n.* passion, irritation, anger *calmness* 4. *n.* humor, disposition, mood.

temperamental *adj.* touchy, irritable, sensitive, moody *calm*, *serene*, *unruffled*, *placid*.

temperate *adj.* dispassionate, calm, moderate, restrained *immoderate*, *extreme*.

tempest *n.* gale, violence, storm, hurricane.

temporary *adj.* momentary, short-lived, transient, passing *fixed*, *everlasting*, *permanent*, *eternal*, *perpetual*.

tempt *v.* seduce, lure, attract, persuade, induce, entice, invite *repel*.

tenacious *adj.* persevering, steadfast, stubborn, diligent, obstinate.

tenant *n.* resident, occupier, dweller, occupant.

tend *v.* 1. lean, verge, incline 2. protect, watch, guard, look after, care for.

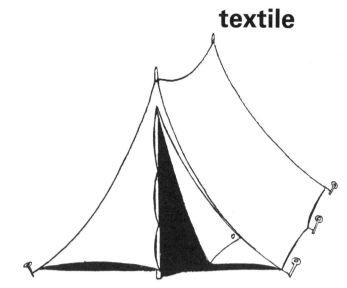

Tents

Tense

tendency *n.* trend, inclination, susceptibility, bias.

tender 1. *adj.* kind, loving, gentle, compassionate *unkind*, *hard-hearted*, *heartless*, *tough*, *callous* 2. *adj.* delicate, soft *hard* 3. painful, sensitive 4. *v & n.* bid, offer, proffer.

tense *adj.* strained, tight, rigid, stretched *relaxed* TENTS.

tenuous *adj.* small, thin, fragile, slender *strong*.

term *n.* 1. expression, name, word, phrase 2. period, time, interval, season.

terminate *v.* finish, cease, end, stop, conclude, close *begin*, *commence*, *start*, *inaugurate*.

terrible *adj.* horrible, horrid, vile, frightful, fearful, dreadful *pleasant*.

terrify *v.* horrify, frighten, shock, alarm, scare *reassure*.

territory *n.* domain, region, district, country, area, quarter.

terror *n.* panic, fear, fright, dread, horror, alarm.

terse *adj.* curt, concise, laconic, short, brief *diffuse*, *fluent*.

test 1. *v.* question, examine, try 2. *n.* trial, quiz, experiment, proof.

testy *adj.* cross, peevish, snappish, fretful, touchy *pleasant*.

text *n.* 1. clause, verse, passage, sentence 2. subject, topic, theme.

textile *n.* fabric, cloth, material.

texture

texture *n.* surface, grain, pattern.

thank *v.* acknowledge, give thanks, appreciate, be grateful.

thankful *adj.* indebted, grateful, beholden, obliged **ungrateful**.

thankless *adj.* unappreciated, ungrateful, heedless, inconsiderate **grateful**.

thaw *v.* melt, dissolve, defrost, liquefy **solidify**, **freeze**.

theatrical *adj.* showy, dramatic.

theft *n.* stealing, pilfering, larceny, robbery.

theme *n.* topic, thesis, subject, text.

theory *n.* hypothesis, opinion, conjecture, speculation.

therefore *adv.* 1. accordingly, thus, consequently 2. for that reason, then, thence.

thick *adj.* 1. solid, gross, dumpy, bulky, dense, squat **thin**, **slim** 2. viscous, sticky, stodgy, gummy, syrupy **watery**.

thief *n.* burglar, crook, robber, pilferer.

thin *adj.* 1. watery, weak, diluted 2. slim, lean, lank, slender, skinny, meager, narrow **thick**, **fat**, **plump**, **stout**, **wide**, **portly**.

thing *n.* object, body, substance, being creature.

think *v.* 1. meditate, speculate, reflect, muse 2. believe, conclude, consider, fancy, suppose.

thirsty *adj.* arid, dry, parched, desiccated **satisfied**.

thorn *n.* prickle, bramble, spine, barb.

thorough *adj.* total, complete, perfect, entire **careless**, **haphazard**, **slapdash**.

thought *n.* 1. notion, fancy, reflection, idea, meditation 2. conclusion, judgment.

thoughtful *adj.* 1. prudent, mindful, attentive, considerate, kind **mean**, **rash**, **thoughtless** 2. pensive, reflective, studious.

thoughtless *adj.* careless, neglectful, heedless, regardless **thoughtful**, **kind**, **careful**, **considerate**.

thrash *v.* punish, flog, whip, beat.

thread *n.* filament, string, fiber, cord.

threaten *v.* 1. loom, forebode, impend 2. intimidate, menace, denounce.

threshold *n.* 1. outset, start, beginning, verge **end** 2. gate, entrance, door.

thrifty *adj.* careful, frugal, saving, sparing **prodigal**, **spendthrift**, **wasteful**, **extravagant**, **improvident**.

thrill 1. *n.* joy, excitement, kick 2. *v.* agitate, stimulate, excite, delight, titillate.

thrive *v.* increase, prosper, flourish, grow, succeed **languish**, **expire**.

throb *v.* & *n.* pound, thump, pulse, beat.

throng 1. *v.* flock, swarm, cluster, crowd 2. *n.* horde, crowd, host, multitude.

throttle *v.* suffocate, choke, stifle, strangle.

throw *v.* & *n.* thrust, toss, fling, pitch THROE.

thrust *v.* & *n.* stab, attack, push, assault, shove, pass.

thump *v.* & *n.* strike, rap, whack, punch, knock, beat.

thwart *v.* contravene, hinder, frustrate, oppose, obstruct **encourage**, **help**, **assist**.

ticket *n.* slip, pass, note, sticker, voucher, permit, label.

tickle *v.* 1. gladden, please, delight, amuse 2. touch, titillate, stroke.

tide *n.* stream, current, flow, ebb TIED.

tidings *n.* news, information, advice, word, notification.

tidy *adj.* orderly, trim, neat **untidy**, **disheveled**, **slovenly**.

Tie   Tie

tie 1. *n*. bond, link 2. *n*. necktie, cravat 3. *v*. knot, link, bind, connect, fasten **untie**, **loosen**.

tight *adj*. 1. stingy, closefisted, mean 2. secure, firm, close, taut, close-fitting **loose**, **slack**.

till 1. *n*. cashbox, cash register, safe 2. *v*. plow, cultivate.

tilt *v*. & *n*. incline, slope, slant.

timber *n*. lumber, wood, planks, logs, boards.

time 1. *n*. tempo, beat, meter, measure 2. *n*. age, term, period, interval, spell 3. *v*. measure, regulate THYME.

timely *adj*. prompt, opportune, convenient, early, punctual **untimely**, **inconvenient**.

timid *adj*. coy, shy, diffident, fearful, bashful, shrinking **bold**, **forward**, **confident**, **fearless**.

tinge *v*. & *n*. color, tint, stain, dye, hue.

tingle *v*. prickle, sting, itch.

tinker *v*. cobble, mend, fix, repair, patch.

tinkle *v*. ring, jingle, jangle, clink.

tint *v*. & *n*. tinge, color, stain, hue.

tiny *adj*. small, little, puny, wee **large**, **huge**, **enormous**, **colossal**, **big**, **immense**, **massive**, **monumental**.

tip 1. *n*. top, point, extremity, peak, end **bottom** 2. *n*. information, clue, advice, hint 3. *n*. reward, gratuity, gift 4. *v*. tilt, incline, lean.

tipsy *adj*. drunk, befuddled, inebriated **sober**.

tire *v*. weaken, fatigue, exhaust, weary **exhilarate**, **refresh**, **invigorate**.

tiresome *adj*. boring, exhausting, arduous, dull, annoying **interesting**.

title *n*. 1. right, deed, claim 2. designation, heading, name.

toil 1. *n*. work, exertion, labor, drudgery 2. *v*. drudge, labor, work **relax**, **loll**.

token *n*. symbol, souvenir, sample, mark, memento, keepsake.

tolerable

tolerable *adj.* sufferable, endurable, acceptable **insufferable, intolerable**.

tolerate *v.* admit, endure, permit, allow **discourage**.

toll 1. *n.* duty, impost, tax 2. *v.* ring, chime, peal.

tomb *n.* grave, vault, sepulcher, crypt.

tone *n.* 1. noise, sound, note 2. color, shade, hue 3. intonation, expression, accent.

tongue *n.* speech, dialect, language.

tonic *n.* refresher, medicine, restorative.

too *adv.* also, as well, additionally.

tool *n.* implement, instrument, utensil TULLE.

top *n.* 1. acme, peak, pinnacle, summit, apex **bottom, base** 2. cap, lid, stopper.

topic *n.* question, theme, matter, subject.

topple *v.* tumble, overturn, fall.

torch *n.* light, lamp, lantern, flashlamp.

torment 1. *n.* agony, torture, pain 2. *v.* pain, pester, torture, annoy, distress **soothe**.

torrent *n.* deluge, downpour, stream, flood.

torture 1. *v.* distress, pain, agonize **comfort, soothe** 2. *n.* torment, anguish, pain, agony.

toss *v.* hurl, fling, throw, cast, pitch, heave, chuck, sling.

total 1. *n.* amount, sum, whole 2. *adj.* full, complete, entire **part**.

totter *v.* reel, falter, stagger.

touch 1. *n.* feeling contact 2. *n.* suggestion, taste, hint, tinge 3. *v.* handle, finger, feel 4. *v.* regard, affect, concern *The king was touched by the loyalty of his subjects* 5. *v.* impress, affect, stir.

touchy *adj.* cross, peevish, irritable, testy, snappy **calm, collected, agreeable**.

tough *adj.* leathery, hardy, strong, severe, firm **weak, tender, vulnerable**.

tour *n.* trip, visit, journey, excursion, expedition.

tourist *n.* traveler, visitor, sightseer, pilgrim.

tournament *n.* game, match, contest.

tow *v.* drag, pull, draw, tug, haul TOE.

tower *n.* spire, steeple, turret, minaret, belfry.

town *n.* city, municipality, place, borough, metropolis.

toy 1. *n.* trinket, plaything, game 2. *v.* play, dally, trifle.

trace 1. *v.* sketch, delineate, draw 2. *v.* track, hunt, follow 3. *n.* vestige, mark, remains, sign.

track 1. *n.* road, path, trail, route, way 2. *n.* trace, footprint, trail 3. *v.* trail, hunt, follow, trace.

tract *n.* region, district, area TRACKED.

trade *n.* 1. occupation, craft, employment 2. business, traffic, barter, commerce.

tradition *n.* folklore, custom, convention, usage.

traffic *n.* 1. exchange, trade, sale, commerce 2. transport, freight, transit, movement.

tragedy *n.* disaster, catastrophe, calamity **comedy, farce**.

tragic *adj.* sad, unfortunate, shocking, miserable, dreadful **comic**.

trail 1. *v.* draw, pull, drag 2. *v.* track, hunt, trace, follow 3. *n.* scent, path, track.

train 1. *n.* chain, succession, series 2. *n.* staff, retinue, followers 3. *v.* drill, instruct, educate, teach.

trait *n.* characteristic, peculiarity, feature, attribute.

traitor *n.* rebel, spy, betrayer, deserter, renegade.

Tramp

tramp 1. *n*. vagrant, loafer, hobo, vagabond 2. *v*. walk, journey, march.

Tramp

tranquil *adj*. quiet, peaceful, calm, serene, still ***disturbed***, ***upset***, ***agitated***, ***frantic***, ***restless***.

transaction *n*. business, deal, negotiation.

transcend *v*. surmount, excel, exceed, surpass.

transfer 1. *n*. removal, change, shift 2. *v*. make over, assign, consign, confer 3. *v*. convey, carry, transmit, move.

transform *v*. convert, change, alter ***retain***.

transgress *v*. offend, disobey, sin, err, infringe, overstep ***obey***.

transient *adj*. temporary, fleeting, brief, passing ***permanent***.

transmit *v*. remit, forward, dispatch, remit, send.

transparent *adj*. 1. obvious, evident 2. lucid, clear, translucent ***opaque***.

transport 1. *n*. carriage, transportation, conveyance, 2. *v*. convey, carry, bear, fetch.

trap 1. *v*. catch, ensnare 2. pitfall, snare, ambush.

trash *n*. junk, waste, rubbish, refuse, garbage, litter.

travel 1. *n*. touring, journeying, passage, movement 2. *v*. ramble, journey, voyage, tour.

treacherous *adj*. disloyal, traitorous, unfaithful, false ***loyal***, ***faithful***.

tread 1. *v*. & *n*. step, tramp 2. *v*. walk, ambulate, plod, trample.

treason *n*. disloyalty, treachery, betrayal ***faith***, ***loyalty***.

treasure 1. *v*. value, prize, cherish 2. *n*. wealth, riches, money, cash.

treat 1. *n*. entertainment, pleasure, delicacy 2. *v*. feast, entertain 3. *v*. handle, manage, use 4. *v*. doctor, nurse, medicate, minister to.

treatment *n*. handling, usage.

treaty *n*. alliance, agreement, negotiation, pact.

tremble *v*. shudder, quake, quiver, shake.

tremendous

tremendous *adj.* 1. marvelous, remarkable, superb **ordinary** 2. immense, vast, huge, enormous 3. fearful, awful, terrible, horrid.

tremor *n.* agitation, quivering, shaking, trembling.

trench *n.* trough, gully, ditch, moat, channel, dugout.

trend *n.* direction, tendency, fashion, inclination, vogue, mode.

trespass 1. *n.* sin, crime, fault 2. *v.* intrude, infringe, encroach 3. *v.* sin, offend, transgress.

trial *n.* 1. examination, test, action, ordeal 2. affliction, suffering, trouble.

tribe *n.* clan, race, family, dynasty, breed, sect.

tribute *n.* 1. payment, donation, tax subscription 2. praise, compliment, admiration.

trick 1. *n.* caper, antic, jest 2. *n.* fraud, wile, deceit, trickery, deception 3. *v.* deceive, cheat, delude, defraud.

trickle *v. & n.* dribble, drip, leak, drop, flow.

tricky *adj.* 1. delicate, complicated, difficult 2. sly, cunning, wily **forthright**, **frank**.

trifle 1. *n.* bauble, plaything, nothing, knickknack 2. *v.* play, toy, dally, fiddle.

trifling *adj.* frivolous, slight, trivial, worthless, petty **important**.

trim 1. *v.* decorate, adorn, ornament 2. *v.* prune, clip, lop 3. *adj.* compact, snug, tidy, neat **untidy**.

trip 1. *n.* tour, jaunt, excursion, voyage 2. *v.* stagger, stumble 3. *v.* hop, dance, skip.

trite *adj.* banal, corny, common, ordinary, stale, dull, hackneyed **original**, **uncommon**.

triumph 1. *v.* prevail, succeed, win **lose**, **fail** 2. *n.* success, victory, conquest **defeat**.

trivial *adj.* slight, paltry, trifling, unimportant, petty, small **important**, **grave**, **momentous**, **serious**, **substantial**.

troop 1. *v.* collect, march, throng 2. *n.* squad, band, company, throng TROUPE.

trophy *n.* memento, prize, souvenir, award.

trouble 1. *n.* adversity, difficulty, annoyance **happiness** 2. *v.* distress, pester, disturb, vex, annoy 3. *v.* bother, inconvenience **appease**.

truce *n.* respite, peace, cessation, armistice, interval.

true *adj.* 1. valid, real, actual, genuine **erroneous** 2. faithful, honest, steady, upright **untrue**, **false**.

trunk *n.* 1. proboscis, snout 2. stock, stem, stalk, body 3. case, chest, box.

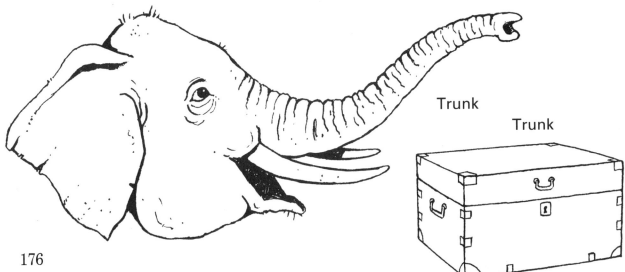

Trunk

Trunk

trust 1. *v.* credit, rely on, believe in 2. *n.* faith, belief, confidence, hope, reliance **distrust, mistrust, doubt, misgiving, suspicion**.

trusty *adj.* strong, reliable, trustworthy, firm **unreliable**.

truth *n.* honesty, fact, sincerity, reality, veracity **falsehood, fallacy, fib**.

try 1. *n.* experiment, attempt, trial 2. *v.* prove, test, examine 3. *v.* endeavor, aim, attempt, strive.

trying *adj.* difficult, irksome, wearisome, troublesome.

tuck *v.* fold, stow, pack, insert, gather.

tuft *n.* cluster, knot, crest, bunch.

tug *v.* haul, pull, drag, draw.

tumble *v.* sprawl, plunge, stumble, fall, topple.

tumult *n.* disturbance, uproar, commotion, affray, row **peace**.

tune *n.* refrain, melody, song, air, strain.

tunnel *n.* gallery, corridor, channel, passage, shaft, cavern, cave.

turbulent *adj.* disorderly, riotous, wild, unruly, violent **calm, peaceful, quiet, mild, pacific**.

turn 1. *n.* spell, stint, chance *It's my turn to throw the dice* 2. *n.* rotation, revolution 3. *v.* rotate, spin, revolve 4. *v.* alter, divert, reverse, change *After four blocks, you turn left* 5. *v.* curve, twist, bend 6. *v.* sour, spoil TERN.

tussle *v. & n.* struggle, scuffle, conflict.

tutor *n.* instructor, teacher.

twaddle *n.* prattle, nonsense, chatter, balderdash.

twinge *n.* gripe, pain, pang, ache.

twinkle *v.* glitter, sparkle, flash, wink.

twirl *v.* revolve, whirl, turn.

twist 1. *n.* curve, bend 2. *v.* writhe, contort, distort 3. *v.* encircle, twin, interweave, wind.

twitch *v. & n.* snatch, shake, jerk, shudder.

type 1. *n.* style, class, group, kind, brand, sort 2. *n.* typeface, font, character 3. *v.* typewrite.

typical *adj.* distinctive, representative, characteristic, symbolic **odd**.

tyrant *n.* oppressor, dictator, despot, autocrat.

ugly *adj.* 1. unsightly, hideous, frightful, plain **attractive, beautiful, bonny, gorgeous, handsome, lovely, pretty** 2. beastly, nasty, unpleasant, unwelcome.

ultimate *adj.* eventual, last, extreme, final **first**.

umpire *v. & n.* judge, referee.

unable *adj.* incompetent, incapable, powerless, ineffective **able**.

unaccustomed *adj.* unfamiliar, unused, new, unexpected, remarkable **accustomed**.

unadorned *adj.* plain, unembellished, simple **fancy, ornate**.

unaffected *adj.* artless, naïve, simple, natural, plain **haughty**.

unanimous *adj.* united, harmonious, agreeing, uniform, congruous **disagreeing**.

unassuming

unassuming *adj.* unpretentious, modest, retiring, humble **vain**, **showy**, **pompous**, **arrogant**.

unaware *adj.* insensible, heedless, oblivious, ignorant **aware**, **conscious**.

unbiased *adj.* fair, impartial, disinterested, neutral **biased**.

uncanny *adj.* creepy, strange, weird, mysterious.

uncertain *adj.* dubious, unsure, unreliable, doubtful **aware**, **certain**, **inevitable**, **sure**.

uncivilized *adj.* savage, barbarous, brutal, wild, **civilized**, **refined**.

uncomfortable *adj.* uneasy, nervous, upset, displeasing, troubled, distressing **comfortable**, **cozy**.

uncommon *adj.* strange, singular, rare, queer, unusual, odd **ordinary**, **prevalent**, **rife**.

unconscious *adj.* 1. ignorant, unaware 2. senseless, insensible **conscious**.

unconventional *adj.* odd, informal, eccentric, unusual **conventional**, **orthodox**.

uncouth *adj.* clumsy, awkward, boorish, coarse, loutish, vulgar, rude, unrefined **genteel**, **courteous**, **suave**.

uncover *v.* reveal, expose, disclose, unmask **cover**, **conceal**, **obscure**.

undaunted *adj.* fearless, courageous, bold, intrepid, brave **meek**, **fearful**.

under *prep.* underneath, beneath, below **above**, **over**.

undergo *v.* endure, experience, bear, suffer, sustain.

underhand *adj.* unfair, dishonest, secret, fraudulent, sly **open**, **honest**, **direct**.

underneath *prep.* below, under, beneath, neath **above**.

understand *v.* 1. comprehend, discern, know, see, grasp **misunderstand** 2. hear, learn.

undertake *v.* try, venture, attempt, set about, essay.

undesirable *adj.* unacceptable, unwelcome, unpleasant, objectionable **desirable**.

undignified *adj.* improper, unseemly, inelegant **dignified**.

undo *v.* untie, dismantle, unfasten, open, loosen **do**, **assemble**.

undress *v.* strip, divest, disrobe, unclothe, unveil, expose **dress**.

unearth *v.* discover, uncover, disclose, find, dig up.

unearthly *adj.* eerie, weird, queer, supernatural, strange.

uneasy *adj.* anxious, restless, disturbed, worried **calm**, **comfortable**.

unemployed *adj.* idle, jobless, unoccupied, inactive, out-of-work **employed**.

Uniform

unequal *adj.* irregular, uneven, inadequate, disproportionate *equal*, *equivalent*.

uneven *adj.* odd, rough, irregular, jagged *even*, *flat*, *level*, *smooth*.

unexpected *adj.* surprising, unforeseen, sudden, abrupt, chance *expected*, *anticipated*.

unfair *adj.* unequal, unjust, biased, partial *fair*, *just*, *impartial*.

unfaithful *adj.* treacherous, deceitful, faithless, false *devoted*, *faithful*, *staunch*.

unfamiliar *adj.* new, novel, different, unusual, unknown, ignorant *familiar*.

unfasten *v.* separate, undo, open, detach, untie, unlock *attach*.

unfit *adj.* incapable, incompetent, unsuitable, unqualified *fit*, *suitable*.

unfold *v.* disclose, clarify, open, decipher, reveal, unroll *fold*, *withhold*.

unforeseen *adj.* sudden, unanticipated, unexpected *expected*.

unforgettable *adj.* memorable, remarkable, outstanding, exceptional *ordinary*.

unfortunate *adj.* unhappy, luckless, hapless, *fortunate*, *lucky*.

unfriendly *adj.* hostile, unkind, malevolent, aloof, cold, surly *friendly*, *hospitable*.

ungainly *adj.* uncouth, loutish, clumsy, awkward, gawky *graceful*.

ungrateful *adj.* unthankful, selfish, thankless *grateful*, *thankful*.

unhappy *adj.* sad, miserable, melancholy, distressed, downcast, wretched *happy*, *glad*.

unhealthy *adj.* unwell, ill, sickly, infirm *healthy*, *sound*, *well*.

uniform 1. *n.* outfit, costume, suit, livery, habit 2. *adj.* constant, alike, regular, unchanging *irregular*.

Uniform uniforms

unimportant *adj.* trivial, petty, insignificant, slight, trifling *grave*, *momentous*, *prominent*, *substantial*, *urgent*.

union *n.* 1. combination, junction 2. league, association, alliance 3. concord, agreement *disunity*.

unique *adj.* single, unprecedented, rare, single, exceptional *common*, *ordinary*.

unite *v.* connect, attach, join, combine, associate *divide*, *separate*, *sever*, *isolate*, *part*.

unity *n.* concord, agreement, oneness, harmony, singleness *discord*.

universal *adj.* total, all, unlimited, entire, general, whole *local*, *particular*.

unjust *adj.* ruthless, unfair, merciless, biased *just*, *merciful*.

unkind *adj.* unfeeling, cruel, heartless, pitiless, mean *kind*, *tender*.

unknown *adj.* mysterious, obscure, unexplored, hidden, mystic *known*.

unlike *adj.* dissimilar, opposite, different *alike*.

unlikely *adj.* improbably, impossible, implausible *likely*, *probable*.

unlucky *adj.* unsuccessful, disastrous, unfortunate *lucky*, *fortunate*.

unnatural *adj.* 1. artificial, forced, stilted, strained 2. irregular, abnormal, unusual, uncommon *natural*.

unnecessary *adj.* needless, pointless, useless, superfluous *indispensable*, *essential*.

unoccupied *adj.* empty, uninhabited, vacant, idle, open *occupied*, *inhabited*.

unpleasant *adj.* offensive, sour, horrible, unpleasing, repulsive, obnoxious *pleasant*.

unpopular *adj.* unliked, unloved, friendless, disliked *popular*.

unprincipled *adj.* dishonest, tricky, wicked, villainous, vicious *honest*.

unqualified *adj.* 1. incompetent, incapable, unfit *qualified*, *eligible* 2. absolute, utter, downright, unconditional *My time at school was not an unqualified success.*

unravel *v.* unfold, extricate, disentangle, decipher, interpret, solve, explain *tangle*.

unreal *adj.* artificial, false, imaginary, spurious, mock, fantastic, sham, fake, phantom *actual*, *real*.

unreasonable *adj.* absurd, outrageous, irrational, extreme, immoderate, unwise, foolish *reasonable*.

unreliable *adj.* fickle, undependable, untrustworthy, inconstant *infallible*, *reliable*, *solid*, *trusty*.

unrest *n.* disturbance, disquiet, turmoil, trouble, stir, agitation, commotion *calm*.

unrivaled *adj.* matchless, incomparable, unequaled, peerless.

unruffled *adj.* placid, serene, calm, quiet, tranquil, peaceful *temperamental*.

unruly *adj.* mutinous, wild, turbulent, riotous, disobedient *obedient*, *orderly*.

unsafe *adj.* hazardous, insecure, dangerous, perilous *safe*.

unscrupulous *adj.* reckless, unprincipled, corrupt, ruthless *honest*, *moral*.

unseemly *adj.* unfit, vulgar, improper, indecent, unbecoming *seemly*, *proper*, *suitable*.

unselfish *adj.* generous, liberal, magnanimous, free *greedy*, *inconsiderate*.

unsettle *v.* disconcert, unhinge, derange, confuse, disturb **steady**.

unsightly *adj.* hideous, ugly, deformed, disagreeable **attractive**, **pretty**.

unskilled *adj.* awkward, inept, inexperienced, inexpert **expert**, **practical**, **proficient**, **ingenious**.

unsophisticated *adj.* naïve, raw, natural, inexperienced, simple, artless, ingenuous **experienced**, **sophisticated**.

unsound *adj.* 1. incorrect, wrong, false 2. imperfect, decayed, defective **reliable** 3. flimsy, thin, feeble, weak 4. sickly, poorly, diseased **sound**.

unsuitable *adj.* inept, improper, inappropriate, unfit **proper**, **right**, **suitable**.

untidy *adj.* slovenly, sloppy, disheveled, unkempt **tidy**, **neat**, **smart**, **trim**, **immaculate**.

untrue *adj.* 1. disloyal, treacherous, unfaithful **true**, **faithful**, **loyal** 2. erroneous, false, incorrect, wrong **right**.

unusual *adj.* extraordinary, rare, queer, uncommon, special, abnormal **common**, **commonplace**, **everyday**, **ordinary**, **regular**, **standard**.

unwary *adj.* hasty, rash, imprudent, heedless, careless **wary**.

unwell *adj.* ill, sick, ailing.

unwieldy *adj.* bulky, clumsy, unmanageable, ponderous, heavy **manageable**.

unwilling *adj.* opposed, loath, reluctant, averse **willing**, **ready**.

unworthy *adj.* worthless, insignificant, inferior, incompetent **respectable**, **worthy**.

uphold *v.* maintain, aid, support, back, sustain, defend.

upkeep *n.* maintenance, support, provision.

upright *adj.* 1. honorable, good, honest, just, virtuous **base**, **corrupt**, **sinful**, **indecent** 2. perpendicular, vertical, erect **horizontal**.

Unsuitable

uproar *n.* commotion, racket, din, tumult, disturbance, rumpus.

upset *v.* 1. startle, bother, disconcert, perturb **calm**, **pacify**, **soothe** 2. invert, overturn, overthrow, capsize.

urban *adj.* suburban, civic, metropolitan, municipal **rural**.

urbane *adj.* courteous, polished, polite, suave, elegant, civil.

urge *v.* 1. plead, beseech, beg, entreat **dissuade**, **discourage** 2. drive, force, push, stimulate, impel, spur, incite, press 3. *n.* desire, impulse.

urgent *adj.* important, persistent, pressing, immediate, insistent **unimportant**.

use 1. *v.* apply, employ, utilize *misuse* 2. *v.* consume, exhaust, expend 3. *v.* exercise, practice 4. *n.* application, employment 5. *n.* usage, habit, custom 6. *n.* benefit, utility advantage.

useful *adj.* serviceable, helpful, handy, beneficial *useless*.

useless *adj.* valueless, unserviceable, futile, worthless, fruitless *helpful*, *useful*.

usual *adj.* normal, regular, customary, common, habitual, familiar, frequent *abnormal*, *extraordinary*, *queer*, *rare*, *special*, *unusual*.

usurp *v.* appropriate, seize, take control, take over, assume *abdicate*.

utensil *n.* instrument, implement, appliance, tool.

utmost *adj.* last, uttermost, extreme, ultimate, farthest.

utter 1. *v.* say, speak, articulate, express 2. *adj.* entire, total, absolute, complete.

vacant *adj.* 1. unoccupied, empty, void, unfilled *occupied*, *full* 2. unthinking, stupid, thoughtless *intelligent*.

vacuum *n.* emptiness, void.

vagabond *n.* outcast, tramp, vagrant, beggar.

vague *adj.* doubtful, indefinite, uncertain, obscure, dim, hazy *specific*, *distinct*, *tangible*.

vain *adj.* 1. arrogant, conceited, haughty, supercilious *humble*, *unassuming* 2. futile, useless, worthless, unavailing *successful* VANE, VEIN.

valiant *adj.* gallant, fearless, brave, heroic, daring, courageous, intrepid *cowardly*, *afraid*, *fearful*.

valid *adj.* good, genuine, sound, effective, weighty, real *invalid*, *fake*, *counterfeit*, *void*.

valley *n.* vale, glen, dale, dell, ravine, dingle *hill*.

valor *n.* boldness, heroism, bravery, courage, daring *cowardice*.

valuable *adj.* 1. important, worthy, estimable 2. costly, precious, expensive *worthless*.

value *n.* 1. merit, importance, worth 2. cost, price.

van *n.* truck, wagon, vehicle, car.

vandal *n.* destroyer, wrecker, barbarian, savage.

vanish *v.* fade, disappear, evaporate, dissolve, go away *appear*.

vanity *n.* pride, conceit, arrogance *humility*, *modesty*.

vanquish *v.* overcome, beat, conquer, defeat, subdue *yield*.

vapor *n.* fog, haze, steam, mist, fume.

variable *adj.* inconstant, changeable, unsteady, shifting *constant*.

variety *n.* 1. class, type, kind, sort, species 2. diversity, difference, assortment.

various *adj.* several, many, diverse, different, numerous.

vary *v.* deviate, differ, change, alter *continue*.

vast *adj.* colossal, wide, huge, measureless, enormous, immense *minute*.

Vault

vault 1. *n.* crypt, tomb, catacomb 2. *n.* coffer, deposit, safe 3. *v. & n.* jump, leap, bound.

veer *v.* change, swerve, shift, turn.

vehement *adj.* passionate, enthusiastic, impetuous, eager, hot, ardent *apathetic*, *cool*.

vehicle *n.* conveyance, carriage, automobile, car, truck.

veil *v.* 1. hide, cover, mask 2. *n.* curtain, screen, gauze, shade VALE.

vein *n.* 1. seam, course, streak, current 2. mood, humor, character, bent *The play was in much lighter vein than I expected* VAIN, VANE.

velocity *n.* swiftness, quickness, speed.

venerate *v.* honor, reverence, respect *dishonor*.

vengeance *n.* retaliation, reprisal, revenge, reprisal.

venom *n.* 1. toxin, virus, poison 2. rancor, acrimony, malice, spite, grudge.

vent 1. *v.* utter, discharge, emit, express, gush, squirt 2. *n.* outlet, hole, opening, duct.

ventilate *v.* 1. aerate, fan, winnow, air 2. examine, discuss, consider,

venture *v & n.* chance, hazard, gamble, risk.

verbal *adj.* spoken, oral, unwritten *written*.

verdict *n.* judgment, sentence, decision, finding, opinion.

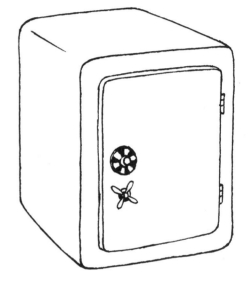

Vault

verge 1. *v.* lean, tend, incline, bear 2. *n.* brink, edge, margin, rim.

verify *v.* attest, prove, confirm, authenticate.

versatile *adj.* capable, adaptable, flexible, variable, skilled.

verse *n.* rhyme, poem, stanza, strophe, couplet.

version *n.* rendering, interpretation, translation.

vertical *adj.* plumb, perpendicular, erect, upright *horizontal*.

very *adv.* remarkably, excessively, highly, extremely.

vessel

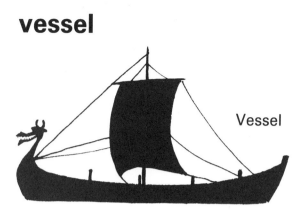

Vessel

Vessel

vessel *n.* 1. boat, ship, craft 2. container, utensil, receptacle.

vestige *n.* hint, sign, evidence, residue, indication.

veteran *n.* adept, master, expert, old hand, doyen *recruit*.

veto 1. *n.* denial, refusal, prohibition *approval* 2. *v.* forbid, prohibit, refuse, deny *approve*.

vex *v.* worry, tease, pester, annoy, harass, torment *please*.

vibrate *v.* shake, tremble, oscillate, quiver, quake, quaver.

vice *n.* 1. evil, corruption, wickedness, sin *virtue* 2. clamp, cramp.

vicinity *n.* proximity, neighborhood, nearness *distance*.

vicious *adj.* 1. brutal, cruel, savage, ruthless 2. immoral, corrupt, mischievous, wicked, sinful *virtuous*, *kind*, *good*.

victim *n.* loser, scapegoat, sufferer, dupe, prey, butt.

victor *n.* vanquisher, winner, conqueror *loser*.

victory *n.* success, conquest, triumph, superiority *defeat*.

view 1. *n.* judgment, opinion, belief 2. *n.* scene, vista, prospect 3. *n.* vision, sight, survey 4. *v.* see, behold, survey, scan, witness.

vigilant *adj.* wakeful, watchful, alert, careful *negligent*, *careless*.

vigor *n.* might, vitality, strength, power, energy, force, might *weak*, *weakness*.

vigorous *adj.* energetic, active, quick, brisk, robust *languid*.

vile *adj.* mean, offensive, wicked, disgusting, sinful, obnoxious, base, despicable *worthy*.

villain *n.* scoundrel, rascal, rogue, knave *hero*.

vim *n.* punch, vitality, vigor, drive *weakness*.

vindicate *v.* uphold, free, acquit, defend, justify *denounce*.

vindictive *adj.* malicious, spiteful, revengeful, unforgiving *forgiving*.

violate *v.* 1. outrage, defile, abuse 2. trespass, infringe, transgress, break.

violent *adj.* furious, turbulent, passionate, raging, fiery *gentle*, *mild*.

virgin 1. *adj.* pure, chaste, untouched, fresh 2. *n.* girl, lass, maiden, maid, damsel.

virile *adj.* robust, manly, forceful, male, masculine *effeminate*.

virtual *adj.* essential, implicit, substantial, implied.

virtue *n.* morality, integrity, goodness, excellence, distinction, uprightness *vice*, *fault*.

virtuous *adj.* righteous, chaste, upright, good, excellent, honest *vicious*, *wicked*.

visible *adj.* apparent, clear, perceptible, evident, discernible *hidden*, *imperceptible*, *invisible*.

vision *n.* 1. appearance, apparition, specter, ghost 2. seeing, sight 3. foresight, perception *Candidates for this job need to be people of vision.*

visit *v. & n.* stay, call, stop.

visitor *n.* caller, guest, patron, pilgrim, tourist.

vital *adj.* necessary, essential, critical, indispensable *unessential*, *deadly*.

vivacious *adj.* merry, lively, pleasant, sprightly, cheerful *dull*.

vivid *adj.* brilliant, intense, clear, lucid, bright *dull*.

vocal *adj.* said, outspoken, spoken, uttered, oral.

vocation *n.* career, profession, occupation, employment, calling, business, work.

vociferous *adj.* loud, noisy, blatant, clamorous *silent*.

vogue *n.* custom, style, fashion, mode.

voice *n.* speech, language, articulation, utterance, tone.

void 1. *adj.* invalid, useless, null, ineffectual *valid* 2. *adj.* vacant, empty, unoccupied *full* 3. *n.* vacuum, emptiness, space.

volatile *adj.* 1. lively, buoyant, airy 2. changeable, fickle, flighty *steady*, *constant* 3. gaseous, evaporable *dense*.

volume *n.* 1. book, tome, publication 2. capacity, bulk, contents, amount, dimensions.

voluntary *adj.* gratuitous, optional, free, unforced *compulsory*, *forced*, *involuntary*.

vomit *v.* disgorge, puke, retch, belch, emit, spew.

vote 1. *v.* elect, select, choose 2. *n.* election, ballot, choice, suffrage.

vouch *v.* guarantee, attest, declare, affirm.

voucher *n.* certificate, receipt, coupon.

vow 1. *v.* swear, dedicate, assert, pledge 2. *n.* pledge, promise, guarantee.

voyage *n.* trip, journey, tour, cruise.

vulgar *adj.* coarse, rude, crude, unrefined, common, ordinary, rustic *polite*, *refined*, *genteel*, *elegant*.

vulnerable *adj.* sensitive, defenseless, susceptible, exposed *protected*, *impregnable*, *tough*.

wad *n.* packet, plug, bunch, pack, batch, bundle, wedge.

wag 1. *n.* wit, joker, humorist 2. *v.* shake, flap, vibrate, wave.

wage 1. *v.* conduct, engage in, undertake *The war was waged over a border dispute* 2. *v.* pledge, stake, bet.

wages *n.* pay, earnings, salary, remuneration.

wagon *n.* vehicle, truck, carriage, van, buggy.

wail *v. & n.* cry, lament, howl, moan.

wait 1. *v.* delay, linger, stay, remain, tarry *depart* 2. *v.* serve, attend 3. *n.* holdup, delay WEIGHT.

waiter *n.* servant, steward, attendant.

waive *v.* renounce, forego, relinquish, defer *demand*, *insist*, *claim* WAVE.

wake *v.* rouse, stir, awaken *sleep*, *doze*.

walk

walk 1. *v.* stroll, march, tread, step, go, hike, promenade 2. *n.* step, carriage, gait 3. *n.* promenade, stroll 4. *n.* pathway, trail, promenade.

wallow *v.* grovel, flounder, roll, writhe.

wan *adj.* ashen, pale, pallid, pasty, haggard *robust*.

wand *n.* baton, scepter, stick, mace, rod, truncheon.

wander *v.* deviate, stray, ramble, rove, swerve, roam.

wane *v.* diminish, lessen, decrease, recede *wax* WAIN.

want 1. *n.* need, requirement, necessity, desire 2. *n.* penury, poverty 3. *v.* desire, crave, require, wish, need.

Watch the time

ward *n.* 1. district, division, quarter 2. room, chamber, apartment 3. dependent, pupil, minor WARRED.

wardrobe *n.* 1. cupboard, closet 2. clothing, clothes, raiment.

warm 1. *v.* cook, heat *cool* 2. *adj.* tepid, heated, sunny, hot *cold*, *chilly*, *cool*, *frigid*, *frosty* 3. *adj.* cordial, hearty, friendly.

warn *v.* admonish, give notice, caution, inform WORN.

warning *n.* omen, caution, advice, notice.

warp *v.* bend, contort, twist.

warrant 1. *n.* commission, voucher, authority, permit 2. *v.* assure, guarantee, attest.

warrior *n.* fighter, hero, soldier, champion.

wary *adj.* watchful, cautious, careful, chary *imprudent*, *unwary*.

wash 1. *n.* bathing, cleansing, washing 2. *v.* scrub, clean, launder, cleanse.

waste 1. *n.* rubbish, garbage, refuse 2. *n.* loss, depletion, decay 3. *v.* misuse, lavish, spend, squander, dissipate *save* 4. *v.* pine, perish, wither, dwindle *preserve* WAIST.

wasteful *adj.* lavish, thriftless, spendthrift, extravagant *economical*, *productive*, *thrifty*.

Watch

wanton *adj.* 1. lustful, unchaste, immoral *chaste*, *modest* 2. needless, reckless, careless *heedful* 3. frisky, sportive, playful.

war *n.* battle, hositility, combat, conflict *peace* WORE.

watch 1. *v.* regard, look at, observe, view 2. *n.* patrol, vigil, guard.

water *v.* moisten, sprinkle, irrigate, wet.

wave 1. *n.* surge, undulation, ripple, billow 2. *v.* motion, brandish, flicker, flourish WAIVE.

waver *v.* fluctuate, hesitate, doubt, flicker, quiver ***determine***.

wax 1. *v.* swell, increase, grow, gain ***wane***, ***dwindle***, ***ebb*** 2. *n.* resin, cere, mastic, polish.

way *n.* 1. mode, method, style, manner 2. route, road, track, path WEIGH.

wayward *adj.* contrary, naughty, perverse, disobedient, willful, wanton ***obedient***.

weak *adj.* 1. infirm, feeble, delicate, sickly ***strong***, ***powerful***, ***hale***, ***hearty***, ***lusty***, ***mighty***, ***robust***, ***rugged***, ***stalwart*** 2. unsafe, unsound, frail 3. undecided, irresolute ***resolute*** 4. watery, diluted, thin.

wealth *n.* fortune, riches, abundance, treasure, affluence, possessions ***poverty***, ***poor***.

wealthy *adj.* affluent, rich, prosperous, well-off ***destitute***, ***poor***, ***penniless***.

wear *v.* 1. use, corrode, impair, rub, consume, waste 2. bear, have on, don WARE.

weary 1. *v.* tire, exhaust, fatigue 2. *adj.* tired, exhausted, fatigued.

weather *n.* climate, conditions, temperature.

weave *v.* plait, interlace, braid.

web *n.* tissue, netting, membrane, textile, cobweb.

wed *v.* marry, unite, espouse, betroth ***divorce***.

wee *adj.* tiny, small, little, diminutive ***large***, ***big***, ***huge*** WE.

weep *v.* lament, sob, cry, shed tears.

weigh *v.* 1. consider, ponder, deliberate 2. balance, measure, gauge WAY.

weight *n.* 1. influence, power, importance 2. burden, heaviness, load ***lightness*** WAIT.

weird *adj.* strange, uncanny, supernatural, unearthly ***natural***.

welcome 1. *n.* reception, greetings, salutation 2. *v.* receive, greet ***banish***, ***bar***.

welfare *n.* advantage, profit, happiness, success, benefit ***loss***, ***misfortune***.

well 1. *adv.* fully, thoroughly, amply, certainly 2. *adv.* justly, rightly, satisfactorily 3. *adj.* hale, hearty, fortunate, healthy ***ill***, ***indisposed***, ***sick***, ***unhealthy*** 4. *n.* source, spring, fountain.

wet *adj.* 1. moist, damp, rainy, humid ***dry***, ***arid***, ***parched*** 2. *v.* dampen, soak, moisten.

whack *v. & n.* strike, bang, hit, rap, slap, beat.

wharf *n.* pier, quay, dock, landing stage.

wheedle *v.* flatter, persuade, cajole, coax.

whet *v.* excite, rouse, sharpen, stimulate.

whiff *n.* aroma, perfume, puff, blast, odor, smell.

Web

187

whim

whim *n.* quirk, humor, caprice, fancy, notion.

whine *v. & n.* whimper, cry, moan.

whip 1. *n.* strap, scourge, lash 2. *v.* strike, flog, beat, lash, scourge.

whirl *v.* twist, spin, rotate, revolve.

whisk *v.* hasten, brush, rush, speed.

whisper *v. & n.* mumble, murmur, mutter *roar*.

whole *adj.* complete, undivided, total, entire *part*, *partial*, *fraction*, *scrap*, *fragment* HOLE.

wholesome *adj.* nourishing, nutritious, healthy, beneficial *unwholesome*.

wicked *adj.* sinful, immoral, bad, depraved, evil, villainous *virtuous*.

wide *adj.* ample, spacious, broad, extensive, vast *narrow*, *thin*.

wield *v.* control, handle, manipulate, brandish, use.

wife *n.* spouse, mate.

wild *adj.* 1. savage, untamed, undomesticated *tame*, *domestic* 2. reckless, imprudent, madcap 3. violent, disorderly, turbulent.

will 1. *n.* resolution, determination, decision 2. *n.* legacy, testament 3. *v.* choose, wish, desire, elect.

willful *adj.* stubborn, perverse, obstinate *involuntary*.

willing *adj.* ready, agreeable, disposed, inclined *unwilling*, *reluctant*, *involuntary*.

wilt *v.* droop, sag, wither.

wily *adj.* sly, subtle, artful, crafty, cunning *straightforward*.

win *v.* achieve, gain, succeed, procure, triumph, acquire *lose*.

wind (rhymes with pinned) *n.* breeze, draft, air, gust.

wind (rhymes with kind) *v.* twine, twist, turn, coil WINED.

wink *v.* squint, blink.

wipe *v.* stroke, mop, clean, rub.

wire *n.* 1. telegram, telegraph 2. electric cable.

wisdom *n.* sagacity, judgment, intelligence, brains, sense *folly*.

wise *adj.* erudite, sensible, learned, sage, intelligent *uneducated*, *foolish*, *ignorant*.

wish 1. *n.* desire, will, intention 2. *v.* direct, express, bid, mean 3. *v.* want, crave, long for, desire.

wistful *adj.* thoughtful, yearning, reflective, longing.

wit *n.* 1. fun, sparkle, humor 2. intelligence, understanding *ignorance* 3. comedian, wag, humorist.

witch *n.* enchantress, sorceress, hag.

withdraw *v.* 1. recede, retire, abandon, retreat *stand*, *maintain*, *attack* 2. recall, disavow, recant.

wither *v.* wilt, fade, droop, shrivel, dry *bloom*.

withhold *v.* restrain, suppress, retain, keep back *grant*, *allot*, *supply*.

withstand *v.* confront, resist, thwart, oppose, endure *yield*.

witness 1. *v.* observe, see, notice, attest *disprove* 2. *n.* collaborator, beholder, spectator.

witty *adj.* droll, alert, humorous, funny, amusing, sprightly.

wizard *n.* sorcerer, diviner, magician, conjuror.

woe *n.* agony, trouble, sorrow, torture, grief, distress *happiness*.

woman *n.* wife, girl, lady, female *man*.

wonder 1. *n.* curiosity, spectacle, phenomenon 2. *n.* awe, amazement, astonishment 3. *v.* stare, marvel 4. *v.* question, ponder, meditate.

wonderful *adj.* amazing, startling, marvelous, astonishing, miraculous, astounding *ordinary*.

wood *n.* 1. log, timber, lumber, stick, plank 2. forest, thicket, grove, copse, timberland WOULD.

word *n.* 1. phrase, statement, utterance, term 2. promise, pledge 3. tidings, news.

work 1. *n.* labor, toil, effort *recreation* 2. *n.* job, employment 3. *n.* achievement, production, performance *The art society held an annual show of student's work* 4. *v.* operate, function, run 5. *v.* labor, toil, drudge, act *rest*, *play*.

world *n.* globe, planet, earth.

worry 1. *v.* fret, chafe, grieve 2. *v.* harass, bother, tease, annoy, vex 3. *n.* trouble, anxiety, vexation *comfort*, *joy*.

worsen *v.* decline, fail, deteriorate, sink *improve*, *mend*, *recover*, *reform*.

worship 1. *v.* idolize, respect, adore, revere, venerate *detest* 2. *n.* reverence, adoration, homage.

worth *n.* virtue, cost, value, integrity, merit *worthlessness*.

worthless *adj.* unworthy, useless, trifling, paltry, valueless *worthy*, *valuable*, *invaluable*.

worthy *adj.* excellent, deserving, honest, meritorious *unworthy*, *worthless*.

wound 1. *n.* harm, hurt, damage, injury 2. *v.* damage, harm, hurt, injure *heal*.

wrangle *v. & n.* squabble, brawl, dispute, quarrel, tiff.

wrap *v.* enfold, cover, enclose, envelop RAP.

wrath *n.* rage, ire, fury, anger *serenity*.

wreck 1. *n.* ruin, desolation, destruction 2. *v.* destroy, shatter, strand, founder *reconstruct*.

wrench *v.* jerk, strain, tug, twist.

wrestle *v.* fight, struggle, battle, strive.

wretched *adj.* distressed, miserable, unhappy, forlorn *happy*, *fortunate*.

wring *v.* wrest, twist, squeeze RING.

A writer

A writer

wrinkle *v. & n.* pucker, twist, crease, furrow, fold.

write *v.* scrawl, record, scribble, inscribe, pen RIGHT, RITE, WRIGHT.

writer *n.* scribe, author, composer, clerk, secretary, penman.

writhe *v.* contort, squirm, twist, wriggle.

wrong 1. *n.* evil, sin, wickedness 2. *n.* unfairness, injustice 3. *v.* abuse, maltreat, injure 4. *adv.* falsely, improperly 5. *adj.* unfair, unjust 6. *adj.* false, inaccurate, incorrect *correct*, *accurate* 7. *adj.* wicked, sinful, bad, improper *right*, *good*, *proper*.

wry *adj.* crooked, twisted, askew, contorted RYE.

yap *v.* cry, bark, yelp.

yard *n.* 1. gauge, measure, scale 2. compound, square, enclosure, court, grounds, park.

yarn *n.* 1. tale, story, fable, 2. fiber, wool, thread.

yawn *v.* open wide, gape.

yearn *v.* desire, crave, long for, hanker.

yell *v. & n.* scream, shout, screech, shriek.

yield 1. *n.* crop, harvest, product 2. *v.* abandon, give way, relinquish, surrender *keep*, *retain*, *conquer*, *defy*, *overcome*, *vanquish* 3. *v.* confer, impart, produce, bear.

yoke *n.* link, bondage, servitude, chain, bond YOLK.

young *adj.* immature, youthful, juvenile *old*, *aged*, *mature*.

youth *n.* 1. childhood, youthfulness, immaturity, adolescence 2. lad, youngster, stripling, boy *adult*.

zany *adj.* foolish, funny, droll, clownish.

zeal *n.* devotion, passion, enthusiasm, ardor, fervor.

zenith *n.* top, acme, apex, summit, peak, pinnacle.

zero *n.* nothing, nil, naught, null.

zest *n.* appetite, savor, relish, gusto, delight.

zone *n.* belt, district, region, area, climate, quarter, section, department, territory.

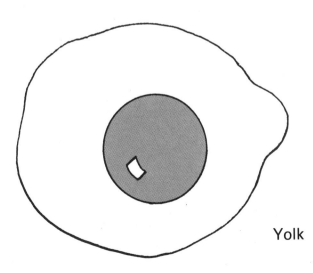

Yolk

Yoke

THE
SPELLING
CHECKLIST

*   refer to main dictionary for
explanation of differences

**   differences are explained in the
footnote

abscess
absence
accede
accelerate
*accept (see except)
*access (see excess)
accessible
accidentally
accommodation
accumulate
accurately
**acetic (see ascetic)
ache
achieve
acquaintance
acquire
acquit
across
adaptation
address
adequate
adolescent
advertise
advertisement
advice
advise
aerial
*affect (see effect)
aggravated
aggressor
aghast
agreeable
aisle (see isle)
alcohol
allege
allot, allotted
**all ready (see already)
all right
**allude (see elude)

already
altogether
amount
analysis
analyze
anchor
anonymity
anonymous
anxiety
appall, appalling
apparatus
apparently
appearance
appropriate
aquatic
arbitrary
Arctic
argument
article
artisan
ascend
*ascent (see assent)
**ascetic (see acetic)
assassinate
*assent (see ascent)
assess
associate
athlete
atrocious
attach
attitude
author
auxiliary
awkward

bachelor
balloon
**baring (see bearing)
barrenness

basically
battalion
beautiful
beggar
beginning
believe
benefited
besiege
bicycle
bigoted
boisterous
*bridal (see bridle)
*bridle (see bridal)
budget
buoy
burglar
business

calendar
campaign
**capital (see capitol)
**capitol (see capital)
career
careful, carefully
carriage
casualty
catarrh
category
caterpillar
cede
ceiling
cemetery
*cereal (see serial)
changeable
chaos
character
chief
children's
choose
chose
cigarette
cinnamon
circuit
*cite (see sight and site)
collaborate
colleague
college

*colonel (see kernel)
colossal
column
coming
commemorate
commission
committee
comparatively
comparison
competent
*complement (see compliment)
completely
*compliment (see complement)
concede
conceive
concentrate
condemn
conjuror
conscientious
conscious
consistent
conspiracy
contemporary
continuous
controlled
coolly
correspondence
corroborate
*council (see counsel)
*counsel (see council)
counterfeit
courageous
courteous
criticism
cynicism

**dairy (see diary)
deceit
deceive
*decent (see descent)
decision
defendant
defense
defensible
definite
democracy
*descent (see decent and dissent)

*desert (see dessert)
desiccated
desperate
detached
deteriorate
deterrent
develop, developed
development
device
devise
diarrhea
diary
*die (see dye)
difference
dilapidate
dilemma
disappear
disappoint
disastrous
discipline
dissatisfied
*dissent (see descent)
disservice
dissolve
doesn't
**dual (see duel)
duly
*dye (see die)
*dyeing (see dying)
*dying (see dyeing)

echoes
ecstasy
eerie
*effect (see affect)
eighth
elegant
**elicit (see illicit)
*eligible (see illegible)
eliminate
**elude (see allude)
embarrassed
**emigrate (see immigrate)
emperor
endeavor
enormous
enroll, enrolled

enthusiasm
**envelop (see envelope)
**envelope (see envelop)
evenness
exaggerate
exceed
*except (see accept)
*excess (see access)
exhilarate
exuberant

familiar
feasible
February
fiery
fluorescent
focused
foreigner
forfeit
**formally (see formerly)
**formerly (see formally)
forth (see fourth)
forty
fourteen
fourth (see forth)
friend

gaiety
gauge
gesture
gnaw
goddess
**gorilla (see guerrilla)
government
grammar
grandeur
grievous
guarantee/or
guaranty
guard
**guerrilla, guerilla (see gorilla)

handkerchief
harass
height
heir

194

heroes
*hoard (see horde)
**holy (see wholly)
hoping
*horde (see hoard)
hygiene

*idle (see idol)
*idol (see idle)
*illegible (see eligible)
**illicit (see elicit)
immediately
**immigrate (see emigrate)
independence, independent
inoculate
install, installment
intercede
interrupt
irregularly
irresistible
*isle (see aisle)
isn't
**its (see it's)
**it's (see its)

jealous
jeweler, jewelry

knowledge

ladies
laid
leisure
liaison
library
lieutenant
liquefy
*loose (see lose)
*lose (see loose)
lovable

maintenance
manageable
maneuver
*marshal (see martial)
*martial (see marshal)

meant
medicine
mediocre
men's
**miner (see minor)
miniature
**minor (see miner)
miscellaneous
mischievous
misspell
moccasin
monastery
murmured
**muscle (see mussel)
**mussel (see muscle)

**naval (see navel)
**navel (see naval)
necessary
nephew
niece
ninety
ninth
no one
noticeable

oblige
occasion
occurred
overrun

paid
palm
parallel, paralleled
paralyze
parliament
pastime
pavilion
perceive
pharaoh
piece
pigeon
*plain (see plane)
*plane (see plain)
playwright
pneumonia
precede

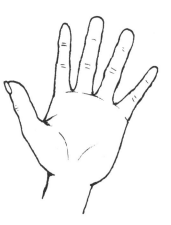

preferred
pretense
prevalent
*principal (see principle)
*principle (see principal)
privilege
procedure
proceed
professor
**profit (see prophet)
prominent
propeller
**prophet (see profit)
protrude
pursue

quiet
quite

**rain (see reign and rein)
*raise (see raze)
*raze (see raise)
recede
receive
recipe
recommend
recurrence
reference
referred
**reign (see rain and rein)
**rein (see rain and reign)
relieve
religious
rendezvous
renown
rhyme
rhythm
*right (see rite and write)
*rite (see right and write)

sacrilegious
satellite
scenery
schedule
scissors

seize
separate
sergeant
**serial (see cereal)
severely
sheriff
siege
sieve
*sight (see cite and site)
silhouette
sincerely
*site (see cite and sight)
soothe
source
sovereign
*stair (see stare)
*stare (see stair)
*stationary (see stationery)
*stationery (see stationary)
*straight (see strait)
*strait (see straight)
subtle
succeed
success
succumb
superintendent
supersede
suppress
surprise
syllable
symbol
symmetry

**their (see there and they're)
**theirs (see there's)
*there (see their and they're)
**there's (see theirs)
**they're (see their and there)
thorough
through
tongue
tragedy
twelfth

unanimous
unnecessary
until

*vain (see vane and vein)
*vane (see vain and vein)
*vein (see vain and vane)
vengeance
villain

**weather (see whether)
weird
**whether (see weather)
**wholly (see holy)
**who's (see whose)

**whose (see who's)
wintry
withhold
woolen
woolly
women's
*write (see right and rite)
wrought

yacht
**your (see you're)
**you're (see your)

✳✳

**acetic: an acid, usually referred to as "acetic acid"
ascetic: means "abstemious" or "self-denying"

all ready: "everyone prepared"
already: (one word) an adjective, meaning "by this time"

all right: always spelled as two words, not "alright"

allude: means "to refer to"
elude: means "to dodge or avoid"

baring: means "making bare"
bearing: means "manner"

dairy: means "a place for buying milk or butter"
diary: means "a day-to-day record book"

elicit: means "to draw out"
illicit: means "illegal"

emigrate: means "to move to another country"
immigrate: means "to come from another country"

envelop: means "to enfold"
envelope: means "a wrapper or cover"

formally: means "strictly or properly"
formerly: means "previously"

gorilla: means "an ape"
guerrilla: means "a rebel or fighter"

holy: means "sacred"
wholly: means "entirely"

its: is the possessive pronoun for "it"
it's: means "it is"

miner: means "an underground worker"
minor: means "a young person"

muscle: means "fibrous tissue of the body"
mussel: means "a shellfish"

naval: means "relating to the navy"
navel: means "the belly-button"

profit: means "benefit"
prophet: means "one who foretells the future"

197

rain: means "falling water"
reign: means "the rule of a monarch"
rein: means "the strap of a horse"

cereal: means "edible grain"
serial: means "a story told in parts"

their: is the possessive pronoun for "they"
there: means "at that place"
they're: means "they are"

theirs: means "what belongs to them"
there's: means "there is"

who's: means "who is"
whose: means "of whom"

your: is the possessive pronoun for "you"
you're: means "you are"